G000058544

jQuery 1.4 Animation Techniques
Beginner's Guide

Quickly master all of jQuery's animation methods and build a toolkit of ready-to-use animations using jQuery 1.4

Dan Wellman

[PACKT] PUBLISHING
open source
community experience distilled

BIRMINGHAM - MUMBAI

jQuery 1.4 Animation Techniques
Beginner's Guide

Copyright © 2011 Packt Publishing

All rights reserved. No part of this book may be reproduced, stored in a retrieval system, or transmitted in any form or by any means, without the prior written permission of the publisher, except in the case of brief quotations embedded in critical articles or reviews.

Every effort has been made in the preparation of this book to ensure the accuracy of the information presented. However, the information contained in this book is sold without warranty, either express or implied. Neither the author, nor Packt Publishing, and its dealers and distributors will be held liable for any damages caused or alleged to be caused directly or indirectly by this book.

Packt Publishing has endeavored to provide trademark information about all of the companies and products mentioned in this book by the appropriate use of capitals. However, Packt Publishing cannot guarantee the accuracy of this information.

First published: March 2011

Production Reference: 1140311

Published by Packt Publishing Ltd.
32 Lincoln Road
Olton
Birmingham, B27 6PA, UK.

ISBN 978-1-849513-30-2

www.packtpub.com

Cover Image by Filippo (Filosarti@tiscali.it)

Credits

Author
Dan Wellman

Reviewers
Shaiful Islam
Ben Nadel
Cyril Pierron

Acquisition Editor
Sarah Cullington

Development Editor
Roger D'souza

Technical Editor
Conrad Sardinha

Indexer
Hemangini Bari

Editorial Team Leader
Akshara Aware

Project Team Leader
Priya Mukherji

Project Coordinator
Sneha Harkut

Proofreader
Aaron Nash

Production Coordinator
Melwyn D'sa

Cover Work
Melwyn D'sa

Foreword

Since the first jQuery homepage in 2006, an interactive example introduced visitors to jQuery with a single line of code, and a button to run that code. When clicked, it added a class to a hidden paragraph, and animated that paragraph to become visible.

Today, in late 2010, the API documentation has 15 methods listed in the Effects category. These provide built-in animations for fading and sliding, as well as various ways to create custom animations. When combined with color and class animations and custom easings that jQuery UI provides, there are even more ways to create animations.

A good rule of thumb for using animations is to use slides when showing elements within the pageflow, and fades for overlays, like a tooltip. But that's just a rule of thumb, and with all the tools available there's a lot more opportunity to improve interactions, as well as messing them up.

With that in mind, a full book on animations starts to make a lot of sense. It makes even more sense when also taking into account upcoming technologies which aren't bound to jQuery directly, like CSS3 animations or animated canvas drawings.

As a tech reviewer I've worked with Dan on his jQuery UI 1.6 and jQuery UI 1.7 books. At the time the jQuery UI team was still figuring out the scope and exact direction of the project, including several direction changes at the time when Dan was writing the first book. Despite these challenges Dan did a great job providing documentation and extensive examples on how to use and combine the widgets and interactions jQuery UI provides.

With this book Dan brings his experience in writing on jQuery topics to teach you when and how to use animations to create better user experiences. I hope it serves you well.

Jörn Zaefferer

jQuery UI development lead, plugin author, and QUnit maintainer

About the Author

Dan Wellman is an author and web developer based on the South coast of the UK. By day he works alongside some of the most talented people he has had the pleasure of calling colleagues, for a small, yet accomplished digital agency called Design Haus. By night he writes books and tutorials on a range of frontend topics. He is hopelessly addicted to jQuery. His life is enriched by four wonderful children, a beautiful wife, and a close circle of family and friends. This is his fifth book.

I would like to thank the hugely supportive and patient editorial team at Packt, without whom this book would not exist. I would also like to thank the reviewers, especially Ben Nadel and Cyril Pierron, who put aside their own personal projects and dedicated countless hours to ensuring the book's technical accuracy. I'd also like to say a big Hey! to some of my closest friends, in no particular order; Andrew Herman, Steev Bishop, Aaron Matheson, Eamon O'Donoghue, James Zabiela, Mike Woodford, and John Adams.

About the Reviewers

Shaiful Islam completed his graduation in Computer Science and Engineering (CSE) from IIUC (International Islamic University Chittagong), and loves web development and PHP.

He is a Software Engineer, with three years of experience in web development and a keen lover of web technology. He also loves CSS, JQuery, CodeIgniter, Cakephp, and Zend Framework, which showed him the way to develop his career in web development and the programming field.

His motto is: **Work through best approach, commitment, skill, and keep smiling.**

Currently he is working for "bGlobal Sourcing LLC" as a Software Engineer.

> I would like to thank all of my friends, colleagues, and those senior brothers who reviewed this type of book before and from whom I got inspiration. Special thanks to everyone at Packt Publishing.

Ben Nadel is the chief software engineer at Epicenter Consulting, a Manhattan-based web application development firm specializing in innovative custom software that transforms the way its clients do business. He is also an Adobe Community Professional as well as an Adobe Certified Professional in Advanced ColdFusion. In his spare time, he blogs extensively about all aspects of obsessively thorough web application development at http://www.bennadel.com/.

Cyril Pierron is an engineer, a web addict, tech savvy, and life curious. He started programming at age 8, and has been working in telecommunications for the past 12 years. He is married and a father of a lovely baby girl.

I would actually like to thank Twitter which gave me the opportunity to see Packt Publishing message when they were looking for reviewers. Obviously thanks to the Packt Publishing team for giving me the chance to work on one of their titles. Lots of thanks to Dan Wellman who I actually followed on Twitter previously to realizing I was reviewing one of his books. This is an amazing piece that draws inspiration and Dan is the most cheerful, open minded, and supportive person. Finally thanks to my wife who showed quite some patience and support when I kept working on this book after hours.

www.PacktPub.com

Support files, eBooks, discount offers and more

You might want to visit www.PacktPub.com for support files and downloads related to your book.

Did you know that Packt offers eBook versions of every book published, with PDF and ePub files available? You can upgrade to the eBook version at www.PacktPub.com and as a print book customer, you are entitled to a discount on the eBook copy. Get in touch with us at service@packtpub.com for more details.

At www.PacktPub.com, you can also read a collection of free technical articles, sign up for a range of free newsletters and receive exclusive discounts and offers on Packt books and eBooks.

http://PacktLib.PacktPub.com

Do you need instant solutions to your IT questions? PacktLib is Packt's online digital book library. Here, you can access, read and search across Packt's entire library of books.

Why Subscribe?

- Fully searchable across every book published by Packt
- Copy and paste, print and bookmark content
- On demand and accessible via web browser

Free Access for Packt account holders

If you have an account with Packt at www.PacktPub.com, you can use this to access PacktLib today and view nine entirely free books. Simply use your login credentials for immediate access.

For Pat Spacagna, the greatest mother-in-law I could have wished for. You are fondly remembered, but sorely missed. May you rest in peace always.

Table of Contents

Preface

jQuery is a cross-browser JavaScript library designed to simplify the client-side scripting of HTML, and is the most popular JavaScript library in use today. Using the features offered by jQuery, developers are able to create dynamic web pages. This book will act as a resource for you to create animation and advanced special effects in your web applications, by following the easy-to-understand steps mentioned in it.

jQuery 1.4 Animation Techniques: Beginner's Guide will allow you to master animation in jQuery to produce slick and attractive interfaces that respond to your visitors' interactions. You will learn everything you need to know about creating engaging and effective web page animations using jQuery. The book uses many examples and explains how to create animations using an easy, step-by-step, beginner's guide approach.

This book provides various examples that gradually build up the reader's knowledge and practical experience in using the jQuery API to create stunning animations. The book starts off by explaining how animations make your user interface interactive and attractive. It explains the various methods used to make the element being animated appear or disappear. It provides a set of steps to create simple animations and show fading animations.

You can later learn how to make complex animations by chaining different effects together as well as how to halt a currently running application. You will find out how to slide your animation elements and learn to create custom animations that can be complex and specialized.

You will find out how to obtain and set up the jQuery UI—the official user interface library for jQuery. This book will tell you how to animate a page's background image, and will teach you how to make images scroll in a certain direction and at a certain speed depending on the movement of the mouse pointer.

What this book covers

Chapter 1, Introduction covers the basics including downloading jQuery and setting up a development area, a brief history of animation on the Web, when and where not to use animation, how animation can enhance an interface, and the animation methods exposed by jQuery. A basic example of animation is also covered.

Chapter 2, Fading Animations looks at the fading family of animation methods including fading elements in and out, fade toggling, triggering animations with `show()`, `hide()`, and `toggle()`, and fading an element to a specific opacity.

Chapter 3, Managing Animations covers the animation queue and the methods jQuery provides for managing it. We see how to clear the queue, how to add functions to it, and how to clear it. We see how to add a delay between queued items and how to prevent animations building up in the queue when they are not required.

Chapter 4, Sliding Animations looks at jQuery's sliding animation and covers how to slide elements in an out of view and how to toggle the slide based on their current state. We also look at how CSS positioning can affect animations and how to avoid a common pitfall when using these methods in a drop-down menu.

Chapter 5, Custom Animations focuses on the `animate()` method, which jQuery provides for us as a means of creating custom animations not already predefined. This extremely powerful method allows us to animate almost any CSS-style property to easily create complex and attractive animations.

Chapter 6, Extended Animations with jQuery UI looks at the additional effects added by jQuery UI, the official UI library built on top of jQuery. We look at each of the 14 new effects as well as covering the easing functions built into the library.

Chapter 7, Full Page Animations looks at animations that form the main focus of the page. Techniques we cover include animating page scroll, creating a parallax effect, and creating basic stop-motion animations.

Chapter 8, Other Popular Animations looks at some common types of animations found on the web including proximity animations triggered by the mouse pointer, animated headers, and a modern-day equivalent to the marquee element.

Chapter 9, CSS3 Animations covers how we can use CSS3 to create attractive animations driven by the latest CSS transforms and how jQuery can be used to make the process easier, including the latest cssHooks functionality.

Chapter 10, Canvas Animations looks at the HTML5 canvas element and shows how it can be used to create stunning animations without the use of Flash or other proprietary technologies. The book closes with an in-depth example teaching how to create an interactive game using nothing but HTML and JavaScript.

What you need for this book

To get the most out of this book you should have some knowledge of frontend development, preferably including JavaScript. Experience with jQuery is also preferable, but is not essential as all techniques used in the book are discussed in full.

You should have a computer capable of running the latest browsers and preferably an Internet connection. A code editing development software package will be of help, but again is not essential provided you have a text editor of some description.

Who this book is for

This book is written for web designers and frontend developers who already have good knowledge of HTML and CSS, and some experience with jQuery. If you want to learn how to animate the user interface of your web applications with jQuery, then this book is for you.

Conventions

In this book, you will find several headings appearing frequently.

To give clear instructions of how to complete a procedure or task, we use:

Time for action – heading

1. Action 1
2. Action 2
3. Action 3

Instructions often need some extra explanation so that they make sense, so they are followed with:

What just happened?

This heading explains the working of tasks or instructions that you have just completed.

You will also find some other learning aids in the book, including:

Pop quiz – heading

These are short multiple choice questions intended to help you test your own understanding.

Have a go hero – heading

These set practical challenges and give you ideas for experimenting with what you have learned.

You will also find a number of styles of text that distinguish between different kinds of information. Here are some examples of these styles, and an explanation of their meaning.

Code words in text are shown as follows: "The `fadeIn()` and `fadeOut()` methods perform the least complex animations available via jQuery".

A block of code is set as follows:

```
$("#fader").fadeOut(function() {
  console.log($(this).queue());
}).fadeIn().fadeOut().fadeIn();
```

When we wish to draw your attention to a particular part of a code block, the relevant lines or items are set in bold:

```
subMenuParent.mouseenter(function() {
  $(this).find("ul").toggle("fast");
});
```

New terms and **important words** are shown in bold. Words that you see on the screen, in menus or dialog boxes for example, appear in the text like this: "In this case, we clear the whole canvas, removing the space ship and any surviving aliens, and print the text **GAME OVER!** to the center of the canvas".

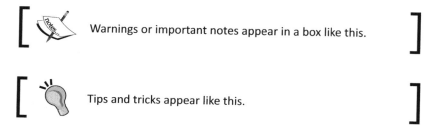

Warnings or important notes appear in a box like this.

Tips and tricks appear like this.

Reader feedback

Feedback from our readers is always welcome. Let us know what you think about this book—what you liked or may have disliked. Reader feedback is important for us to develop titles that you really get the most out of.

To send us general feedback, simply send an e-mail to feedback@packtpub.com, and mention the book title via the subject of your message.

If there is a book that you need and would like to see us publish, please send us a note in the **SUGGEST A TITLE** form on www.packtpub.com or e-mail suggest@packtpub.com.

If there is a topic that you have expertise in and you are interested in either writing or contributing to a book, see our author guide on www.packtpub.com/authors.

Customer support

Now that you are the proud owner of a Packt book, we have a number of things to help you to get the most from your purchase.

Downloading the example code

You can download the example code files for all Packt books you have purchased from your account at http://www.PacktPub.com. If you purchased this book elsewhere, you can visit http://www.PacktPub.com/support and register to have the files e-mailed directly to you.

Errata

Although we have taken every care to ensure the accuracy of our content, mistakes do happen. If you find a mistake in one of our books—maybe a mistake in the text or the code—we would be grateful if you would report this to us. By doing so, you can save other readers from frustration and help us improve subsequent versions of this book. If you find any errata, please report them by visiting http://www.packtpub.com/support, selecting your book, clicking on the **errata submission form** link, and entering the details of your errata. Once your errata are verified, your submission will be accepted and the errata will be uploaded on our website, or added to any list of existing errata, under the Errata section of that title. Any existing errata can be viewed by selecting your title from http://www.packtpub.com/support.

Piracy

Piracy of copyright material on the Internet is an ongoing problem across all media. At Packt, we take the protection of our copyright and licenses very seriously. If you come across any illegal copies of our works, in any form, on the Internet, please provide us with the location address or website name immediately so that we can pursue a remedy.

Please contact us at copyright@packtpub.com with a link to the suspected pirated material.

We appreciate your help in protecting our authors, and our ability to bring you valuable content.

Questions

You can contact us at questions@packtpub.com if you are having a problem with any aspect of the book, and we will do our best to address it.

1
Introduction

Welcome to the jQuery 1.4 Animation Techniques: Beginner's Guide book. Over the course of the book we'll look at each and every method that produces or controls animations available in the jQuery JavaScript library. We'll see how the methods are used, the arguments they are able to accept, and the different behavior they produce. We'll also look at how to use a range of accompanying resources including selected jQuery plugins and the jQuery UI library.

In this introductory chapter, we'll look at the following topics:

◆ A brief history of animation on the Web
◆ Why animating your UIs is important
◆ Animation methods provided by jQuery
◆ The template file used by each of the examples
◆ A basic animation example

Animation on the Web

In 1989 Compuserve released GIF89A, an enhanced version of the popular GIF image format which allowed a sequence of frames to be stored as a single image and played by supporting software.

The GIF format was already popular on what passed for the Internet in those days (remember, the World Wide Web didn't even exist until 1991) due to its small file size, lossless compression, and wide support. The enhanced version, which allowed animations that anyone could create themselves provided they had supporting software, quickly became popular also.

In addition to animated GIFs, browser vendors added support for proprietary HTML elements that handled animation natively, such as the `<blink>` and `<marquee>` elements, which added different animated effects to text.

Neither of these elements was particularly attractive or successful and the W3C, as well as leading industry accessibility and usability experts, advised against their use in most cases. Different browsers at the time supported one or the other of these elements but not both. Both elements were added by their respective vendors as part of the original browser wars.

In the late 1990s, popular browsers added support for a technique known as Dynamic HTML (DHTML), which allowed scripting languages to modify the contents of a page after the page had loaded. DHTML wasn't any single technology, but rather a collection of techniques (JavaScript, CSS, the DOM, and so on) that worked together to enable a basic level of interactivity and/or animation.

In fact, DHTML made it possible to create quite advanced animations, but restrictions in the early implementations of the required technologies, as well as hugely varying browser support, made DHTML tricky at best.

This era also saw the release and rise of Flash (and Shockwave, a competing technology that was eventually subsumed by Macromedia), a vector and raster graphics format that allowed audio and video streaming, frame-by-frame animation, and a host of other features. Flash quickly became popular and at the time of writing is still the number one format for web-based video, browser-based gaming, and advertising.

Gradual standardization of the DOM across (most) browsers, as well as the rise of JavaScript libraries such as jQuery, which abstracted away the differences that remained between browsers, have opened up animation to a much wider range of people than ever before. The term DHTML isn't often used these days because of its connotations with poor support between browsers, but the underlying principles and techniques that drive many interactive and animated sites remain similar.

Today, in addition to the animations made plausible and accessible by JavaScript libraries we have much newer, much more exciting possibilities with CSS3 and native HTML elements such as the `<canvas>` element, which provides complete pixel-level control over an area of the page. We'll be looking at some CSS3 animation techniques, as well as the `<canvas>` element in more detail towards the end of the book. Flash-based animation is on the decline for the first time this century, and new technologies are poised on the horizon.

The power of animated UIs

Modern operating systems use animations constantly to engage their users and to create a more compelling computing experience. Used in the right way, animations provide assistance to the users of the system, to lead and guide them through different tasks, provide context or feedback, and reinforce positive actions.

A good example of this is the way that applications are minimized in Windows 7, or OSX—the application appears to squish down into the icon on the taskbar/dock, which shows the user where to go when they want to return to the application. It's the simple details like this that can be the most effective.

Good animations can lend an air of sleek professionalism to an interface and make it appear more advanced or more modern. Apple's iPhone (or iPad) is a perfect example—the seamless use of subtle animations and transitions within the operating system and its applications allow the user to connect with the device in a profoundly satisfying and immersive way. Anything that appears or disappears is faded smoothly in or out, and menus and content panels slide in or out from the top or the sides. Sudden events can unsettle or distract users, but a well-timed animation can help to make them aware that something is happening or something is about to happen.

Be warned however—badly executed, clumsy, or overly pointless animations can do the opposite, making your interface appear basic, poorly designed, or inferior. No animation can be better than poor animation. Even if your application works perfectly, superfluous animations can leave your users feeling frustrated and cause them to forgo your application or website.

Desktop computers and a rapidly growing number of mobile and hand-held devices are easily powerful enough to handle quite complex animations, and with integrated hardware acceleration and more refined CSS3 and HTML5 making its way into the latest browsers, the possibilities of what can be achieved on the Web are increasing exponentially.

When to use animations

Animations can make a great impression and enhance the user experience in the following situations:

- When showing or hiding windows, pop ups, and content panels
- When something is moved to a different area of the window or page
- When something has changed state on the page as a result of the action of the user
- When something is transitioning between different states
- To lead the user to a specific call to action or bring their attention to something important

When not to use animations

Too many animations or animations in unnecessary places can be damaging. Try and avoid animations, or at least give them serious consideration, in the following situations:

◆ When an action needs to be repeated very frequently by the user

◆ Where the capabilities of the devices known to use the system are likely to be incapable of displaying the animation adequately

◆ On time-sensitive actions or processes

Bear in mind that these are guidelines only, not laws which must be obeyed at all costs, and they are certainly not definitive. There are few situations where animations should never, ever be used and few situations where they must always be used.

Use your judgment to determine whether an animation is suitable for your application or page and its intended audience. If possible, give your users the chance to enable or disable animations based on their own personal preferences.

Animation checklist

Before implementing an animation in our pages or applications, consider the following checklist of questions:

◆ Is the animation appropriate for your target users?

◆ Is the animation practical?

◆ Does the animation add value or enhance the user experience?

◆ Will the animation run at appropriate speeds on the devices that are most likely to be used?

If you can answer yes to all of the above, the animation will probably be a positive feature. If you answered no to any of these questions, you probably need to stop and think about what you are trying to achieve by adding the animation, and whether or not it could be better achieved in some other manner.

Animating with jQuery

jQuery provides a range of animation methods natively, without the use of additional effects libraries or plugins. There are however, many plugins contributed from the online community, including jQuery UI, the official UI library for jQuery, which extend jQuery's animation capabilities. Natively, jQuery provides methods that add sliding and fading behavior with minimal configuration, and which work cross-browser. It also exposes methods related to managing the animation queue, and provides a means for creating custom animations that work on almost all numerical CSS styles. Over the course of this book, we'll look at every animation method that the library contains in detail. These methods are listed below:

- `animate()`
- `clearQueue()`
- `delay()`
- `dequeue()`
- `fadeIn()`
- `fadeout()`
- `fadeTo()`
- `fadeToggle()`
- `hide()`
- `queue()`
- `show()`
- `slideDown()`
- `slideToggle()`
- `slideUp()`
- `stop()`
- `toggle()`

All in all, it gives us a powerful and robust environment to easily add almost any type of animation that we can conceive.

Animation is also a popular theme for plugins, with many available plugins that bring different types of animations to our fingertips, for instant implementation with minimal configuration. We'll look at several plugins later in the book.

The template file

Each of the example files we'll create throughout the course of this book will rely on a common set of elements. Rather than repeatedly showing these same elements in every single code section and example in the book, I'll show you them just once now:

```
<!DOCTYPE html>
<html lang="en">
  <head>
    <meta charset="utf-8">
    <title></title>
    <link rel="stylesheet" href="css/.css">
      <!--[if lte IE 8]>
```

```
      <script src=
        http://html5shiv.googlecode.com/svn/trunk/html5.js"></script>
      <![endif]-->
  </head>
  <body>
    <script src="js/jquery.js"></script>
    <script>
      (function($){


      })(jQuery);
    </script>
  </body>
</html>
```

Downloading the example code

You can download the example code files for all Packt books you have purchased from your account at http://www.PacktPub.com. If you purchased this book elsewhere, you can visit http://www.PacktPub.com/support and register to have the files e-mailed directly to you.

Save a copy of this file now and call it template.html. This is the base file that we'll use for every single example, so when we start working through the examples and I say "add the following markup to the <body> of the template file", I mean insert it directly between the opening <body> tag and the first <script> tag in the template file, as shown above. Whenever we add any JavaScript to the template file, it will be added within the anonymous function in the second <script> tag.

Let's just take a look at what the template file contains. We start out with the HTML5 doctype declaration as we'll be using plenty of HTML5 elements in our examples. We also set the lang attribute of the <html> element to en, and <meta> tag with its charset attribute to utf-8, neither of which are strictly required but are nevertheless best practice.

Next comes an empty <title> element, to which we can add the name of each example, and a <link> element with an incomplete href, ready for us to add the name of the stylesheet that each example will use.

Because current versions (prior to version 9) of Internet Explorer don't support any HTML5 elements, we need to use Remy Sharp's html5shiv script to make this browser use them correctly. We can link to the online version of this file for convenience using a conditional comment that targets all versions of IE lower than version 9. Feel free to download html5.js and store it locally if you plan on playing with the examples in IE while disconnected from the Internet.

To get the most out of the examples throughout the book, it would probably be wise to upgrade to the latest stable release versions of the most common browsers, which at the time of writing are Firefox 3.6.13, Chrome 9.0, Safari 5.03, and Opera 11, although expect these to change quite rapidly.

At the time of writing, Internet Explorer 9 is available in beta release and is scheduled to go to full release at some point in early 2011. IE9 does support a lot of HTML5 and CSS3, so using the `html5shiv` file may not be required.

The `<body>` of the page is empty except for some `<script>` tags. We'll obviously use jQuery in every example, so the first tag links to that. The current version of jQuery is 1.5 at the time of writing (but like the browser versions, this is likely to change pretty quickly!).

In the second `<script>` tag we have an empty function, into which all of the example JavaScript code we write will go. We pass the `jQuery` object into our anonymous function and alias it to the `$` character. Although not strictly necessary (except in the example where we create a jQuery plugin), this is another good habit to get into.

Creating a project folder

So that's the template file that we'll be referring to and using in the code examples throughout the book. Let's also take a moment to look at the folder structure that the example files use. Create a project folder and call it `jquery-animation` or similar. Within this, create three new folders and call them `css`, `img`, and `js`.

The HTML pages we create will go into the `jquery-animation` folder alongside the subfolders. All of the CSS files we create will go into the `css` folder and all of the images that we use in the examples will go into the `img` folder. The jQuery library and any additional script files we use or create will go into the `js` folder. This is also the directory structure you'll find if you download and unpack the accompanying code archive containing all of the examples.

A basic animation example

Let's look at a basic example of the kind of animation that can help reassure our visitors that something is happening. If the user performs an action, and the results are not displayed immediately, feedback that their action is in the process of being executed is a helpful use of animation. This is what we will end up with at the end of the example:

In the previous screenshot we can see the loading indicator centered beneath the trigger `<button>`. It features three separate loading bars which sequentially light up to show that something is happening. Each bar is styled slightly differently.

Time for action – creating an animated loader

In this example we'll create a simple animated loading indicator that we can start when a particular process is initiated, and stop once the process has completed.

1. Open up the template file that we just looked at and add the following `<button>` to the `<body>` of the page (this should go before the `<script>` elements):

```
<button id="go">Initiate the action</button>
```

2. Next, in the empty function in the second `<script>` element at the bottom of the page, add the following code:

```
var loader = $("<div></div>", {
    id: "loader"
}).css("display", "none"),
bar = $("<span></span>").css("opacity", 0.2),
loadingInterval = null;

for (var x = 0; x < 3; x++) {
bar.clone().addClass("bar-" + x).appendTo(loader);
}

loader.insertAfter("#go");

function runLoader() {
  var firstBar = loader.children(":first"),
  secondBar = loader.children().eq(1),
  thirdBar = loader.children(":last");

  firstBar.fadeTo("fast", 1, function(){
    firstBar.fadeTo("fast", 0.2, function() {
      secondBar.fadeTo("fast", 1, function() {
        secondBar.fadeTo("fast", 0.2, function() {
          thirdBar.fadeTo("fast", 1, function() {
            thirdBar.fadeTo("fast", 0.2);
          });
        });
      });
    });
  });
```

```
  };

$("#go").toggle(function() {
  loader.show();
  loadingInterval = setInterval(function() {
    runLoader(); }, 1200);
}, function() {
  loader.hide();
  clearInterval(loadingInterval);
});
```

3. Save the file as `loading.html` in the main project folder (`jquery-animation`). Finally, we'll need to add a few basic styles to the example. Create a new file in your text editor and add to it the following code:

```
#loader { margin:10px 0 0 36px; }
#loader span {
  display:block; width:6px; float:left; margin-right:6px;
  border:1px solid #336633; position:relative;
  background-color:#ccffcc;
}
#loader .bar-0 { height:15px; bottom:-20px; }
#loader .bar-1 { height:25px; bottom:-10px; }
#loader .bar-2 { height:35px; margin-right:0; }
```

4. Save this file in the `css` folder as `loading.css`.

What just happened?

The `<button>` hardcoded onto the page is used to show and hide the loading animation. This is done purely for the purpose of this example. In an actual implementation, we'd show the loading animation at the start of a load operation, when new content was being added to the page for example, and then hide it again once the operation was complete.

The first thing we do inside the outer function is set some variables. We create a new `<div>` element as a container for the loader, using an object literal as the second argument to the `$()` (`jQuery()`) method to give it an `id` of `loader`. We then set its style to `display:none` with jQuery's `css()` method so that it is not immediately visible.

We also create a new `<span>` element, which will be used as a template to create the three individual loading bars. We set its opacity to `0.2` (20% opaque), also using the `css()` method. jQuery normalizes this style for us so that it works correctly in Internet Explorer. The last variable, `loadingInterval` will be used to store the `id` of an interval so that we can clear the interval when we need to. We set this to `null` initially as the interval has not yet been set.

Once our variables have been defined and initialized, we then execute a short `for` loop, with just three iterations. Within this loop we clone the span element we created, give it a class name for styling purposes, and then append it to the container. Once the three loading bars have been added to the container, we insert the container after the `<button>`.

Next we define a function called `runLoader`. This is the function that will be repeatedly called by the interval. The function doesn't run until the button is clicked. Within this function we cache the selector for each of the three individual bars and then run a series of nested functions.

We first increase the first loading bar to full opacity using the `fadeTo()` jQuery animation method. This method takes a string indicating the speed of the animation as its first argument, the opacity that the element should be faded to as its second argument, and a callback function as the third argument. The callback function is executed as soon as the animation ends.

In the callback function, we then fade the first loading bar back to its original opacity of 0.2. We supply another callback function to this method call, and within this callback function we animate the second loading bar to full opacity, and then back to its original opacity. The process is repeated for the third loading bar.

Finally, we use the jQuery `toggle()` method to add two functions which will be executed alternately each time the `<button>` is clicked. In the first function, we show the loader and then set the interval that repeatedly calls the `runLoader()` function. In the second function, we hide the loader and clear the interval.

Pop quiz – basic animation with jQuery

1. Thinking about what we discussed earlier regarding when and when not to use animations, when would be an appropriate time to use this animation?

    a. When there is a browser-intensive operation taking place

    b. When there is a delay between something being requested from the server and the request returning from the server, but where the processing required by the browser is minimal

    c. As an alternative to a Flash animation

    d. When animated GIF images are not supported

2. What arguments are used with jQuery's `fadeTo()` method?

    a. An integer representing the ending opacity

    b. An object containing configuration options for the animation

c. A string or integer representing the speed or duration of the animation as the first argument, the ending opacity of the target element, and optionally a callback function to be executed when the animation ends

d. No arguments are required

Have a go hero – extending the loading animation

I mentioned that we could use the loading animation when making requests and waiting for a response. Try using it with jQuery's AJAX methods, showing the loader just before making the request, and hiding it again once the response has been processed. The JSONP example, which retrieves images of cats, on the jQuery website (at `http://api.jquery.com/ jQuery.getJSON/`) makes a great test case, although depending on the speed of your connection, the loader may not be visible for very long.

Summary

In this introductory chapter, we looked at a brief history of animation on the Web including how it began, early HTML elements and browser support, the rise of Flash, and the direction it's heading in the not too distant future.

We also looked at how animations can be used in a user interface to enhance the user experience. We saw some guidelines as to when animation should and shouldn't be used and looked at some of the things we should consider when implementing animations.

We closed the chapter with a basic example looking at a loading animation. In this example, we used the `fadeTo()` jQuery method to change the opacity of elements on the page, and a simple interval to "play" the animation. We didn't cover the method in full detail, but we saw one example of how it can be used. We'll look at this method in more detail in the next chapter, which covers all of the fading animations provided by jQuery.

2

Fading Animations

In this chapter we'll be looking at the most basic types of jQuery animations, in which the element being animated gradually appears or disappears. There are several jQuery methods that deal with fading and we'll look at each of them in turn throughout the chapter. These methods are:

`fadeIn()`

`fadeOut()`

`fadeTo()`

`fadeToggle()`

`show()`

`hide()`

`toggle()`

In this chapter, we will learn:

◆ How to create simple animations with the `fadeIn()`, `fadeOut()`, and `fadeToggle()` methods

◆ How to control the ending opacity value of the animation with the `fadeTo()` method

◆ How to create fading animations with the `show()` and `hide()` methods

◆ How to simplify our code with the `toggle()` methods

Fading animations

The `fadeIn()` and `fadeOut()` methods perform the least complex animations available via jQuery. They simply adjust the opacity of selected elements to either show or hide the element, and can be used with no additional configuration. The `fadeToggle()` method is almost as simple, but does provide some basic logic to check the selected element's current state.

Elements that are hidden with `display:none` will be set to their correct display type, (either `display:block` for block-level elements or `display:inline` for inline elements) where possible at the start of a `fadeIn()` animation.

An element's natural display type is used wherever possible, so hidden `<li>` elements are set to `display:list-item`, and hidden `<td>` elements are set to `display:table-cell`. IE however, has been known to have issues fading `<tr>` elements. In IE8 (and lower) for example, the `<tr>` is shown immediately when the `fadeIn()` method is used, even with a large duration.

Elements that are set to `display:block` (or are set to another display type but nevertheless visible on the page) will be set to `display:none` at the end of a `fadeOut()` animation. Elements will switch between their visible and non-visible states when the `fadeToggle()` method is used.

Elements that are to be shown using the `fadeIn()` method must be initially hidden with `display:none`; while elements that are hidden with `visibility:hidden`; for example, will remain hidden at the end of the animation.

In their simplest forms, these methods can be used without any additional configuration. We can simply call the methods on any collection of selected elements without using any arguments:

```
jQuery(elements).fadeIn();
jQuery(elements).fadeOut();
jquery(elements).fadeToggle();
```

When no arguments are provided, the animations will have the default duration of 400 milliseconds and the default easing of `swing`.

Configuring the animations with arguments

With arguments, the fading methods may take the following form, (square brackets denote optional arguments):

```
jQuery(elements).fadeIn([duration], [easing], [callback]);
jQuery(elements).fadeOut([duration], [easing], [callback]);
jQuery(elements).fadeToggle([duration], [easing], [callback);
```

We can control the duration of the animation using the duration argument to specify either an integer in milliseconds or one of the strings `slow` or `fast`, which are shortcuts for durations of 600 or 200 milliseconds, respectively.

We can also supply `0` as the duration argument, which will effectively disable the animation. It's unlikely that we'd need to do this as it would be more efficient to not use an animation at all, but it is useful to know. I should point out that the fade will still occur; it will just happen over a duration of 0 milliseconds.

The duration argument relates to the length of time the animation takes to run, not the speed of the animation. Therefore, a higher value will mean a slower, longer animation and not a faster, shorter animation.

The easing argument can be changed from its default value of `swing` to `linear`, which causes the animation to progress at the same speed throughout the animation. The default, `swing`, causes the animation to start slowly, speed up slightly, and then slow down towards the end of the animation.

The number of easing types can be greatly increased using plugins. We'll look at the extra easing types added by jQuery UI later in the book.

We may supply a callback function (either a function reference or an anonymous function, with the latter being more common-place). This callback function will be executed after the animation ends for each element in the selection, so it may be triggered more than once if more than a single element is being animated.

jQuery's Unified Animation API

In addition to the fading methods looked at in this chapter, it is worth noting at this stage that *any* of the animation methods exposed by jQuery can accept the strings `slow` or `fast` as the value of the duration argument, and they will always equate to durations of 600 or 200 milliseconds, respectively.

Any other strings that are supplied will be ignored and will cause the animation to take its default duration of 400 milliseconds (as if no duration argument had been supplied). Any integer, representing an actual length of time in milliseconds, can also be supplied.

Additionally, all jQuery animation methods can have easing configured, and all can accept a callback function as an argument. Each of the animation methods work and are used in the same way; it is just the effect which differs. This makes using the methods easy and intuitive.

A useful point to note is that the arguments do not need to all be provided when only the callback function is required. If we don't need to set the duration or easing arguments, we can just supply the callback function and jQuery will still execute it at the end of the animation.

Enhancing simple CSS hover states with fadeIn

It is standard practice to add hover-states for the items in a navigation menu using CSS, but with jQuery we can progressively enhance simple CSS hover states into full-on animations that give a much more attractive and professional effect when hovered.

In this example, we will see how to:

- Disable standard CSS hovers when JavaScript is enabled
- Add the additional HTML markup required for the animations
- Implement attractive `fadeIn()` animations triggered by hovering

We'll end up with a navigation menu in which the hover-states are animated into view instead of being shown instantly, as shown in the following screenshot:

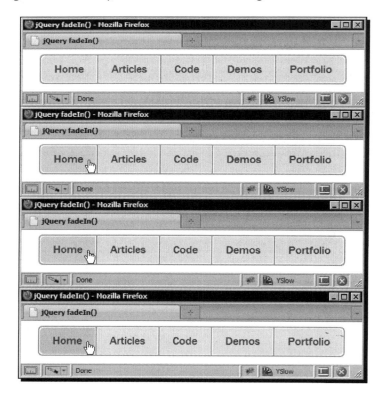

The previous screenshot shows how the hover-state is applied to one of the menu items over a short period of time, instead of instantly, as it would normally be with pure CSS, The animation proceeds from top to bottom in the previous picture.

Time for action – adding the underlying markup and styling

To begin with, we need to create the elements that will be used by the example and the styling to set their visual appearance.

1. Add the following underlying markup for our navigation menu to the template file we created in *Chapter 1, Introduction*:

```
<nav>
  <ul class="purecss">
    <li><a href="#" title="Home">Home</a></li>
    <li><a href="#" title="Articles">Articles</a></li>
    <li><a href="#" title="Code">Code</a></li>
    <li><a href="#" title="Demos">Demos</a></li>
    <li class="last">
      <a href="#" title="Portfolio">Portfolio</a>
    </li>
  </ul>
</nav>
```

2. Save the page in the `jquery-animation` directory as `fadeIn.html`.

3. We'll also need to link to a custom stylesheet for this example. Add the following code to the `<head>` of the page:

```
<link rel="stylesheet" href="css/fadeIn.css">
```

4. Next we should create the stylesheet we just linked to. In a new file, add the following code:

```
body { text-align:center; }
nav {
  display:inline-block;
  font:normal 18px "Nimbus Sans L", "Helvetica Neue", "Franklin
  Gothic Medium", Sans-serif; border:2px solid #aaa; -moz-border-
  radius:7px; -webkit-border-radius:7px; border-radius:7px;
}
nav ul { list-style-type:none; padding:0; margin:0; }
nav li { float:left; border-right:2px solid #aaa; }
nav a {
  display:block; padding:10px 20px; position:relative; color:#333;
```

```
    text-decoration:none; background-color:#eee;
    border:1px solid #fff;
}
nav span {
    display:none; width:100%; height:33px; padding-top:10px;
    position:absolute; top:0; left:0; background-color:#ccc;
}
nav .purecss a:hover { background-color:#ccc; }
nav li.first a {
    -moz-border-radius:7px 0 0 7px;
    -webkit-border-top-left-radius:7px;
    -webkit-border-bottom-left-radius:7px;
    border-radius:7px 0 0 7px;
}
nav li.first span {
    -moz-border-radius:7px 0 0 7px;
    -webkit-border-top-left-radius:7px;
    -webkit-border-bottom-left-radius:7px;
    border-radius:7px 0 0 7px;
}
nav li.last { border-right:none; }
nav li.last a {
    -moz-border-radius:0 7px 7px 0;
    -webkit-border-top-right-radius:7px;
    -webkit-border-bottom-right-radius:7px;
    border-radius:0 7px 7px 0;
}
nav li.last span {
    -moz-border-radius:0 7px 7px 0;
    -webkit-border-top-right-radius:7px;
    -webkit-border-bottom-right-radius:7px;
    border-radius:0 7px 7px 0;
}
```

5. Save this file as `fadeIn.css` in the `css` folder within our project folder.

What just happened?

We use the HTML5 `<nav>` element as the logical container for our navigation menu. The menu itself is created from a simple unordered list, where each link is made from an anchor element within a list item. This is the simple, semantic structure that will be rendered by default. Additional enhancements will be made in our script.

Most of the styles we used in this example are purely for the layout and appearance of this example and can be changed to suit your implementational requirements. What's important is that the hover states for the navigation links are provided using the class name `pure-css` attached to the outer `<ul>` element.

We do use a CSS3 style in this example, which some readers may not be familiar with. We'll be looking at CSS3 in much more detail towards the end of the book but, we'll cover this one for the benefit of those that have not used it before.

The CSS3 style we used was the `border-radius` style, which gives the element rounded corners in supporting browsers. Few browsers currently support the true `border-radius` CSS3 style property (at the time of writing, only Opera supports this style property natively), but Firefox and Webkit-based browsers do support it with their vendor-prefixes, `-moz-` and `-webkit-` respectively.

Internet Explorer 8 and below do not support the `border-radius` style property, or any variant of it, and these browsers do not provide their own vendor-prefixes to use. However, the menu itself and the example code, still work perfectly in these browsers. The only difference is, they have square corners and not rounded ones.

If this is acceptable, then everything is fine, and you have super-simple rounded corners without the additional HTTP request(s) and payload that images would require in supporting browsers. If rounded corners are critical to your application or interface, we can always provide these to IE using conditional comments.

Time for action – scripting the animation

Now we just need to add the script that will animate our simple navigation menu.

1. Add the following code within the anonymous function at the bottom of the `<body>`:

```
var ul = $("nav ul");

ul.removeClass("purecss");

ul.find("a").each(function(){
  var a = $(this);
  a.append("<span>" + a.text() + "</span>");
});

ul.find("a").hover(function() {
  $(this).find("span").fadeIn("slow");
}, function() {
  $(this).find("span").hide();
});
```

What just happened?

The first thing we did was cache a reference to the `<ul>` located inside our `<nav>` element. We'll be referencing it several times so it is more efficient to only select it from the DOM a single time. For performance reasons, it is generally best to minimize the number of DOM operations that are carried out.

We then remove the `purecss` class from the element so that our standard CSS hover states are no longer effective. We use JavaScript to do this so the basic hovers still work if JavaScript is disabled in the browser.

Next we insert a new `<span>` element into each of the anchors. We'll perform the animation on each of these `<span>` elements so that anchors themselves remain clickable and functional. As the `<span>` elements are styled to fit exactly within their parent `<a>` elements, we also add the text from the anchor into the `<span>`.

Finally, we use jQuery's `hover()` method to attach `mouseover` and `mouseout` event handlers to the `<a>` elements. This method accepts two functions; the first is executed on `mouseover`, the second on `mouseout`.

In the first function, we select the `<span>` inside the `<a>` that was hovered on and call the `fadeIn()` method specifying the slow string. In the second function, we simply hide the `<span>` again. When we run the page in a browser, we find that the hover states are activated when we hover over the list items. It's a great effect, and one I use frequently when building clients' sites. In this example, we have a potential issue in that the link text is duplicated in the `<span>` elements that are added to each link. It would be trivial to hide the link text when the `<span>` is made visible, which we could do using a callback function supplied as an argument to the `fadeIn()` method.

Pop quiz – using fadeIn

1. Which strings can be passed into the method as the first argument?

    a. The strings `short` or `long`, which refer to the duration of the animation

    b. The strings `low` or `high`, which refer to the opacity that the element is faded to

    c. The strings `slow` or `fast`, which refer to the duration of the animation

    d A hexadecimal string specifying the `background-color` of the element

2. What else can be passed into the method?

    a. A string specifying the easing function to use for the animation, and a callback function to be executed once the animation ends

    b. An object containing additional configuration options

    c. An array containing additional configuration options

    d. A callback function to be executed at the start of an animation and a callback function to be executed at the end of the animation

Have a go hero – doing more with fadeIn

In this example, we used the `fadeIn()` method to show the hidden `<span>` elements on `mouseover`, but hide the element straight away on `mouseout`. Have a go at extending the example so that the elements are faded out on `mouseout` instead of being hidden straight away using the `fadeOut()` method.

Fading elements out

The `fadeOut()` method is syntactically identical to `fadeIn()` in that it accepts the same arguments and adjusts the opacity of the selected element, except that with the `fadeout()` method, the target element is hidden instead of being shown. Let's look at this method in action with a brief example.

When elements need to be removed from the page, using a subtle fade out can be much more effective than just removing the element in question. We may have an overlay of some description, like a dialog box for example, on the page which can be closed by the visitor. Instead of having it disappear instantly, we can animate its disappearance smoothly.

In this example, we'll look at the following aspects of using `fadeOut()`:

◆   Hiding an element with the `fadeOut()` method

◆   Using a numerical argument to control the duration

◆   Running additional code once the animation completes

This is how our dialog will disappear from the page:

In the previous screenshot, we see the dialog gradually fading from view once the `<button>` has been clicked. The animation proceeds from top to bottom in the previous image.

Time for action – creating the dialog

We'll start again by creating the underlying markup that the dialog is built with and add any necessary styling.

1. First, add the following code to the `<body>` in a fresh copy of the template file:

```
<div id="dialog">
<header>A dialog box of some description</header>
Lorem ipsum etc, etc.
<footer><button>Ok</button></footer>
</div>
```

2. We'll also need to link to a stylesheet in the `<head>` of the page:

```
<link rel="stylesheet" href="css/fadeOut.css">
```

3. Save this page as `fadeOut.html` in the main project folder. The code for the stylesheet is as follows:

```css
#dialog {
    background-color:#fff; width:300px; padding:10px;
    font:normal 14px "Nimbus Sans L", "Helvetica Neue", "Franklin
        Gothic Medium", Sans-serif;
    border:1px solid #aaa; -moz-border-radius:7px;
    -webkit-border-radius:7px; border-radius:7px;
    -moz-box-shadow:2px 2px 5px #000;
    -webkit-box-shadow:2px 2px 5px #000;
    box-shadow:2px 2px 5px #000;
}
#dialog:after {
    content:""; height:0; display:block; clear:both;
    visibility:hidden;
}
#dialog header {
    display:block; padding-bottom:5px; margin-bottom:10px;
    font-weight:bold; font-size:16px; border-bottom:1px solid #aaa;
}
#dialog footer {
    display:block; padding-top:10px; margin-top:10px;
    border-top:1px solid #aaa;
}
#dialog button { float:right; }
```

4. Save this in the `css` folder as `fadeOut.css`. To perform the `fadeOut()` animation, we'll need just a tiny bit of JavaScript. Inside the anonymous function in the second `<script>` element at the bottom of the `<body>`, add the following code:

```
$("#overlay button").click(function() {

  $("#overlay").fadeOut(500, function() {

    $(this).remove();
  });
});
```

What just happened?

In our code, we attach a click handler to the `<button>` using jQuery's `click()` helper method. The anonymous function we specify as an argument is executed whenever the button is clicked. Within this function we select the dialog using its `id` and call the `fadeOut()` method on it using a numerical argument of `500` milliseconds instead of one of the acceptable strings.

We also specify a callback function as the second argument to the `fadeOut()` method. As there is only a single element in the selection (the element with an `id` of `overlay`), this function will be executed only once. Inside this callback function, the `this` keyword is set to the current element, so we can easily manipulate it from within the callback.

All the function does is remove the dialog from the DOM. This behavior would be appropriate when the element to be removed was a one-time-only dialog that would either not be shown again during the current session, or would be generated again from scratch by the system when required.

We'll see the dialog when we load the page. In a proper implementation, it would probably be centered in the viewport and be absolutely positioned so that it appears to float above the page (additionally the CSS3 shadow that we used would reinforce this impression). It would also more than likely be modal, so the underlying page would be obscured, or otherwise shielded from interaction, until the dialog is closed.

To avoid unnecessary cluttering of the example however, our dialog is alone on an empty page. Clicking the `<button>` will cause the dialog to fade away and then be removed from the page.

The animation is fairly quick and less jarring than instantaneous removal of the dialog, but I should point out that fading animations can often annoy users if they are too frequent, take too long to complete, or are felt to be completely unnecessary.

For example, the application may generate a large number of dialogs during any single session and if the user has to repeatedly wait half a second every time they close a dialog, they may perceive that the animation is wasting their time or otherwise acting as a barrier to their interaction.

I believe it is best to pass control of whether the animation is used or not back to the visitor, and provide an option to disable the animation if the system is going to be generating them on a regular basis. This way, users will be able to remove the effect if they do feel that it is a barrier.

Pop quiz – using fadeOut

1. What happens if the integer `0` is supplied as the value of the duration argument?

    a. The animation occurs instantly

    b. The animation runs at the default speed of 400 milliseconds

    c. Animations with jQuery are disabled globally

    d. A script error is thrown

2. How can we access the element that was animated within a supplied callback function?

    a. The callback function is passed a reference to the element that was animated

    b. By reselecting it from the DOM

    c. Using the jQuery property `animatedElement`

    d. Using the `this` keyword (optionally wrapped in jQuery functionality (`$(this)`)

Have a go hero – doing more with fadeout

A popular implementation that makes use of fade-out animations is a "growl" style messaging system where feedback is provided in the form of messages that pop up in the viewport before fading away; why not create your own growl style messaging system that utilizes the `fadeOut()` method.

Fading PNGs in IE

In the previous examples, we've looked at fading in and out using CSS background colors to illustrate the effect. We could easily extend it to include background images instead, which generally work just as well, if not better, with this effect.

One thing to watch out for when using background images in conjunction with fading animations however is that problems can be encountered with the display of the images when the animations are viewed in Microsoft's Internet Explorer.

It is known as the black-border problem and causes a black aura to be displayed around the image when a PNG with alpha-transparency (semi-opacity) is used as the background image. It really only affects IE8 as there are work-arounds that can be used to fix the issue in both IE7 and IE6.

Here's a screenshot of the problem:

The previous screenshot shows a `fadeout()` animation in progress. The jagged black border around the logo is the issue we face in IE and is caused by Microsoft's proprietary `filter` properties, which jQuery uses to set the opacity (and produce the fade) in IE.

There are several different fixes for this issue including:

◆ Fading the container of the element instead of the element directly

◆ Giving the container, or the element that is faded, a background color

Whichever solution works best will depend on the situation at hand. An alternative solution, but which only fixes the issue in both IE6 and IE7, involves using the `DD_BelatedPng.js` library, to display alpha-transparent PNGs using VML. Unfortunately this doesn't work in IE8, so sometimes a combination of fixes may be required.

The following screenshot shows an image in IE8 fading out correctly:

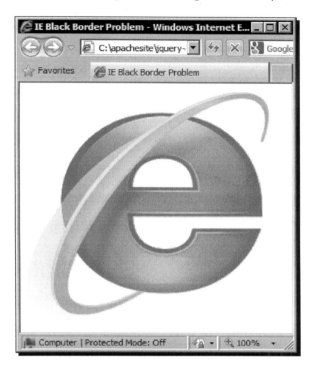

We can see in the previous screenshot that there are no black borders around the image while it is fading out in IE8. In this example, I put the PNG into a container, set the background-color of the container to white, and faded out the container.

Using fadeToggle() for convenient state-checking logic

The fadeToggle() method exposed by jQuery will either fade an element in, or fade it out depending on the current state of the element. Elements that are visible will be faded out, while elements that are hidden will be faded in.

When elements are faded out with fadeToggle(), they will automatically be set to display:none at the end of the animation so that the element doesn't affect the layout of the page.

Time for action – showing and hiding with fadeToggle()

As before, we first create the HTML markup and CSS styling required by the example.

1. Open up a new copy of the template file and add the following code to the `<body>` of the page:

```
<form>
  <label for="name">Enter your name:
    <input id="name" name="name" type="text">
    <span id="help"></span>
    <span id="helpText">Your name. You know, the thing that people
      call you by</span>
  </label>
</form>
```

2. Save this page as `fadeToggle.html`. Next we need to add a few styles. In a new page in your text editor, add the following code:

```
form { width:280px; margin:100px auto; position:relative; }
input { margin-left:5px; }
#help {
  display:block; width:16px; height:16px; margin-top:3px;
  float:right; cursor:pointer;
  background:url(../img/help.png) no-repeat;
}
#helpText {
  display:none; width:100px; height:75px; padding:12px 18px;
  position:absolute; left:115px; top:-90px;
  font:normal 12px "Nimbus Sans L", "Helvetica Neue",
    "Franklin Gothic Medium", Sans-serif;
  background:url(../img/bubble.png) no-repeat;
}
```

3. Save this file as `fadeToggle.css` in the `css` folder. Finally, let's add the script that will make the example work. Within the anonymous function in the second `<script>` element, add the following code:

```
$("#help").click(function() {
  $("#helpText").fadeToggle();
});
```

What just happened?

On the page we have a simple `<form>` containing a label, an `<input>`, and a couple of `<span>`elements. The first `<span>` is used as an icon, while the second `<span>` contains help text to prompt the user for the value the `<input>` expects.

The CSS is used mostly to lay out the example page, and to give the `<span>` elements their required sizing and background images. The most important rule is setting the help text to `display:none`, although this isn't actually critical like when using the `fadeIn()` method as the `fadeToggle()` method will work on both visible and hidden elements.

In the script we simply call the `fadeToggle()` method on the second `<span>` each time the first `<span>` is clicked. The page will alternately show and hide the help text on each click of the help icon.

With this method, the natural display style of elements is not maintained. When our `helpText <span>` is shown, it will have its `display` set to `block`, as opposed to a `<span>` element's natural `display` type `inline`. In this example, this actually helps us—if the `<span>` were set to its natural `inline` display, our widths and padding would not work correctly. But it is something we need to be aware of when using the method.

Here's how the page should look after clicking the icon the first time:

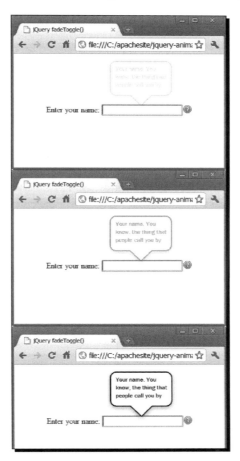

In the previous screenshot, we see our help text gradually fading into view. Once the icon is clicked a second time, the animation will be shown in reverse, with the element going from full opacity to full transparency.

Pop quiz – using fadeToggle()

1. Why should we use caution when using `fadeToggle()`?

   a. Because elements still affect the flow of the page once they have been faded out

   b. Because of the black border problem in Internet Explorer

   c. Because the natural display style of an element is not always maintained, so inline elements will be set to `display:block` when they are faded in

   d. Because the method does not check the current state of the element it is called on

Have a go hero – extending fadeToggle()

In this example we faded an element that has an alpha-transparent PNG as its background image. This means that the page will suffer from the black border problem in all current versions of IE. Have a go at using one of the fixes described earlier in the chapter to fix the problem.

Greater opacity control with fadeTo()

With the `fadeTo()` method we can use the same arguments as before, but we can also control the final opacity of the element that is being animated. This is very useful for situations where we don't want to fade an element all the way in or out.

Unlike the `fadeIn()` or `fadeOut()` methods, the `fadeTo()` method must be supplied with both a duration and an ending opacity at least. The duration argument accepts the same values as with the `fadeIn()`, `fadeToggle()`, and `fadeOut()` methods.

The ending opacity is provided as the second argument and should be a decimal number between the integers 0 and 1, which represents the percentage of opacity, with 0 being fully transparent, and 1 being fully opaque. 50% opacity is therefore specified as `0.5`.

If easing is required, this should be provided as the third argument and can take the strings `swing` (the default) or `linear`, like the other methods we have looked at so far. A callback function to be executed for each selected element may also be supplied.

The `fadeTo()` method is used in the following way:

```
jQuery(elements).fadeTo(duration, ending-opacity, [easing],
    [callback]);
```

Animating to partial opacity

In this example we have a table in which certain rows can be removed. When one of the rows is selected for removal by the user, we can animate the row to partial opacity while requesting confirmation of the removal. In this section we will cover the following topics:

◆   The required arguments of the `fadeTo()` method

◆   Setting a specific ending opacity

◆   A work-around for fading table-rows in IE

Once a table row has been faded, it will appear like this:

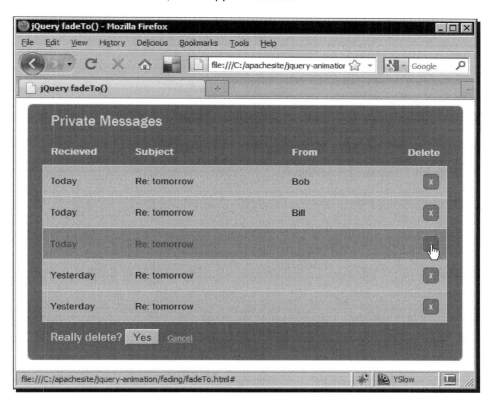

The middle row of the table shown in the previous screenshot has been faded to 50 % opacity.

Time for action – creating the example page

This example requires significantly more HTML than before, although we still add this, as well as the styling first.

1. Begin by adding the following example markup to our template file:

```
<div id="messageList">
  <header>Private Messages</header>
  <table summary="This table lists the personal messages you
                  have received">
  <tr><th class="rec">Recieved</th><th class="sub">Subject</th><th
    class="from">From</th><th class="del">Delete</th></tr> <tr><td
    class="rec">Today</td><td class="sub">Re: tomorrow</td><td
    class="from">Bob</td><td class="del"><a href="#" title="Delete
    Message">x</a></td></tr>
    <tr><td class="rec">Today</td><td class="sub">Re:
      tomorrow</td><td class="from">Bill</td><td class="del">
      <a href="#" title="Delete Message">x</a></td></tr>
    <tr><td class="rec">Today</td><td class="sub">Re:
      tomorrow</td><td class="from"></td><td class="del">
      <a href="#" title="Delete Message">x</a></td></tr>
    <tr><td class="rec">Yesterday</td><td class="sub">Re:
      tomorrow</td><td class="from"></td><td class="del">
      <a href="#" title="Delete Message">x</a></td></tr>
    <tr><td class="rec">Yesterday</td><td class="sub">Re:
      tomorrow</td><td class="from"></td><td class="del">
      <a href="#" title="Delete Message">x</a></td></tr>
  </table>
</div>
```

2. Save this page as `fadeTo.html` in the main project folder.

3. To create the stylesheet for this example, add the following code in a new file in your text editor:

```
#messageList {
  width:540px; padding:10px 20px; margin:auto;
  font:normal 14px "Nimbus Sans L", "Helvetica Neue", "Franklin
    Gothic Medium", Sans-serif;
  background-color:#666; border:1px solid #aaa;
  -moz-border-radius:7px; -webkit-border-radius:7px;
  border-radius:7px;
}
#messageList header {
  color:#eee; padding-left:10px; font-size:20px;
}
```

```
#messageList table {
  border-collapse:collapse; margin:10px 0; background-color:#666;
}
#messageList th, #messageList td {
  width:100px; padding:10px; color:#eee; text-align:left;
  border-bottom:1px solid #eee;
}
#messageList td { background-color:#ccc; color:#000; }
#messageList th.sub { width:220px; }
#messageList th.del { text-align:right; }
#messageList table a {
  padding:0 7px 2px; float:right; background-color:#ea3c37;
  color:#fff; text-align:center; text-decoration:none;
  border:1px solid #990000; -moz-border-radius:5px;
  -webkit-border-radius:5px; border-radius:5px;
}
.confirm { color:#eee; font-size:16px; }
.confirm button { margin:0 10px; }
.confirm a { font-size:12px; color:#ffcaca; }
```

4. Save this as `fadeTo.css` in the `css` folder.

What just happened?

The underlying HTML is relatively simple; we have an outer containing `<div>` within which reside a HTML5 `<header>` element and a `<table>`. Each row of the `<table>` corresponds to a received message. Don't forget to link to the `fadeTo.css` file in the `<head>` of the new page, as we have in previous examples.

As with previous examples, the CSS we use for this example is purely arbitrary and is used simply to make the example presentable. We use the CSS3 rounded corner style property again, to give a nice effect to the widget. Once again, these styles won't work in IE, but the worst that will happen is that it will have square corners.

Time for action – adding the behavior

Finally we can add the script that will make it all work. In the empty function at the bottom of the `<body>` element, add the following:

```
var messageList = document.getElementById("messageList"),
  messages = $("table", messageList),
  confirmDiv = $("<div></div>", {
    "class": "confirm",
    text: "Really delete?"
```

[39]

```
  }),
  remove = $("<button></button>", {
    id: "delete",
    text: "Yes"
  }).appendTo(confirmDiv),
  cancel = $("<a></a>", {
    href: "#",
    id: "cancel",
    text: "Cancel",
    title: "Cancel"
  }).appendTo(confirmDiv),

  deleteRow = function(e) {

    e.preventDefault();

    $(this).closest("tr").fadeTo(400, 0.5, function() {

      $(this).addClass("pre-delete");
      confirmDiv.clone().insertAfter(messages);
      messages.find("a").unbind();
    });
  };

  messages.find("a").click(deleteRow);

  $("#delete, #cancel").live("click", function(e) {
    e.preventDefault();

    if (this.id === "delete") {
      messages.find(".pre-delete").fadeTo(400, 0, function() {
        $(this).remove();
      });
    } else {
      messages.find(".pre-delete").removeClass("
        pre-delete").fadeTo(400, 1, function() {
        var el = $(this);
        if (el.css("filter")) {
          el[0].style.removeAttribute("filter");;
        }
      });
    }

    $(".confirm", messageList).remove();

    messages.find("a").click(deleteRow);
  });
```

What just happened?

Our script is a little longer than those in previous examples, but still relatively simple; let's step through what happens. First we get a reference to the outer container for our message widget. We get the element using the standard JavaScript `document.getElementById()` function. We can use this DOM node as a context for jQuery methods to make selecting elements from the DOM faster. Selecting elements by class name is not very efficient (even with jQuery), so being able to pass in a DOM node to a jQuery selector to tell jQuery where to begin for searching for the element makes our queries much faster than searching through the entire document each time we want to get an element using its class name.

We also store a reference to the `<table>` element as we'll need to refer to this element throughout the script. Instead of creating a new jQuery object and selecting the element each time we need to manipulate it, we create a single jQuery object representing the element (notice how we use our `messageList` variable as a context for the selection) and store it in a variable for use as many times as we require with no additional overhead.

Next we create a series of new elements for use later in the script. We create a container `<div>` and give it some attributes including a class name and some text. Note that the word `class` is surrounded with quotation marks to prevent Internet Explorer throwing script errors.

We also create a new `<button>` element and a new `<a>` element and give both of these some attributes too. The new button and anchor elements are appended to the new container. These elements are not added to the page however, they are kept in memory for use later on in the script.

Next we add an inline function stored in the `deleteRow` variable, which is used to handle clicks on the delete icons in each row of the `<table>`. Within this function we first use the `preventDefault()` JavaScript method to prevent the delete link being "followed" by the browser and jumping back to the top of the page. We then select the closest parent `<tr>` element and call the `fadeTo()` method specifying a duration of 400 milliseconds (the default) and an ending opacity of `0.5`.

We also supply a callback function that is executed when the animation ends. We use this function to add a class name to the row so that we can easily refer to it later on. We then create a copy of the container element (including the child elements we added to it) that we created at the start of the script using jQuery's `clone()` method. Copying these elements from memory is much more efficient than creating them from scratch each time the function is executed. The copy of the container is then inserted into the widget after the `<table>`.

To prevent other messages being selected for deletion (and a build-up of confirmation messages), we unbind the click handler from the delete links in each row. We don't need to select the links from the DOM at this point. We use the `messages` variable (containing a reference to the `<table>`) and jQuery's `find()` method to select the links without needing to create a new jQuery object.

Next we pass a reference to the `deleteRow` function that we just defined to jQuery's `click()` event-helper method. We don't provide the `deleteRow` function itself as an argument to the `click()` method this time, as it is easier and less repetitive to pass the function reference to the methods instead of defining it several times.

We then add a click handling function to the `<button>` and the `<a>` elements that exist in the confirmation panel and are inserted each time a delete icon is clicked. We use the `live()` method here so that we don't have to rebind to each handler whenever one of these elements are created.

Whether the `<button>` or the **Cancel** link is clicked, we first check the `id` of the clicked element (accessible via the `this` keyword) to determine which element was clicked. Because all we are checking is the `id` of the element, we don't need to wrap the `this` keyword in jQuery functionality (`$()`).If the `id` is `delete`, we know the button was clicked and can proceed with fading out the `<tr>` so that it is completely transparent, and then removing it from the page altogether using a callback function supplied as an argument to the `fadeTo()` method.

If the `id` is `cancel`, we know that the `<a>` element was clicked. In this case, we stop the browser from following the link with `preventDefault()`, remove the `pre-delete` class name from the `<tr>`, and then fade it back to full opacity.

We also use a callback function for this method too. Within it we check whether the element that was faded contains a `filter` style property, and if it does, we remove the `filter` attribute from the element. This fixes the issue with aliased text in IE which affects elements after they have been faded.

This is all we need to make our `fadeTo()` example work as intended in most browsers. Whenever one of the delete icons is clicked, the corresponding row is animated to 50% opacity and the confirmation is then displayed.

This requires the action be confirmed or canceled. When the **Cancel** link is clicked, the row is animated back to full opacity. When the `delete` `<button>` is clicked, the row is animated all the way to full transparency and then removed from the page.

Pop quiz – using fadeTo

1. Which arguments must be provided when using the `fadeTo()` method?

   a. The duration and easing arguments

   b. The ending opacity

   c. A callback function

   d. The duration and ending opacity

2. What format can these arguments take?

   a. They must be strings

   b. They must be arrays or objects

   c. They may be either strings or integers

   d. They must be functions that return the value in string format

Have a go hero – doing more with fadeTo

A great application of the `fadeTo()` method is when it is combined with a modal overlay. Often when a pop-up dialog is displayed, the underlying page is screened with a semi-transparent PNG. Instead of using an image why not obscure the underlying page by fading an element that covers the entire visible area of the page to semi-transparency instead.

Fading table-rows in Internet Explorer

If we run the previous example in any current version of IE (8 or below), we see that the example fails. Fading `<tr>` elements in IE simply does not work. However, all is not lost, with just a few tweaks and minor changes to the code we can get the example working in IE as well.

Time for action – fading table-rows in IE

This time we'll change the script slightly so that it works as intended in Internet Explorer.

1. Change the contents of the last `<script>` element in the `fadeTo.html` file that we created in the last example so that it appears like this (new or changed code is shown in bold):

```
var messageList = document.getElementById("messageList"),
  messages = $("table", messageList),

  confirmDiv = $("<div></div>", {
    "class": "confirm",
    text: "Really delete?"
  }),
  remove = $("<button></button>", {
    id: "delete",
    text: "Yes"
  }).appendTo(confirmDiv),
    cancel = $("<a></a>", {
    href: "#",
    id: "cancel",
```

```
        text: "Cancel",
        title: "Cancel"
    }).appendTo(confirmDiv),

    deleteRow = function(e) {

  var selector = (window.ActiveXObject) ? $(this).closest("tr").
  children() : $(this).closest("tr");

  selector.fadeTo(400, 0.5, function() {

        $(this).addClass("pre-delete");

    if(!$(".confirm").length) {
        confirmDiv.clone().insertAfter(messages);
        }

        messages.find("a").unbind();
      });
    };

messages.find("a").click(deleteRow);

$("#delete, #cancel").live("click", function(e) {

  if (this.id === "delete") {
    messages.find(".pre-delete").fadeTo(400, 0, function() {
      $(this).remove();

    if (window.ActiveXObject) {
      messages.find("tr").each(function() {
        var row = $(this);

        if(!row.children().length) {
          row.remove();
        }
      });
    }
      });
    } else {
      e.preventDefault();
      messages.find(".pre-delete").removeClass("pre-
        delete").fadeTo(400, 1, function() {
```

```
      var el = $(this);
      if (el.css("filter")) {
        el.css("filter", "");
      }
    });
  }

  $(".confirm", messageList).remove();
  messages.find("a").click(deleteRow);
});
```

2. Save the new file as `fadeToIE.html` in the main project folder.

What just happened?

Let's look at what changed in the new version of this example. The first difference is that in the `deleteRow` function, we store a reference to the element that we are going to fade in a variable called `selector` (storing jQuery objects in a variable like this is commonly known as caching a selector).

We check for the presence of the `ActiveXObject` on the `window` object. This object will only exist in IE and so is a useful thing to check for if we are looking to target just IE. If the object is found, we select the `<td>` elements within the target row instead of the row itself. If the object is not found, we select the `<tr>` itself (as we did in the previous example).

The other changes are in the click handler for the delete and cancel elements. All we do is check for the `ActiveXObject` again and if found, check each `<tr>` element to find which one is empty. One of the rows will be empty because it is the `<td>` elements that get removed in IE. The empty row is then removed.

We have also added a callback function to the animation when the **Cancel** link is clicked. When IE animates the `<td>` elements to half opacity, the `clearType` effect that IE uses for font-smoothing is removed. This is a consequence of the `filter` being applied, which is how jQuery sets the opacity in IE.

Within the new callback function, we check for the presence of the `filter` attribute, and if it is found, we set to an empty string to disable it. The text will then return to its anti-aliased state.

When we run the new version of the file in IE we should find now that it works as expected in all current versions. Even though we are fading the individual cells in IE instead of the rows, visually it is the same. Because of the conditional checking we do, this version of the example should continue to work in other browsers such as Firefox, Chrome, or Safari as well.

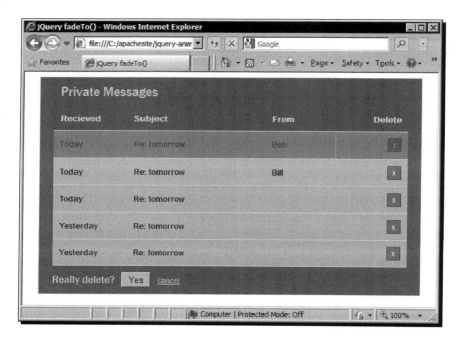

As we can see in the previous screenshot, the fades are now working in IE. However, IE still doesn't like fading the <td> elements. It displays a border between the **From** and **Delete** columns, even though these cells do not have a border style set on them. IE8 also loses borders when the element is faded back to full opacity. This is not a problem in IE7, and can be fixed in IE8 by removing the background-color from the <td> elements.

Showing and hiding

By default, jQuery's show(), hide(), and toggle() methods show or hide the selected element by manipulating its display style property. This is an instantaneous effect and does not constitute an animation.

Usually these methods do not take any arguments, but we can trigger an animation by supplying an additional argument which represents either the duration, or the easing of the animation. We can also add a callback function in keeping with the animation methods we have looked at so far.

The methods can take the following format:

```
jQuery(elements).show(duration, [easing], [callback]);
jQuery(elements).hide(duration, [easing], [callback]);
```

These animations are a step-up in complexity from simple fading because instead of just animating the opacity of the selected elements, the width and height of the element are animated too. Syntactically, the methods are very similar however.

This means that the selected elements will grow in size as they appear, or shrink as they disappear. We have little direct control over this however, and can set only the duration or easing of the animations.

The direction in which the selected element will grow or shrink can be manipulated indirectly via CSS however. If the selected element is positioned using its `left` and `top` style properties, the animation will proceed from the top-left corner, growing to the right and down. If it is positioned using its `right` and `bottom` style properties, it will grow up and to the left instead.

When an animation is not proceeding in the way in which you expect, it is always worth ruling out any interference from CSS. Styles can affect how an element is animated, so if you aren't getting errors in the JavaScript console, always check that the CSS isn't the cause of unexpected behavior. I have lost count of the hours spent checking and rechecking scripts, only to find that a tiny tweak to the CSS fixes the problem entirely.

Like the `fadeIn()` method, elements that are to be animated using the `show()` method should initially be hidden with `display:none`. Elements being shown will be set to `display:block`, or whatever other display mode is acceptable for the element in question.

Flyout submenus with jQuery's show/hide logic

Let's take a look at a basic example of the `show()` and `hide()` methods in action. We'll create a simple vertical navigation menu which features fly-out submenus that are animated in and out of view. We'll look at the following aspects of these methods:

◆ How to trigger an animation using the `show()` or `hide()` methods

Our fly-out menu will be displayed like this:

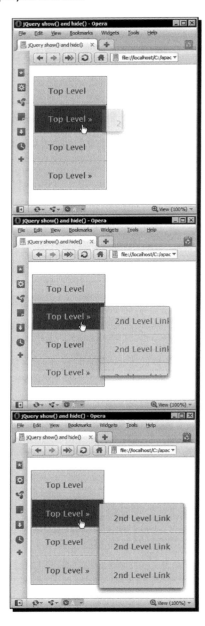

In the previous screenshot, we see the submenu fade in as well as grow outwards as the mouse pointer hovers over a top-level menu item. As before, the animation proceeds from the top to the bottom in the screenshot.

Time for action – animations with show/hide

It's always easiest to add any required HTML and basic CSS first, before adding any behavior with JavaScript, and this example is no exception.

1. Add the following markup to the `<body>` of the template file:

```
<nav>
  <ul>
    <li><a href="#" title="Top Level Link">Top Level</a></li>
    <li><a href="#" title="Top Level Link">Top Level &raquo;</a>
      <ul>
        <li><a href="#" title="2nd Level Link">2nd Level
          Link</a></li>
        <li><a href="#" title="2nd Level Link">2nd Level
          Link</a></li>
        <li><a href="#" title="2nd Level Link">2nd Level
          Link</a></li>
      </ul>
    </li>
    <li><a href="#" title="Top Level Link">Top Level</a></li>
    <li class="last"><a href="#" title="Top Level Link">Top Level
      &raquo;</a>
      <ul>
        <li><a href="#" title="2nd Level Link">2nd Level
          Link</a></li>
        <li><a href="#" title="2nd Level Link">2nd Level
          Link</a></li>
        <li><a href="#" title="2nd Level Link">2nd Level
          Link</a></li>
      </ul>
    </li>
  </ul>
</nav>
```

2. Save this file as `showHide.html`. The following CSS should go into a new file:

```
nav {
  font:normal 18px "Nimbus Sans L", "Helvetica Neue", "Lucida Sans
    Unicode", Sans-serif;
}
nav a {
  display:block; padding:20px 30px; text-decoration:none;
  background-color:#ddd; color:#333; border:1px solid #fff;
}
nav a:hover { background-color:#333; color:#ddd; }
```

```
nav ul {
  padding:0; float:left; list-style-type:none;
  border:1px solid #666;
}
nav ul li { position:relative; border-bottom:1px solid #666; }
nav ul li.last { border-bottom:none; }
nav ul ul {
  display:none; position:absolute; top:10px; left:150px;
  z-index:999; -moz-border-radius-bottomleft:7px;
  -moz-border-radius-bottomright:7px;
  -webkit-border-bottom-left-radius:7px;
  -webkit-border-bottom-right-radius:7px;
  border-bottom-left-radius:7px; border-bottom-left-radius:7px;
  -moz-box-shadow:0px 4px 10px #666;
  -webkit-box-shadow:0px 4px 10px #666;
  box-shadow:0px 4px 10px #666;
}
nav ul ul li a { white-space:pre; }
nav ul ul li:last-child a {
  -moz-border-radius-bottomleft:7px;
  -moz-border-radius-bottomright:7px;
  -webkit-border-bottom-left-radius:7px;
  -webkit-border-bottom-right-radius:7px;
  border-bottom-left-radius:7px; border-bottom-left-radius:7px;
}
```

3. Save this in the `css` folder as `showHide.css` and don't forget to link to it in the `<head>` of the page.

4. Finally, we need to add the jQuery methods that will show and hide our submenus when appropriate. Add the following code to the anonymous function at the bottom of the `<body>`:

```
var subMenuParent = $("nav ul ul").parent();

subMenuParent.mouseenter(function() {

  $(this).find("ul").show("fast");

});

subMenuParent.mouseleave(function() {

  $(this).find("ul").hide("fast");

});
```

What just happened?

The simple markup for this example consists of the `<nav>` container element and a series of nested unordered lists.

As I mentioned, the way in which the selected element grows when it is acted upon by the `show()` method is dictated by the CSS positioning that it uses. In this case, we'd like the menu to grow down and to the right, so we position the submenus using their `top` and `left` properties. The submenus are also hidden initially with `display:none;` as is required for an element to be shown with the `show()` method.

In the script, we first select each of the nested `<ul>` elements and then navigate up to their respective parent `<li>` elements. We then use the `mouseleave()` and `mouseenter()` event helper method to attach the events. This is so that only list items containing submenus will have the listeners attached.

In the anonymous functions supplied to these listeners, we navigate down to the nested `<ul>` and call the `show()` or `hide()` method as appropriate, triggering an animation by supplying the string `fast`.

When we run this page in a browser, we should find that hovering the mouse pointer over one of the list items that contain a submenu cause the submenu to be animated into full size and opacity.

Pop quiz – using show and hide

1. Which argument should be provided to trigger animations when using the `show()` or `hide()` methods?

   a. A callback function

   b. An object containing the duration and easing for the animation

   c. An integer or string specifying the duration of the animation, and/or a string specifying the easing

   d. An array containing the duration and easing for the animation

2. How is the direction of growth in the animated element controlled?

   a. By its CSS positioning properties

   b. By setting a property of the jQuery object

   c. By passing an object containing values for left and top properties into the method

   d. It cannot be controlled

Animated toggling

jQuery provides a `toggle()` method, which can be used in several different ways depending on which arguments are passed to it. Normally it is used to execute two or more functions alternately, but like the `show()` or `hide()` methods, it can be used to create animations when a duration or easing is supplied as an argument.

When animations are required from the `toggle()` method, we should simply supply a duration and/or an easing argument, which may take the same numerical or string based format as the other animation methods we have looked at so far.

The same rules about CSS positioning also apply to the `toggle()` method, so the direction of animation is easy to customize. The duration argument may be of string or integer types, and a callback function may be provided if required. The easing argument should be in string format.

The `toggle()` method works in a similar way to the `fadeToggle()` method that we looked at earlier in the chapter. It contains logic that checks the current state of the element and either shows, or hides the element based on this.

The method should be seen merely as a convenient short-cut that may be beneficial in some basic situations. From a performance perspective, the `show()` and `hide()` methods are marginally more efficient as there is no internal check on the current visibility of the element being animated. It is effectively a combination of the `show()` and `hide()` methods.

Time for action – replacing show and hide with toggle

In this example, we'll change our `showHide.html` page so that the submenus are displayed (or hidden) with `toggle()` instead of using `show()` and `hide()`.

1. All that needs to change is the script:

```
subMenuParent.mouseenter(function() {

    $(this).find("ul").toggle("fast");

});

subMenuParent.mouseleave(function() {

    $(this).find("ul").toggle("fast");

});
```

2. Save the changes as `toggle.html`.

3. We should find when we run the page that it works in the same way as it did using the `show()` and `hide()` methods. In this example, using the `toggle()` method has done nothing for us; we haven't reduced our own code at all.

4. In some applications, if we were using the click event to either show or hide an element for example, we would be able to reduce the complexity of our event handlers and rely on `toggle()` to do it for us.

Have a go hero – doing more with toggle

Why not change the last two examples so that the vertical `<nav>` menu uses click events instead of hover events. You'll get to see when `toggle()` can be used to simplify your code.

Summary

In this chapter, we looked at some of jQuery's most basic animation methods. The fade class of methods are the simplest animation methods found in jQuery, animating nothing except the opacity of the selected element(s).

The `show()`, `hide()`, and `toggle()` methods can also be used to perform animations but alter the dimensions of the element as well as its opacity. All of these methods are simple to use and require few or no additional configuration in order to run.

We looked at the following methods in this chapter:

- `fadeIn()`
- `fadeOut()`
- `fadeTo()`
- `fadeToggle()`
- `show()`
- `hide()`
- `toggle()`

We also covered the following points:

◆ The fade methods work by altering the opacity and display properties of the selected elements. All methods may accept an optional duration argument in string or integer format except for the fadeTo() method, with which the argument is mandatory.

◆ Transparent PNGs in IE can end up with unsightly black borders when they are faded in or out with jQuery, but there are ways to avoid the issue in all current versions of IE. We also saw that fading table elements can cause problems in IE.

◆ By default, the show(), hide(), and toggle() methods occur instantaneously. However, they can all be used to create animations by supplying a duration and/ or easing argument(s).The duration argument may take integers representing milliseconds, or the strings slow or fast which correspond to durations of 600 or 200 milliseconds.

◆ All animations have a default easing of swing, although we can change this to linear for an animation that proceeds at a uniform pace.

◆ CSS can have a huge impact on how animations proceed, as we saw when we looked at how to control the direction that the selected elements grow or shrink when using show() or hide().

One thing to note with all of the fading animations is that it can cause issues with clearType text in IE; clearType is disabled when the animation runs so any text in the element being animated becomes aliased. There are several different work-arounds for this issue which involve removing the filter attribute once the animation has run.

Now that we've covered the most basic types of jQuery animations and got an idea about how they run, we can move on to look at the animation queue and the methods we have at our disposal for managing it.

3
Managing Animations

Like most of the methods that jQuery makes available to us, the effect, or animation, methods can be chained together in sequence, like this:

```
jQuery(elements).fadeIn().slideDown()
```

When several animation methods, such as `fadeIn()`, *and so on, are chained together and called on the same element or collection of elements, they are placed into a queue to be executed one after the other in series rather than all executing simultaneously in parallel. The standard animation queue created for an animated element is called* `fx`, *although custom queues can easily be created.*

jQuery gives us several methods that make working with and manipulating an element's `fx` queue extremely easy. These methods include:

- ◆ `clearQueue()`
- ◆ `delay()`
- ◆ `dequeue()`
- ◆ `queue()`
- ◆ `stop()`

The techniques that we'll learn in this chapter include:

- ◆ Viewing the items in an element's queue
- ◆ Counting the items in an element's queue
- ◆ Preventing queued effects from executing
- ◆ Delaying the start of the next effect in the queue

- Replacing the existing queue with a new queue
- Calling the next function in a custom queue
- Stopping the current effect without executing the rest of the queue
- Globally disabling all animations
- Changing the frame rate of animations globally

The jQuery object itself also contains several properties that can be useful when working with animations. These include:

- `jQuery.fx.off`
- `jQuery.fx.interval`

 The queue is not restricted to storing animation methods; other methods can also be added to the queue. We will only be looking at the `queue()` method from an animation perspective here.

Working with the queue

When several effects are chained together, the first effect is begun straight away. The remaining effects are stored as functions in an array in the element's `fx` queue. As the effects are stored in an array, we can call standard JavaScript array methods on it to manipulate it, and examine its properties to find out additional information about it.

We can determine how many functions are in the queue by looking at the `length` property of the array, or we can call standard functions such as `push()`, `pop()`, or `reverse()` on it to perform various operations on the items (functions) in the array. It is unlikely that this would be required in most normal situations however.

An important point to note about the queue is that the first effect method called on an element *does not* get stored in the queue, so the length of the queue at the start of the operation will always be one less than the total number of effect methods called on the element.

The queue executes on a first-in-first-out basis, with the last function stored in the queue executing last. The default `fx` queue for an animated element will run automatically and each function contained within it will be called automatically by jQuery. The string `inprogress` is used as the first item in the default `fx` queue as a flag indicating that the queue is currently being run.

A custom queue that we create ourselves will not run automatically and we must ensure that each item in the queue is executed one after the other. jQuery provides several ways of doing this including the dequeue() method, which executes the next function in the queue, and a callback function that we can pass into functions in the queue. We'll look at both of these techniques later in the chapter.

Viewing the queue

To view the queue we simply call the queue() method; no arguments are required but we can optionally supply the queue name if it differs from the default fx. When the method is called, it returns an array containing the remaining functions in the queue. The queue() method may be used in the following form:

```
jQuery(elements).queue([queue name], [new queue], [callback]);
```

In addition to the name of the queue, we can also supply either a new queue, or a single callback function. The new queue, if supplied, should take the form of an array of functions. The new queue will replace the existing queue entirely. Passing an empty array to the queue() method will clear the queue. A callback passed to the queue() method will be added to the end of the queue and executed last after the functions originally in the queue.

A common use of the queue() method is to look at the length property of the returned array to determine how many functions are left to run; but if we need to, we can also look at each function individually by calling the toString() JavaScript function on any item in the array (except for item 0 which will simply display the string inprogress).

Most functions in the returned array are function literals, however, the "next" item in the queue is not available via the queue() method. The contents of item 0 in the default fx queue will always be the string inprogress as this is the animation currently being run.

Time for action - viewing the queue

Let's look at a basic example of the use of the queue() method and the type of results we can expect to obtain.

1. In the <head> of our template file add the following code:

```
<style>
  #fader { width:100px; height:100px; background-color:#000; }
</style>
```

2. Finally, in the anonymous function at the bottom of the second `<script>` element, add the following code:

```
$("#fader").fadeOut(function() {

    console.log($(this).queue());

}).fadeIn().fadeOut().fadeIn();
```

3. Save the page as `queue.html`.

What just happened?

Typically, we'd use an external stylesheet for any styling, but for a single selector and three rules, it seems pointless creating a separate file. In the script we have four effects chained together to form a simple animation in which our `<div>` element is simply faded out and back in twice. We provide a callback function as an argument to the first of our effect methods, within which we call the `queue()` method.

You'll need to use a browser that has a console for this example, such as Firefox. Here's what the output looks like in Firebug:

In the previous screenshot, we can see that the array making up the queue has been output to the console for us to view. There are three items left in the queue when the method is called. The first item in the array is the string `inprogress`. The remaining two items are the queued methods that have not yet run.

If we wish to see how many functions are left in the queue (including the one that is in progress), we could change the `console.log` line to this:

```
console.log($(this).queue().length);
```

This code would show the following output in Firebug's console:

This time our console shows numerically how many items are left in the queue, as shown in the previous screenshot.

We can use other array methods on the queue if we wish (although this would rarely be useful), such as `push()` or `pop()` to add or remove items for example. We can also get a single item from the queue if we wish, by adding square braces and an index number after the call to `queue()`:

```
console.log($(this).queue()[1]);
```

As shown above, this time the value of the second item is output to the console. As I mentioned earlier, we can see the actual contents of the function using the `toString()` JavaScript function:

```
console.log($(this).queue()[1].toString);
```

Running this code produces the following output:

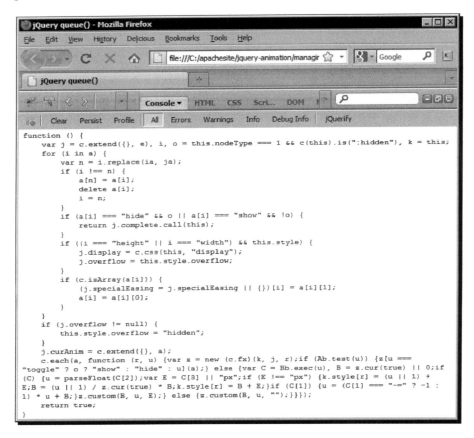

The code shown in the previous screenshot won't make much sense to the casual observer as it's been minified, but it's the contents of jQuery's `fadeout()` method.

Pop quiz – viewing the queue

1. What is the easiest way of determining the number of functions in the queue?

   a. Using the `length()` method

   b. Using the `length` property

   c. Counting them in Firebug

   d. By looking at the `effectsLeftToRun` property of the animated element's `fx` queue

2. What does the `queue()` method return?

    a. A function

    b. A JSON object

    c. An array

    d. The number of effects left to run

Adding a function to the queue

Appending a new function to the end of the queue is a trivial matter and we don't even need to use a new method. We just need to pass the new function, or a function reference, to the `queue()` method as an argument.

When we pass a single function into the `queue()` method and we are working with the default `fx` queue, jQuery will automatically call the function for us using the `dequeue()` method. We haven't looked at the `dequeue()` method yet, but we will cover this a little later in the chapter.

Time for action – adding a single function to the queue

Let's see how easy it is to add a new function to the end of the queue.

1. Update the script in `queue.html` so that it appears as follows:

    ```
    $("#fader").fadeOut(function() {

      $(this).queue(function() {
        $(this).css("backgroundColor", "green");
      });

    }).fadeIn().fadeOut().fadeIn();
    ```

2. Save the new file as `queueAdd.html`.

What just happened?

By supplying a callback function as the optional second argument to the `queue()` method, we add the function to the end of the animation queue. When we run the code in a browser the animation should proceed as normal; then once the effects have run, the `<div>` will turn green.

We don't need to supply the name of the queue unless it differs from the default `fx` queue. In this simple example, we just change the `background-color` of the target element, but in reality a function of any complexity can be appended to the queue.

jQuery handles calling this function for us when we add it to the default `fx` queue. When working with custom queues we will need to dequeue the function manually using the `dequeue()` method, which we'll look at shortly.

Pop quiz – adding new items to the array

1. What is the easiest method of adding a new function to the queue?

    a. Supplying a callback to the `queue()` method

    b. Using the JavaScript `push()` function

    c. Using the `add()` method

    d. Using the `jQuery.fx.queue` property

Using a callback function to keep the queue moving

In the last example, the function that we added to the queue was added as the last function in the queue, so ensuring that the queue kept running was not necessary. Sometimes however we may need to add several functions to the end of the queue, and will therefore need to execute the additional functions ourselves.

Time for action – keeping the queue running

1. Change the `<script>` element at the bottom of the `queueAdd.html` so that it appears as follows (new code is shown in bold):

    ```
    $("#fader").fadeOut(function() {

      $(this).queue(function(next) {
        $(this).css("backgroundColor", "green");
        next();
      }).fadeOut();

    }).fadeIn().fadeOut().fadeIn();
    ```

2. Save this file as `queueInsert.html`.

What just happened?

This time we have chained an extra call to the `fadeout()` method to the end of the `queue()` method inside the callback function for the first `fadeout()` method. We still pass an anonymous function to the `queue()` method, but this time we supply an argument to this function as well.

The argument we supply to the function passed into the `queue()` method is called `next`. jQuery will treat whatever we pass in as a function and all we have to do is call this function from within the callback function and that will make sure the next function in the queue is executed.

The function we pass into the callback function passed to the `queue()` method doesn't have to be identified as `next`, it can be any accepted function name. In this example, we call the next function after setting the `background-color` of the `<div>` to `green`.

This will cause the extra `fadeout()` method to be executed last, so when we run this example in a browser, we should find that the green `<div>` disappears at the end.

Pop quiz – keeping the queue running

1. What can we use to call the next function in the queue when inserting a callback function into the queue using the `queue()` method?

    a. A Boolean value of `true` passed into the callback function as an argument

    b. A string containing the word `next`

    c. A function

    d. An integer of -1

Replacing the queue

Sometimes adding a single function to the end of the queue may not be enough—we may wish to replace the queue entirely. This behavior is also managed entirely by the `queue()` method.

Time for action – replacing the queue

1. We'll update the `queue.html` file once again for this example. We'll need another style rule in the `<style>` element in the `<head>` of the page:

    ```
    #fader span {
      display:none; width:100%; height:100%; position:absolute;
        left:0;
      top:0;
    }
    ```

2. We should also add `position:relative;` to the `#fader` selector.

3. Now change the script at the bottom of the page to this:

```
<script>
  (function($){

    function changeColor(element, newColor) {

      $("<span>").css("backgroundColor",
        newColor).appendTo(element).fadeIn(500, function(){

        element.dequeue();

      });
    }

    var fader = $("#fader");

    var newQ = [
      function() { changeColor(fader, "yellow") },
      function() { changeColor(fader, "orange") },
      function() { changeColor(fader, "green") },
      function() { changeColor(fader, "red") },
      function() { changeColor(fader, "blue") },
      function() { changeColor(fader, "purple") }
    ];

    $("#fader").fadeOut(function() {

      //replace queue
      $(this).queue(newQ);

    }).fadeIn().fadeOut().fadeIn();

  })(jQuery);
</script>
```

4. Save the file as queueReplace.html.

What just happened?

First we define a single function which accepts two arguments. The first is a jQuery object referring to the animated element and the second is a new color.

We then create a new <span> element, set its background-color to the color passed into the function, append it to the element passed in to the function, and then fade it into view.

We pass a callback function into the `fadeIn()` method used with the new `<span>`. In this function, we just call the `dequeue()` method. This is required for the next function in the queue to be executed; if we don't do this, only the first function in our custom queue will be executed.

Next we define our replacement queue, after first caching a selector for the `#fader` element. The new queue is defined as an array where each item consists of an anonymous function which in turn invokes our `colorChange()` function, passing in the cached selector and a CSS color name.

Finally, we call an effect method on the target element and queue up some additional effects as we did before. This time when we call the `queue()` method, we supply our custom queue, which replaces the default `fx` queue created by the chained fade methods.

When we run the page in a browser, we see that the first effect is applied, and then our queue of custom `colorChange` functions is called. The two fade effects that would have been in the default `fx` queue originally are not executed.

Pop quiz – replacing the queue

1. What do we need to pass to the `queue()` method in order to replace the queue?
    a. A string containing a function reference
    b. The `dequeue()` method
    c. An array
    d. A Boolean

2. What is an easy way of clearing the default `fx` queue, other than using the `clearQueue()` method?
    a. Passing the string `clear` to the `queue()` method
    b. Passing the integer `0` to the `queue()` method
    c. Passing the Boolean `false` to the `queue()` method
    d. Passing an empty array to the `queue()` method

Ensuring custom queues iterate correctly

When we create custom queues, the chained methods are not automatically called for us. This is something we need to do manually and is handled using the `dequeue()` method as we saw in the previous example.

When called, it will remove the next function in the queue and execute it. It's a simple method, with few arguments, and is used in a very specific manner. The method may take a single optional argument which is the name of the queue to execute the next function from:

```
jQuery(elements).dequeue([queue name]);
```

The queue name is only required if we are working with a queue other than the default `fx` queue. We didn't need to provide the name of the queue in the previous example in the last section because we replaced the animated element's default `fx` queue. The `dequeue()` method has the same effect as calling the `next()` function that we used to keep the queue moving in the `queueInsert.html` example from the last section.

Time for action – dequeueing functions

Let's change the `queueInsert.html` page so that it uses the `dequeue()` method instead of the `next()` function to keep the queue moving.

1. Change the code in `queueAdd.html` so that it appears as follows:

```
$("#fader").fadeOut(function() {

  $(this).queue(function() {
    $(this).css("backgroundColor", "green").dequeue();
  }).fadeOut();

}).fadeIn().fadeOut().fadeIn();
```

2. Save this version as `dequeue.html`.

What just happened?

This time we do not need to pass anything into the callback function passed to the `queue()` method. We simply chain the `dequeue()` method to the `<div>` after setting its `background-color` to `green`. This has the same effect as before and the green `<div>` will fade out at the end of the animation.

Stopping an animation

The `stop()` method can be used to stop an effect that is currently running on the selected element. In its simplest form, we may call the method without supplying any additional arguments, but if necessary we can supply up to two Boolean arguments. The method takes the following format:

```
jQuery(elements).stop([clear queue], [jump to end]);
```

The first argument clears the element's queue and the second forces the final state of the effect to be applied.

The `stop()` method behaves differently depending on whether there are any additional effects in the `fx` queue.

When the method is called and there are no functions in the queue, any effects that are currently running on the selected element(s) will simply stop and the element will remain in whatever state it reached during the animation.

If there are several functions in the queue however, the current animation will be stopped in whatever state it is in at the time, but then the remaining functions in the queue will be executed.

Take the following code for example:

```
$("#fader").fadeOut(5000).fadeIn().fadeOut().fadeIn();

$("#stop").click(function() {
  $("#fader").stop();
});
```

If the stop element is clicked while the first effect is running, the fader element will flicker as the remaining effects are applied one after the other.

To prevent the queued functions being executed, we can supply `true` as the value of the first argument. To force the element into its final state, we can also supply `true` as the value of the second argument. Both arguments default to `false`.

The `stop()` method can be really useful for preventing animation build-up. If an animation is triggered by clicking a button for example and the button is clicked repeatedly, the animation can run multiple times. Usually this behavior is undesirable and can be prevented using the `stop()` method.

 To see the differences between each variation of the `stop()` method, see the `stopTest.html` file in the accompanying code download for this book.

Time for action – preventing animation build-up using the stop method

In *Chapter 2, Fading Animations*, we used the `fadeIn()` method to enhance CSS hover states, but we didn't hide the hover state using `fadeOut()`. The reason for this is because the animations can quickly build up. If the mouse pointer is moved on and off one of the links repeatedly, the hover state will continue to fade in and out even after the mouse pointer moves away.

Fortunately, we can use the `stop()` method to prevent this from happening. In this section, we'll add `fadeOut()` effects to the navigation menu example from *Chapter 2, Fading Animations* and use the `stop()` method to prevent an effect build-up.

1. In `fadeIn.html`, change the `hover()` method so that it appears as follows:

```
ul.find("a").hover(function() {
  $(this).find("span").stop(true, true).fadeIn("slow");
}, function() {
  $(this).find("span").stop(true, true).fadeOut("slow");
});
```

2. Save this file as `stop.html`.

What just happened?

By calling the `stop()` method directly before applying the `fadeIn()` effect, we ensure that a build-up of effects does not occur and spoil the hover states. In order for the effects to work correctly, we supply `true` as the values of both the *clear queue* and *jump to end* arguments.

Pop quiz – stopping an animation

1. What does the first argument that can be passed to the `stop()` method determine?

    a. Whether or not the method should return `false`

    b. Whether or not the element should be removed from the page

    c. Whether or not the queue should be cleared

    d. Whether or not the queue should be replaced

2. What does the second argument control?

    a. - Whether or not the queue is cleared

    b. Whether or not the method returns the queue as an array

    c. Whether the element should be removed from the page

    d. Whether the element should be set to its final state

Delaying queue execution

As of jQuery 1.4 we can choose to delay the execution of the next function in the queue using the `delay()` method. We need to supply the duration as an argument to the method to tell it how long the delay before the next effect starts should be, and we can optionally supply the name of the queue to delay as an argument as well. The method is used in this format:

```
jQuery(elements).delay(duration, [queue name]);
```

The duration argument may be supplied as an integer representing the length of the duration in milliseconds, just like the effect methods we've covered so far, or it may be one of the strings `slow` or `fast` which correspond to the standard values. If no duration is provided, the queue will not be delayed, and if a string other than `slow` or `fast` is provided, the delay will be the default duration of 400 milliseconds.

The queue does not need to be directly manipulated in order to set a delay. All we need to do is chain the method between our animation methods, so an animation that fades an element in and out several times that required a delay could be constructed like this:

```
$("#fader").fadeOut().delay(2000).fadeIn().fadeOut().fadeIn();
```

Note that the `delay()` method is only supposed to be used with methods or functions in a queue, just like the `stop()` method, and cannot (and is not meant to) replace JavaScript's `setTimeout()` function.

Plugins

There are several great plugins that make working with both the `setTimeout()` and `setInterval()` native JavaScript functions quicker and easier. Just search the plugin repository for **setTimeout**.

Clearing the queue

As well as viewing the queue and manipulating its contents, we can also remove all of the functions from it entirely. jQuery provides the `clearQueue()` method allowing us to easily clear all functions in the specified element's queue.

Like `dequeue()`, this is a simple method that takes just a single optional argument:

```
jQuery(elements).clearQueue([queue name]);
```

This method is generally used with non-animation-based queues, when using the `stop()` method is not possible, and so will not be discussed further.

Passing an empty array to the `queue()` method will also clear the queue.

Useful properties of the jQuery object

The jQuery object contains a couple of properties that we can set which can be useful when creating animations. The jQuery (or $) object contains an `fx` property, which itself contains two properties related to animations which we can manipulate.

This `fx` object is not to be confused with the `fx` queues that are created by default for any element that has more than one animation method called on it in a chain. These individual `fx` queues do not contain the same properties that the jQuery `fx` property contains.

Globally disabling animations

One property of `fx` that we can set is the `off` property. This property contains a Boolean that is set to `false` by default, but which we can set to `true` to globally disable all animations on a page. The property is set using the following syntax:

```
jQuery.fx.off = true;
```

That's all we do need to do. If this is set at any point in our script, all elements that have animation methods attached to them will be set to their final state, as if the animation had already completed.

Changing the default frame rate

The other property of jQuery's `fx` that we can set is the `interval` property. This property accepts an integer and specifies the number of milliseconds between each frame of the animation. By default, it is set to 13, so an animation will have a frame-rate of about 76 frames per second.

To set this property, we just supply a different integer:

```
jQuery.fx.interval = 28
```

Setting the property to 28 like this would make the animation run at about 35 frames per second, making animations run almost half as smoothly.

Note that animations will still run over the same duration of time (whether that is the default 400 milliseconds, or another value set with the duration argument of an animation method) regardless of what this property is set to. However, an interval value that is lower, and therefore has a higher number of frames per second, will make animations appear smoother.

Also note that the lower we set the `interval` property, the more intensive animations will be. While the latest browsers will cope with these increased demands satisfactorily, older or slower browsers will struggle.

There must be no animations running when this property is set for it to take effect. Any animations that are running must be stopped.

Summary

While manipulating an element's `fx` queue directly may not often be required, when we do need to work with it, jQuery makes the process easy and transparent. With a collection of methods at our disposal, we can have full control over how the queue behaves. In this chapter, we looked at the following methods:

◆ `clearQueue()`
◆ `delay()`
◆ `dequeue()`
◆ `queue()`
◆ `stop()`

We also looked at the following properties of the jQuery object:

◆ `jQuery.fx.off`
◆ `jQuery.fx.interval`

In this chapter we found that:

◆ The contents of the queue and the number of items in the queue can be easily obtained using the array that's returned by the `queue()` method. We can also use standard JavaScript array methods, such as `push()` or `pop()`, to interact with the array.

◆ We can supply different arguments to the `queue()` method which make adding a single function to the queue, or replacing the queue entirely, a trivial matter.

◆ When working with custom queues, or when adding more than a single new function to the default `fx` queue, we will need to ensure that the queue keeps running and executing the remaining functions. We can do this using either the `dequeue()` method, or a function passed into a callback function.

◆ The `stop()` method will halt the currently-running animation and can be made to clear the queue and force the element into its final state if necessary using additional arguments.

◆ The `delay()` method allows us to add an interval, or delay, in between queued animations.

◆ The `clearQueue()` method is not designed to work with animations, when using the `stop()` method and `clearQueue` argument is more appropriate.

◆ We can globally disable all animations on a page by setting the `off` property of jQuery's `fx` property to `true`.

◆ We can change the global frame rate of animations using the `interval` property of jQuery's `fx` property.

Now that we've mastered the animation queue, we'll move back to looking at some more of jQuery's built-in effect methods. In the next chapter, we'll look at the sliding group of methods including `slideDown()`, `slideUp()`, and `slideToggle()`.

4

Sliding Animations

Another type of effect that is built into jQuery is the slide effect. Elements can be made to slide vertically so that they appear to open or close depending on their current state. There are three methods related to sliding that are exposed by jQuery:

```
slideDown()
slideUp()
slideToggle()
```

How each of these methods works will be explored thoroughly over the course of this chapter.

Some of the skills we'll learn include:

- ◆ Showing hidden elements with `slideDown()`
- ◆ Hiding visible elements with `slideUp()`
- ◆ How an element's CSS styling can influence sliding animations
- ◆ How we can save code with `slideToggle()`
- ◆ How to add easing effects to sliding animations
- ◆ How to deal with a common usability issue with sliding animations triggered by hover events

You should note that the sliding methods all work with the `display` style property of the selected element(s), and are used to either show or hide the element in question by sliding it open or closed.

Sliding elements into view

When an element is hidden from view using `display:none;` we can easily show the element using the `slideDown()` method. This method may take the following form:

```
jQuery(elements).slideDown([duration], [easing] [callback]);
```

The optional duration argument may take either integer or string formats just like the animation methods we have already looked at, and the default duration of 400 milliseconds will be used when no duration argument is supplied.

As before, an easing function may also be supplied as the second argument, and a callback function, if supplied, will be executed once for each selected element once the animation has completed.

The `slideDown()` method works by changing an element's `display` property from `none` to `block` in the same way that fade animations do. If an element requires a different display mode, such as `inline-block` for example, this will need to be set using the optional callback function, or by using a nested element within the element that has `slideDown()` called on it.

As well as the `display` property, the method also adjusts the target element's `height` property to gradually reveal the hidden element. The `height` of the target element is calculated by jQuery, so things that affect this, such as `padding` or `margin`, can affect how the animation displays as it runs.

Sliding an element that does have padding or margin applied to it can cause the animation to run unusually, with the elements inside the animated element also appearing to move. Padding or margin can also cause animations to be choppy or uneven when being run.

Elements that do not have fixed widths can also cause problems when animated with `slideDown()`, `slideUp()`, or `slideToggle()`. This can also cause a small jump at the end of a slide animation in some browsers.

If `margin` or `padding` *is* required, or if a fixed width is not possible, it is advisable to use a wrapper element in conjunction with the target element to run the animation on, or to give the required padding or margin. All of the sliding methods return the original jQuery object and so are perfectly safe for chaining. Additionally, the sliding effects will be stored in the selected element's `fx` queue when several are chained to a single element.

Time for action – creating a slide-down login form

In this example we'll see how easy it is to implement a login form that slides open when a link is clicked. It's common practice to include a login link at the top of a page, but usually the whole login form isn't shown. Instead, clicking the link will reveal an inline form that is hidden by default. The following screenshot shows how the page will appear with the login form open:

1. To begin with, add the following code to the `<body>` of our template file:

```
<header>
  <ul>
    <li>Already registered?</li>
      <li>
        <a id="login" href="login.html" title="Login">Login</a>
          <form>
            <fieldset>
              <legend>Login Form</legend>
                <label for="username">Username:<input
                  name="username" id="username"></label>
                <label for="password">Password:<input
                  name="password" id="password"
                  type="password"></label>
                <input name="remember" id="remember"
                  type="checkbox"><label for="remember">Remember
                  me:</label>
                  <button type="submit">Login</button>
            </fieldset>
          </form>
      </li>
  </ul>
</header>
```

2. Save the file as slideDown.html in the main project folder.

3. Next let's add the CSS for this example. In a new file in your text editor, add the following code:

```
header {
  display:block;
  font-family:Verdana, Arial, Helvetica, sans-serif;
}
header ul {
  margin:0; position:relative; float:right; list-style-type:none;
  font-size:11px;
}
header ul li { float:left; margin-top:10px; }
header ul li a {
  display:block; margin:-13px 0 0 10px; padding:11px 18px;
  -moz-border-radius:5px; -webkit-border-radius:5px;
  border-radius:5px; font-size:14px; color:#000;
}
header ul li a:hover, header ul li a:focus, header ul li a.on {
  padding:3px 10px; border:8px solid #666; background-color:#fff;
  text-decoration:none;
}
header ul li a.on {
  border-bottom:0; padding-bottom:10px;
  -moz-border-radius-bottomright:0; -moz-border-radius-
    bottomleft:0;
  -webkit-border-bottom-right-radius:0;
  -webkit-border-bottom-left-radius:0; border-bottom-right-
    radius:0;
  border-bottom-right-radius:0; position:relative; z-index:10;
  outline:0;
}
header form {
  display:none; width:260px; border:8px solid #666;
  -moz-border-radius:px; -moz-border-radius-topright:0;
  -webkit-border-radius:5px; -webkit-border-top-right-radius:0;
  border-radius:5px; border-top-right-radius:0;
  position:absolute; right:0; top:27px; z-index:5;
}
header fieldset { margin:0; padding:20px 10px 10px; border:0; }
header legend { display:none; }
header form label { display:block; float:right; font-size:14px; }
header form label:first-child { margin-bottom:10px; }
```

```
header form input {
  display:block; width:148px; margin:-2px 0 10px 8px; float:right;
}
header form input#remember { width:auto; margin:3px 0 0 10px; }
header form button {
  margin:10px -1px 0 0; float:right; clear:right;
}
```

4. Save this stylesheet in the `css` folder as `slideDown.css`.

5. Finally we should add the script that will enable the slide effect. Within the anonymous function in the second `<script>` element, add the following code:

```
$("#login").click(function(e) {

  e.preventDefault();

  $(this).addClass("on").next().slideDown();
});
```

6. When we run the page now, we should see that the hidden form slides open when the login link is clicked:

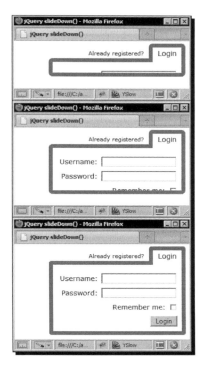

The previous picture shows the menu as it opens. The animation proceeds from top to bottom. Because the `slideDown()` effect is only applied to elements that are hidden, clicking the link while the menu is open will not cause the menu to reopen.

What just happened?

We have a relatively straight-forward collection of elements here. The HTML5 `<header>` element is the natural container for our login elements. The form is part of a simple unordered-list along with a link that will open the form.

Note that the link that will be used to open the login form has its `href` attribute set to a page that contains the login form. This is a simple fallback so that if the visitors have JavaScript disabled, they can still login even if they don't get to see the slide down form.

A lot of the styling is purely presentational and does not affect how the form functions. Similarly, a lot of it is standard positional stuff. What's important is that the form is initially hidden from view with `display:none`, and that the form is positioned using its `top` style property.

We attach a click-handler to the **login** link, which automatically receives the event object (e) as an argument. We use this object to cancel the default behavior of the browser. This prevents the page from jumping to the top when the link is clicked, or following the `href` of the link provided in case JavaScript is disabled. The `preventDefault()` function, which jQuery normalizes to work in IE as well as standard-compliant browsers, handles this for us.

We then add the class name `on` to the link so that our `:hover` styles are persisted when the pointer moves off the link and the form is still open. We then move to the next element after the link, our hidden login form, and call the `slideDown()` method on it with no additional arguments.

Position is important

The position of an element that has `slideDown()` applied to it is very important. The animation will not run correctly if the element uses `absolute` positioning in conjunction with its `bottom` style property to position itself by.

In this situation, the element will appear to slide *up* from the bottom, instead of sliding down as intended. We do not see this behavior with relatively positioned elements however.

Pop quiz – sliding elements down

1. What should be applied to an element before it has the `slideDown()` method called on it?

    a. `visibility:hidden;`

    b. `height:0;`

    c. `display:none;`

    d. `position:static;`

2. What style does an element that has been shown with `slideDown()` end up with?

    a. `display:block;`

    b. `visibility:visible;`

    c. `position:absolute;`

    d. `height:100%;`

Have a go hero – sliding elements down

In our basic example, once the form has been opened it then stays open until the page is reloaded. Add some additional code that fades the login form away after a specified length of time in case it is not interacted with.

Sliding elements out of view

The `slideUp()` method works in exactly the same way as `slideDown()`, except that it hides the target element instead of showing it. The `slideUp()` method accepts the same arguments as `slideDown()` and can be affected by CSS in the same way, so `padding` and `margin` should be taken into account and caution is advised when using `absolute` positioning. The original value of an element's `display` property however, is not a factor when using `slideUp()`.

The method's pattern of usage is as follows:

```
jQuery(elements).slideUp([duration], [easing], [callback]);
```

Time for action – sliding elements up

Let's build on the previous example so that the form slides back up out of view if a **cancel** link is clicked. We can add this link to the underlying markup for the page:

1. In `slideDown.html`, change the form so that it appears as follows (new code is highlighted):

```
<fieldset>
  <legend>Login Form</legend>
  <label for="username">Username:<input name="username"
    id="username"></label>
  <label for="password">Password:<input name="password"
    id="password" type="password"></label>
  <input name="remember" id="remember" type="checkbox"><label
    for="remember">Remember me:</label>
  <a id="cancel" href="#" title="Cancel">Cancel</a>
  <button type="submit">Login</button>
</fieldset>
```

2. Save the new file as `slideUp.html`.

3. We'll also need some more styles in order to stop our new link from picking up the styling of the **login** link. At the end of the `slideDown.css` stylesheet, add the following new selectors and rules:

```
header ul li a#cancel {
  margin:0; padding:0; position:absolute; bottom:14px; left:10px;
  font-size:11px; color:#993333;
}
header ul li a#cancel:hover, header ul li a#cancel:focus {
  border:none; text-decoration:underline; color:#ff0000;
}
```

4. Save the updated file in the `css` folder as `slideUp.css`, and update the `<link>` in the `<head>` of `slideUp.html` to point to the new stylesheet.

5. To add the new behavior, update the `<script>` at the bottom of the page so that it includes the following new code:

```
$("#cancel").click(function(e) {

  e.preventDefault();

  $(this).closest("form").slideUp(function() {
```

```
        $(this).prev().removeClass("on");

    });
});
```

This code should appear within the outer anonymous function, but after the click handler for the **login** link. Now we can close the form while it is opened by clicking the new **cancel** link. When this event occurs, we should see the reverse of the opening animation:

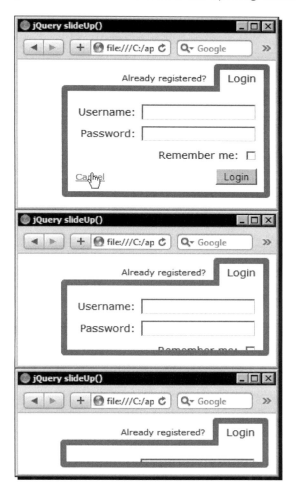

The animation still proceeds from top to bottom, but this time the form ends up hidden when the **Cancel** link is clicked.

What just happened?

We added a new click-handler in much the same way as we did before, including cancelling the default behavior of the browser using the event object (e). In this example, we don't particularly need to do this because the login form is at the very top of the page, so the visitor won't have scrolled down the page at all and there won't be a jump to the top of the page when either the **Login** or **Cancel** links are clicked. However, I have included it here as it is good practice.

We then find the closest parent of the link that is a `<form>` and call the `slideUp()` method on it. This time we also supply a callback function, which is used to remove the `on` class from the **Login** link.

You should notice that the **Cancel** link does not behave like the other elements in the form while the form is sliding open or closed. The link is visible all the time and moves with the bottom of the form as it grows or shrinks (depending on whether the form is opening or closing). The reason for this is simple—it's because the **Cancel** link is positioned absolutely.

We've specifically added the CSS that causes the **Cancel** link to behave in this way, even though it is generally undesirable, as a reminder that CSS can often cause issues when combined with animations.

Pop quiz – sliding elements up

1. What is the only requirement for an element to have the `slideUp()` method called on it?

    a. It should be set to `visibility:visible;`

    b. It should contain a wrapper element

    c. It should have a minimum height of 100 pixels

    d. It should be an element with a display type that naturally renders it visible on the page

Have a go hero – fixing the Cancel link

Have a go at fixing the **Cancel** link so that it is only visible while the form is fully open. The change is simple and requires just a few tweaks to the CSS.

Toggling the slide

The final slide method is `slideToggle()`, which provides rudimentary state-checking in order to determine whether the element should be hidden with `slideUp()` or shown with `slideDown()`, and then applies the relevant effect. Like the `toggle()` method that we looked at earlier, the built-in state checking mechanism is provided as a simple convenience, but there may be situations where we need to provide our own logic.

The `slideToggle()` method may accept the same arguments as the other slide methods, or an object that makes use of easing. For reference, the usage pattern is as follows:

```
jQuery(elements).slideToggle([duration], [easing], [callback]);
```

Time for action – using slideToggle

On the checkout pages of e-commerce sites, it's customary to show the products that are in the visitor's basket so that they know exactly what they're buying. Typically the checkout page (or pages) will be quite long due to the amount of information the visitor will need to enter, especially if it is their first visit to the site.

The page can often end up requesting names, e-mail addresses, and other contact information, payment methods, and more. Hence, it can be useful to hide the contents of the basket and just show a summary, but to allow the basket to be expanded to show the full details of their purchase.

The following screenshot shows how the basket will appear once it has been opened:

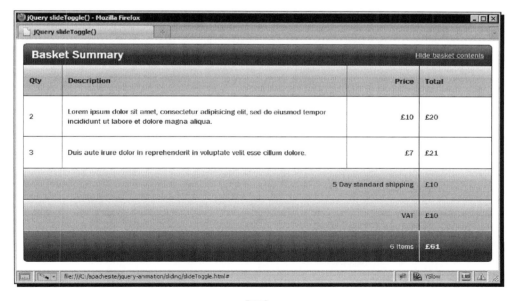

Once the basket area has been expanded, the contents are displayed in full.

1. Let's make a start by creating the underlying HTML. Add the following code to the template file:

```html
<div id="basket">
  <h2>Basket Summary</h2>
    <a id="basketToggle" href="#" title="Display basket
      contents">Show basket contents</a>
  <div id="contents">
    <table>
      <tr><th class="qty">Qty</th><th
        class="desc">Description</th><th
        class="subtotal">Price</th><th
        class="total">Total</th></tr>
      <tr><td class="qty">2</td><td class="desc"></td><td
        class="subtotal">£10</td><td class="total">£20</td></tr>
      <tr><td class="qty">1</td><td class="desc"></td><td
        class="subtotal">£5</td><td class="total">£5</td></tr>
      <tr><td class="qty">3</td><td class="desc"></td><td
        class="subtotal">£7</td><td class="total">£21</td></tr>
      <tr class="summary"><td colspan="3" class="subtotal">5 Day
        standard shipping</td><td class="total">£10</td></tr>
      <tr class="summary vat"><td colspan="3"
        class="subtotal">VAT</td><td class="total">£10</td></tr>
    </table>
  </div>
  <table>
    <tr id="total"><td class="subtotal">6 Items</td><td
      class="total">£66</td></tr>
  </table>
</div>
```

2. Save this page as `slideToggle.html`.

3. Now let's add some basic styling to tidy up and improve the appearance of our example page. In a new file in your text editor, add the following code:

```css
#basket {
  width:860px; margin:auto; position:relative;
  border:1px solid #000; -moz-border-radius:7px;
  -webkit-border-radius:7px; border-radius:7px;
  background-color:#000;

  font:normal 14px "Nimbus Sans L", "Helvetica Neue", "Franklin
    Gothic Medium", Sans-serif;
```

```
}
h2 {
  margin:0; padding:7px 0 7px 14px; -moz-border-radius:7px;
  -webkit-border-radius:7px; border-radius:7px; color:#fff;
  background-image:-moz-linear-gradient(0% 22px 90deg, #222,
    #999);
  background-image:-webkit-gradient(linear, 0% 0%, 0% 50%,
    from(#999), to(#222));
}
#basketToggle {
  position:absolute; right:14px; top:10px; color:#ccc;
}
#basketToggle:hover { color:#fff; }
#basketToggle:active { color:#ddd; }
#basketToggle:focus { outline:none; color:#ddd; }
table {
  width:860px; margin:auto; border-collapse:collapse;
  border-spacing:0;
}
td, th { padding:20px 10px; border:1px solid #000; }
th { border-top:none; }
#contents { display:none; }
#contents table { background-color:#fff; }
.summary td, th {
  background-color:#ccc;
  background-image:-moz-linear-gradient(0% 40% 90deg, #ccc, #fff);
  background-image:-webkit-gradient(linear, 0% 0%, 0% 40%,
    from(#fff), to(#ccc));
}
.qty, .desc { width:50px; text-align:left; }
.qty, #total .subtotal { border-left:none; }
.subtotal, .total { width:112px; }
.subtotal { text-align:right; border-left:0; }
.total { text-align:left; border-right:none; }
.vat .subtotal, .vat .total { border-bottom:none; }
#total .subtotal, #total .total { border-bottom:none; }
#total td { color:#fff; border:1px solid #fff; }
#total .total { border-right:none; font-weight:bold; }
.summary .subtotal, #total .subtotal, .desc { width:auto; }
#total .subtotal, #total .total {
  -moz-border-radius:0 0 7px 7px;
  -webkit-border-radius-bottom-left:7px;
  -webkit-border-radius-bottom-right:7px; border-radius:0 0 7px
    7px;
  background-image:-moz-linear-gradient(0% 70% 90deg, #222, #999);
  background-image:-webkit-gradient(linear, 0% 0%, 0% 70%,
    from(#999), to(#222));
}
```

4. Save this in the `css` folder as `slideToggle.css` and link to the file from the `<head>` of the page we just created.

5. For the final part of the example we can add the script that will toggle the visibility of the contents table. Add the following code to the bottom of the HTML page:

```
var toggler = $("#basketToggle"),
  basketArea = $("#contents"),
  newText = ["", "basket", "contents"];


toggler.click(function(e) {

  e.preventDefault();

  if (!basketArea.is(":animated")) {
    basketArea.slideToggle("slow", function(){
      toggler.text(function(i, text) {

        if (basketArea.is(":visible")) {
          newText[0] = "Hide";
        } else {
          newText[0] = "Show";
        }
        toggler.text(newText.join(" "));
      });
    });
  }
});
```

6. Run the page in your browser now. You should find that you can open or close the contents section of the basket area by clicking the link in the top-right of the container. The basket area should expand like this:

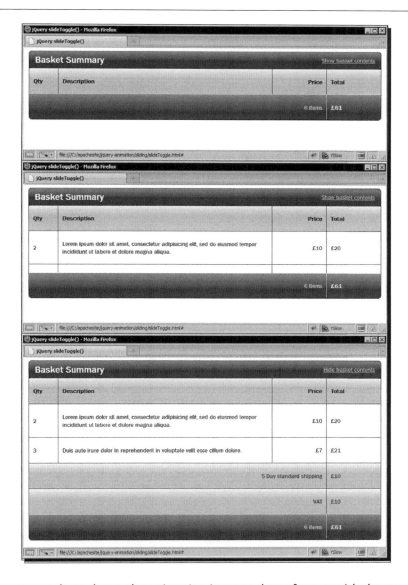

The previous screenshots shows the animation in a top-down format with the start of the animation at the top and the animation nearing the end at the bottom. As we're using the `slideToggle()` method, it is equally valid when running backwards too.

What just happened?

The underlying structures we've placed on the page are pretty straight-forward. To summarize, we basically have two tables, one of which is wrapped in a `<div>`, and an outer container for the whole collection of elements. The table that is wrapped will be hidden when the basket is collapsed. We also have a link at the top of the container which will show or hide the basket contents.

Our JavaScript code is divided into two main sections. In the first section, we cache some jQuery selectors that we'll use a couple of times in the code to save from selecting them one at a time, each time they are required.

We also define a function that we can call whenever we need to change the value of the toggling link. The function sets the text of the link using an anonymous function which returns the new text to add. This is passed to the index of the element in the collection on which the `text()` method was called as the first argument and the second is the original text of the element. We don't need the first argument but we must specify it in order to access the second argument.

The second part of the code is the click handler for the toggle link. It checks that the `<div>` containing the first `<table>` is not already being animated and if not, it calls the `slideToggle()` method, which will either slide the basket open or closed depending on its current state. We use the callback function to update the text of the link once the animation is complete.

The: animated filter

Checking whether an element is already being animated using the `:animated` filter is a quick and easy alternative to the `stop()` method in the previous example in that it only applied the animation if the element was not already animated and therefore prevented a build-up of animations.

Have a go hero – doing more with slideToggle

Have a go at reworking the code so that it uses the `slideDown()` and `slideUp()` methods instead of the `slideToggle()`. It won't make the code any more efficient, but you should get to see roughly how much code the `slideToggle()` method can save you.

Pop quiz – using slideToggle

1. What does the `slideToggle()` method return?

   a. Nothing

   b. The value `true` when the animation ends

   c. The original jQuery object for chaining purposes

   d. A string indicating whether the element is visible or not

2. What arguments can the `slideToggle()` method accept?

   a. The duration and a callback function, or an object

   b. An array containing items specifying the duration, easing and a callback

   c. A collection of strings

   d. A jQuery object containing the selected element

Easing

We discussed easing very briefly in *Chapter 2, Fading Animations* when we saw that each fading method could have an easing type set by passing an argument into the animation method being used. The sliding animations are the same and can also accept an easing type as an argument. Let's take a moment to familiarize ourselves with what easing is exactly and how it can be used with jQuery animations.

Easing is a technique where the speed and/or the direction of animation are changed while the animation is running. Easing can make the animation start off slow and gradually speed up, start up fast and gradually slow down, and a whole host of other effects.

jQuery has two modes of easing built in: `linear` easing and `swing` easing, with `swing` being the default for all types of animations. Sometimes using linear easing can help make a continuous animation run smoother, but the difference between `swing` and `linear` is subtle at best.

There are many more types of easing than the two exposed by jQuery. The `jquery.easing.1.3.js` plugin, written by George McGinley Smith, adapts Robert Penner's original easing equations so that they can be used with jQuery, and makes 30 new types of easing available to us.

 The easing plugin changes the default easing type from `swing` to `easeOutQuad`.

The new types of easing added by the plugin are listed in the following table:

easeInQuad	easeOutQuad	EaseInOutQuad
easeInCubic	easeOutCubic	easeInOutCubic
easeInQuart	easeOutQuart	easeInOutQuart
easeInQuint	easeOutQuint	easeInOutQuint
easeInSine	easeOutSine	easeInOutSine
easeInExpo	easeOutExpo	easeInOutExpo
easeInCirc	easeOutCirc	easeInOutCirc
easeInElastic	easeOutElastic	easeInOutElastic
easeInBack	easeOutBack	easeInOutBack
easeInBounce	easeOutBounce	easeInOutBounce

Time for action – adding easing

The `easeOutBounce` easing type adds a particularly attractive effect when used with `slideDown()` animations.

 The easing plugin can be obtained from `http://gsgd.co.uk/sandbox/jquery/easing/jquery.easing.1.3.js`. A copy of this file is included with the companion download for this book.

In this example, we'll add some easing to our example file.

1. Change the call to the `slideDown()` method in `slideUp.html` so that it appears as follows:

```
$(this).addClass("on").next().slideDown(400, "easeOutBounce");
```

2. Save the changed file as `slideEasing.html`. Don't forget to add a new `<script>` reference to the easing plugin directly after the jQuery reference to avoid a script error.

What just happened?

We supply the name of the easing type we'd like to use as a string. It is the second argument, so to use it we must also supply the first argument. As we don't actually need to change the duration we just supply the default value of 400 milliseconds.

When the login form drops down now, it will appear to bounce a little at the end of the animation. Suddenly our example has physics—the form appears to literally drop down as if pulled upon by gravity and doesn't just stop when it hits its full height, it bounces a little, giving a much more aesthetically pleasing effect.

Easing is a great effect that can be added with the addition of an 8 KB plugin (3.51 KB when minified and with the license moved to an external file) and a very minor tweak to our code. Using it is simple, but its effects can be enormous, transforming a monotonous or otherwise boring animation into one filled with impact and interest.

Using an object literal to add easing

We can also change the format of the arguments we pass into the predefined animation methods in order to use easing. Prior to the easing argument being added to the animation methods (fadeIn(), slideDown(), and so on) in version 1.4.3 of jQuery, this was the de-facto means of using easing with animation methods.

Instead of providing string or numerical arguments (or a callback function), we can provide an object literal where each key refers to the duration, the easing type, and optionally a callback to call when the animation is complete. The usage then becomes as follows:

```
jQuery(elements).slideDown({
  duration: [duration],
  easing: [easing],
  complete: [callback]
});
```

Time for action – using the alternative argument format

This time we'll use the alternative syntax for supplying an easing function.

1. Change the call to the slideDown() method in slideEasing.html so that it appears as follows:

```
$(this).addClass("on").next().slideDown({
  easing: "easeOutBounce"
});
```

2. Save this version of the file as slideEasingObject.html.

What just happened?

By supplying an object literal as the first argument to the slideDown() method, we are able to make use of the easing types provided by the plugin in an alternative syntax. In this example, we omit the duration and complete keys of the object and supply only the name of the easing type as a string.

Have a go hero – using easing

Try out some of the other easing methods that are available via the easing plugin in this, and some of our earlier examples. We'll be using easing where appropriate throughout the remainder of the book, but other than a cursory explanation these won't be focused on in any great detail.

Pop quiz – using easing

1. How many easing types does the easing plugin add?

    a. 20

    b. 30

    c. 17

    d. 48

2. What can we pass into an effect method in the alternative format for using easing?

    a. An object with optional keys specifying the duration, easing type, and a function to call on complete

    b. A string specifying the easing type

    c. An array where the first item is the duration, the second is the easing type and the third is a function to call on complete

    d. An integer specifying the duration of easing

The flicker effect

Sometimes, using `slideDown()` and `slideUp()` animations on the same elements that are triggered when the visitor hovers over an element, such as with a navigation menu for example, can have an impact on the usability of a site. It's important to be aware of what the issue is and how it can be resolved.

Time for action – avoiding the flicker effect

Let's put together a couple of examples so that we can see which situations can cause the problem to arise.

1. Open up the `fadeIn.html` file from Chapter 2, and update the `<nav>` element so that it appears as follows (new code shown in bold):

```
<nav>
  <ul class="purecss">
```

```
  <li class="first"><a href="#" title="Home">Home</a></li>
  <li>
    <a href="#" title="Articles">Articles</a>
    <div class="subnav">
      <ul class="left">
        <li><h2>JavaScript</h2></li>
        <li><a href="#" title="JS Article 1">JS Article
          1</a></li>
        <li><a href="#" title="JS Article 2">JS Article
          2</a></li>
        <li class="last"><a href="#" title="JS Article 3">JS
          Article 3</a></li>
      </ul>
      <ul class="right">
        <li><h2>jQuery</h2></li>
        <li><a href="#" title="jQuery Article 1">jQuery Article
          1</a></li>
        <li><a href="#" title="jQuery Article 2">jQuery Article
          2</a></li>
        <li class="last"><a href="#" title="jQuery Article
          3">jQuery Article 3</a></li>
      </ul>
    </div>
  </li>
  <li><a href="#" title="Code">Code</a></li>
  <li>
    <a href="#" title="Demos">Demos</a>
    <ul class="subnav">
      <li class="first"><a href="#" title="The first demo">The
        first demo</a></li>
      <li><a href="#" title="Another demo">Another demo</a></li>
      <li class="last"><a href="#" title="The third demo">The
        third demo</a></li>
    </ul>
  </li>
  <li class="last"><a href="#"
    title="Portfolio">Portfolio</a></li>
  </ul>
</nav>
```

2. Save the new file as `slideFlicker.html`. We'll also need a new stylesheet for this example (in addition to `fadeIn.css`, which should already be linked to from the original file). In a new file in your text editor, add the following code:

```
nav li { position:relative; }
.subnav {
  display:none; width:100%; margin-left:-2px; border:2px solid
    #aaa;
  border-top:none; -moz-border-radius:0 0 7px 7px;
  -webkit-border-bottom-left-radius:7px;
  -webkit-border-bottom-right-radius:7px; border-radius:0 0 7px
    7px;
  position:absolute; text-align:left;
}
div.subnav { width:244%; }
.subnav ul { float:left; }
.subnav li { float:none; border-right:none; }
.subnav li a { border-bottom:none; font-size:14px; }
.subnav li a:hover { background-color:#ccc; }
.subnav li.first a {
  border-top:none; -moz-border-radius:0;
  -webkit-border-bottom-left-radius:0;
  -webkit-border-top-left-radius:0; border-radius:0;
}
.subnav li.last a {
  border-bottom:1px solid #fff; -moz-border-radius:0 0 7px 7px;
  -webkit-border-top-right-radius:0;
  -webkit-border-bottom-left-radius:7px;
  -webkit-border-bottom-right-radius:7px; border-radius:0 0 7px
    7px;
  }
.subnav .left li a { border-right:none; }
.subnav .left li.last a {
  -moz-border-radius:0 0 0 7px;
  -webkit-border-bottom-right-radius:0; border-radius:0 0 0 7px;
}
.subnav .right li.last a {
  -moz-border-radius:0 0 7px 0; -webkit-border-bottom-left-
    radius:0;
  border-radius:0 0 7px 0;
}
.subnav li h2 {
  margin:0; padding:5px 0; font-size:12px; font-weight:normal;
  text-indent:20px; background-color:#eee;
}
```

3. Save this file as `slideFlicker.css`, and add a link to the file from the `<head>` of `slideFlicker.html` (directly after the link to `fadeIn.css`).

4. Finally, update the second `<script>` element at the bottom of `slideFlicker.html` so that it appears as follows (new code shown in bold):

```
var ul = $("nav ul");

ul.removeClass("purecss");

ul.find("a").each(function() {
  if (!$(this).closest(".subnav").length) {
    var a = $(this);
    a.append("<span>" + a.text() + "</span>");
  }
});

ul.find("a").hover(function() {
  $(this).find("span").fadeIn("slow");
}, function() {
  $(this).find("span").hide();
});

$(".subnav", ul).parent().mouseenter(function() {
  $(this).find(".subnav").stop(true, true).slideDown("fast");
});

$(".subnav", ul).parent().mouseleave(function() {
  $(this).find(".subnav").stop(true, true).slideUp("fast");
});
```

What just happened?

All we've done to the underlying HTML is added a couple of submenus to two of the top level list items in the `<nav>`. One of the submenus is a split menu made up of two `<ul>` elements inside a `<div>`, the other is a single menu built from a standard `<ul>`.

We've also added some new styling, mostly to carry on the theme from the original example. Some of the CSS is used to override previous rules set in the original stylesheet. Mostly the styling is purely for aesthetics, and we use a lot of CSS3 rounded-corner styling, which will not be apparent in all browsers.

For the animations to work as intended, the submenus should initially be hidden from view with `display:none`. For the flicker effect to occur, the submenus should be wider than the parent `<li>` that they are contained within. We've made one of our submenus wider, and the other one the same width so that we can easily see the difference.

In the `<script>`, we've added a simple check when the fading `<span>` elements are added to the page so that the fade effect isn't applied to the submenus (it could easily be adapted to work, but we're looking at a different effect in this particular example).

Following this we attach `mouseenter` and `mouseleave` effect handlers to the parents of any elements with the class `subnav`. In these handlers, we simply find the `subnav` within the element that triggered the event and either show or hide it with a slide effect. The `stop()` method is used to prevent animation build-up, as described in the previous chapter.

Take a look at the page in a browser and note the difference between the two submenus:

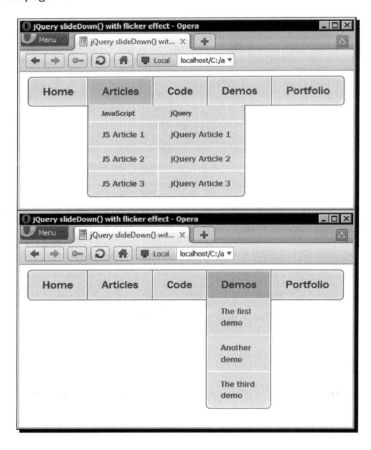

In the previous screenshot, we see both submenus in their expanded, visible states.

The flicker problem arises in part because of the visitor's perception of where the submenu actually is. It is quite clear with the thin submenu where the boundaries of the menu are. The visitor will most likely move their mouse pointer straight down into the submenu when it appears on the page.

With the wider submenu, the visitor may not be quite as sure where they need to move their mouse in order to enter the submenu. Instead of moving straight down from the **Articles** top-level item into the submenu, they may instead move their mouse pointer diagonally down and to the right, thinking that they can enter the second list of links that way.

It is this behavior that produces the flicker effect; try it out yourself—move the mouse pointer diagonally down and to the right when entering the wide submenu. The submenu should flicker on and off wildly.

Time for action – fixing the flicker

In this section we'll see how to prevent the flicker from spoiling the animation.

1. Fixing the problem is relatively easy. Simply update the JavaScript so that it appears as follows (new code again shown in bold):

```
var ul = $("nav ul"),
  timer = null;

ul.removeClass("purecss");
ul.find("a").each(function(){
  if (!$(this).closest(".subnav").length) {
    var a = $(this);
    a.append("<span>" + a.text() + "</span>");
  }
});

ul.find("a").hover(function() {
  $(this).find("span").fadeIn("slow");
}, function() {
  $(this).find("span").hide();
});

$(".subnav", ul).parent().mouseenter(function() {
  clearTimeout(timer);
  $(this).find(".subnav").stop(true, true).slideDown("fast");
});
```

```
function closeIt(el) {
  el.stop(true, true).slideUp("fast");
}

$(".subnav", ul).parent().mouseleave(function() {
  var el = $(this).find(".subnav");
  timer = setTimeout(function() { closeIt(el); }, 100);
});
```

2. Save this new file as `slideFlickerFixed.html`.

What just happened?

First of all, we initialize a new variable at the top of our code. The `timer` variable will be used to store a timeout ID in so that it can be accessed and cleared from within a function. We initially set it to `null` as there is no other appropriate data type for it to temporarily hold. In our `mousenter` event handling function, we first clear the timeout using the ID held in our `timer` variable. The variable may or may not be populated when the handler executes. It is clearing this `timeOut` which is what prevents the flicker effect from occurring.

After our `mouseenter` handler we define a new function, `closeIt()`, which accepts a single argument. The argument will be set to the submenu currently open. The function simply calls the same code from before which closes the submenu by sliding it up.

In our `mouseleave` handler function, we store the currently open submenu in a variable and then use a standard JavaScript `setTimeout()` function to call the `closeIt()` function after a short delay of 100 milliseconds.

We need to use an anonymous function within the `setTimeout()` function to call our `closeIt()` function, so that we can pass in the cached submenu element that the function requires as an argument.

Adding this slight delay with `setTimeout()` fixes the flicker effect entirely. The delay is too short to cause a noticeable delay when the visitor actually moves off of the submenu intentionally. If they accidently move the pointer over the corner of the next top-level link when going diagonally down and to the right to reach the second list of links, when they move back into the submenu it will clear the timeout and the submenu will not close, or flicker.

Pop quiz – fixing the flicker

1. Why was it necessary to use a an anonymous function when calling the `setTimeout()` function in the previous example?

   a. It is the only format accepted by `setTimeout()`

   b. It executes faster

   c. In order to pass in an argument

   d. For fun

Have a go hero – adding a delay before showing a submenu

Usability king Jakob Nielsen advises that a short-delay between the visitor hovering over a navigation menu item and the submenu being displayed, to ensure that the visitor actually wants to see the submenu, should be implemented in common interfaces. Not everyone will agree with this, and there is a danger of the menu feeling unresponsive if the delay is too long.

Update the `flickerFixed.html` file so that there is a short delay before a submenu is shown after its parent menu item is hovered on.

 The article which mentions the timing of displaying submenus can be found at `http://www.useit.com/alertbox/mega-dropdown-menus.html`.

Summary

The sliding family of methods that we looked at over the course of the chapter are the last of jQuery's built-in, predefined animation methods. The methods we looked at in this chapter were:

- `slideDown()`
- `slideUp()`
- `slideToggle()`

We saw that these methods are very similar in how they are used to the other built-in jQuery effect methods, allowing us to specify the same arguments. All that differs is the actual effect. The techniques we learned in this chapter included:

- Showing elements that are hidden using `slideDown()`
- Hiding visible elements with `slideUp()`
- Toggling the visibility of elements with `slideToggle()`

- ◆ Adding easing to jQuery's built-in effects
- ◆ Using the `:animated` filter to test whether an element is currently being animated
- ◆ Fixing a common flickering issue with slide-down submenus
- ◆ How CSS affects sliding elements

We looked at how each of the sliding methods can be used, and also covered easing and how we can easily add these subtle but effective methods to enhance or otherwise improve how the effects appear when they run. The easing types require the inclusion of an external plugin in order to function.

In the next chapter we'll move on to look at the `animate()` method, which allows us to create custom animations which can animate almost any numerical style property of an element.

5

Custom Animations

The predefined effects that we have looked at throughout the book so far are very good at what they do, but they are there to cater for very specific requirements and will sometimes not be enough when more complex animations are needed.

In these situations we can use jQuery's `animate()` *method, which allows us to define custom animations with ease that can be as complex and as specialized as the task at hand requires, and this is what we'll be looking at over the course of this chapter.*

Subjects that we'll cover throughout the course of this chapter will include:

- ◆ Creating custom animations with the `animate()` method
- ◆ Passing arguments to the method
- ◆ Animating an element's dimensions
- ◆ Animating an element's position
- ◆ Creating a jQuery animation plugin

The animate method

All custom animations with jQuery are driven with the `animate()` method. Despite the ability to animate almost any style property that has a numeric value, the method is simple to use and takes just a few arguments. The method may be used in the following way:

```
jQuery(elements).animate(properties to animate,
    [duration],
    [easing],
    [callback]
);
```

The first argument should take the form of an object where each property of the object is a style that we'd like to animate, very similar to how we would use jQuery's `css()` method.

As I mentioned before, this can be any CSS style that takes a purely numerical argument (with the exception of colors, although with the jQuery UI library we can animate colors as well. See *Chapter 6, Extended Animations with jQuery UI* for more information on jQuery UI). Background positions cannot be animated by jQuery natively, but it is quite easy to animate this property manually; see *Chapter 7, Full Page Animations* for more information on this technique.

The duration, easing, and callback arguments take the same formats as those that we used with the fading and sliding methods earlier in the book and are used in exactly the same way.

Per-property easing

As of the 1.4 version of jQuery, we can apply different types of easing to each style property we are animating when using the `animate()` method. So if we are animating both the `width` and `height` of an element for example, we can use `linear` easing for the `width` animation, and `swing` easing for the `height` animation. This applies to the standard easing functions built into jQuery, or any of the easing functions added with the easing plugin that we looked at in *Chapter 4, Sliding Animations*.

To supply easing types to the `animate()` method on a per-property basis, we need to provide an array as the value of the property we are animating. This can be done using the following syntax:

```
jQuery(elements).animate({
    property: [value, easingType]
});
```

An alternative syntax for animate()

Instead of using the duration, easing, and callback arguments individually, we may alternatively pass a configuration object to the `animate()` method containing the following configuration options:

- ◆ `duration`
- ◆ `easing`
- ◆ `complete`
- ◆ `step`
- ◆ `queue`
- ◆ `specialEasing`

The first three options are the same as the arguments would be if we passed them into the method in the standard way. The last three are interesting however, in that we do not have access to them in any other way.

The `step` option allows us to specify a callback function that will be executed on each step of the animation. The `queue` option accepts a Boolean that controls whether the animation is executed immediately or placed into the selected element's queue. The `specialEasing` option allows us to specify an easing function for each individual style property that is being animated, giving us easing on a per-property basis using the alternative syntax.

The pattern for this second method of usage is as follows:

```
jQuery(elements).animate(properties to animate, [configuration
    options]);
```

Like most (but not all) jQuery methods, the `animate()` method returns a jQuery object so that additional methods can be chained to it. Like the other effect methods, multiple calls to `animate()` on the same element will result in an animation queue being created for the element. If we want to animate two different style properties at the same time, we can pass all required properties within the object passed to the `animate()` method as the first argument.

Animating an element's position

The `animate()` method is able to animate changes made to any CSS style property that has a numeric value, with the exception of colors and `background-positions`. In this example, we'll create a content viewer that shows different panels of content by sliding them in and out of view using the `animate()` method.

This type of widget is commonly used on portfolio or showcase sites and is an attractive way to show a lot of content without cluttering a single page. In this example, we'll be animating the element's position.

Time for action – creating an animated content viewer

We'll start again by adding the underlying markup and styling.

1. The underlying markup for the content viewer should be as follows:

```
<div id="slider">
  <div id="viewer">
    <img id="image1" src="img/amstrad.jpg" alt="Amstrad CPC 472">
    <img id="image2" src="img/atari.jpg" alt="Atari TT030">
    <img id="image3" src="img/commodore16.jpg" alt="Commodore 64">
    <img id="image4" src="img/commodore128.jpg" alt="Commodore
      128">
    <img id="image5" src="img/spectrum.jpg" alt="Sinclair ZX
      Spectrum +2">
  </div>
  <ul id="ui">
    <li class="hidden" id="prev">
      <a href="" title="Previous">&laquo;</a></li>
    <li><a href="#image1" title="Image 1" class="active">Image
      1</a></li>
    <li><a href="#image2" title="Image 2">Image 2</a></li>
    <li><a href="#image3" title="Image 3">Image 3</a></li>
    <li><a href="#image4" title="Image 4">Image 4</a></li>
    <li><a href="#image5" title="Image 5">Image 5</a></li>
    <li class="hidden" id="next">
      <a href="" title="Next">&raquo;</a></li>
  </ul>
</div>
```

2. Save the file as `animate-position.html`.

3. Next we should create the base CSS. By that I mean that we should add the CSS which is essential for the content-viewer to function as intended, as opposed to styling that gives the widget a theme or skin. It's good practice to separate out the styling in this way when creating plugins so that the widget is compatible with jQuery UI's Themeroller theming mechanism.

4. In a new file in your text editor add the following code:

```
#slider { width:500px; position:relative; }
#viewer {
  width:400px; height:300px; margin:auto; position:relative;
  overflow:hidden;
}
#slider ul {
```

```
    width:295px; margin:0 auto; padding:0; list-style-type:none;
  }
#slider ul:after {
    content:"."; visibility:hidden; display:block; height:0;
    clear:both;
  }
#slider li { margin-right:10px; float:left; }
#prev, #next { position:absolute; top:175px; }
#prev { left:20px; }
#next { position:absolute; right:10px; }
.hidden { display:none; }
#slide {
    width:2000px; height:300px; position:absolute; top:0; left:0;
  }
#slide img { float:left; }
#title { margin:0; text-align:center; }
```

5. Save this in the `css` folder as `animate-position.css`, and don't forget to link to the new stylesheet from the `<head>` of our page. Run the page in your browser now, before we get into the scripting, so that you can see how the widget behaves without the accompanying script. You should find that any image can be viewed by clicking its corresponding link using only CSS, and this will work in any browser. The previous and next arrows are hidden with our CSS because these will simply not work with JS turned off and the image titles are not displayed, but the widget's core functionality is still fully accessible.

What just happened?

The underlying HTML in this example is very straightforward. We have an outer container for the content-viewer as a whole, then within this we have a container for our content panels (simple images in this example) and a navigation structure to allow the different panels to be viewed.

Some of the elements we've added style rules for in our CSS file aren't hardcoded into the underlying markup, but will be created as necessary when needed. Doing it this way ensures that the content-viewer is still usable even when the visitor has JavaScript disabled.

One important point to note is that the `#slide` wrapper element that we create and wrap around the images has a `height` equal to a single image and a `width` equal to the sum of all image widths. The `#viewer` element on the other hand has both a `width` and a `height` equal to a single image so that only one image is visible at any one time.

With JavaScript disabled, the images will appear to stack up on top of each other, but once the `#slide` wrapper element has been created the images are set to float in order to stack up horizontally.

We'll use easing in this example, so be sure to link to the easing plugin directly after the jQuery reference at the end of the `<body>`:

```
<script src="js/jquery.easing.1.3.js"></script>
```

Time for action – initializing variables and prepping the widget

First we need to prepare the underlying markup and store some element selectors:

```
$("#viewer").wrapInner("<div id=\"slide\"></div>");

var container = $("#slider"),
  prev = container.find("#prev"),
  prevChild = prev.find("a"),
  next = container.find("#next").removeClass("hidden"),
  nextChild = next.find("a"),
  slide = container.find("#slide"),
  key = "image1",
  details = {
    image1: {
      position: 0, title: slide.children().eq(0).attr("alt")
    },
    image2: {
      position: -400, title: slide.children().eq(1).attr("alt")
    },
    image3: {
      position: -800, title: slide.children().eq(2).attr("alt")
    },
    image4: {
      position: -1200, title: slide.children().eq(3).attr("alt")
    },
    image5: {
      position: -1600, title: slide.children().eq(4).attr("alt")
    }
  };

$("<h2>", {
  id: "title",
  text: details[key].title
}).prependTo("#slider");
```

What just happened?

To start with, we first wrap all of the images inside the #viewer <div> in a new container. We'll be using this container to animate the movement of the panels. We give this new container an id attribute so that we can easily select it from the DOM when required.

This is the element that we will be animating later in the example.

Next we cache the selectors for some of the elements that we'll need to manipulate frequently. We create a single jQuery object pointing to the outer #slider container and then select all of the elements we want to cache, such as the previous and next arrows, using the jQuery find() method.

A key variable is also initialized which will be used to keep track of the panel currently being displayed. Finally, we create a details object that contains information about each image in the content viewer. We can store the left position in pixels that the slide container must be animated to in order to show any given panel, and we can also store the title of each content panel.

The title of each panel is read from the alt attribute of each image, but if we were using other elements, we could select the title attribute, or use jQuery's data method to set and retrieve the title of the content.

The <h2> element used for the title is created and inserted into the content-viewer with JS because there is no way for us to change it without using JS. Therefore when visitors have JS disabled, the title is useless and is better off not being shown at all.

The last thing we do in the first section of code is to remove the hidden class name from the next button so that it is displayed.

The previous link (by this I mean the link that allows the visitor to move to the previous image in the sequence) is not shown initially because the first content panel is always the panel that is visible when the page loads, so there are no previous panels to move to.

Time for action – defining a post-animation callback

Next we need a function that we can execute each time an animation ends:

```
function postAnim(dir) {

  var keyMatch = parseInt(key.match(/\d+$/));

  (parseInt(slide.css("left")) < 0) ? prev.show() : prev.hide();

  (parseInt(slide.css("left")) === -1600) ? next.hide() :
    next.show();
```

```
    if (dir) {
      var titleKey = (dir === "back") ? keyMatch - 1 : keyMatch + 1;
      key = "image" + titleKey;
    }

    container.find("#title").text(details[key].title);

    container.find(".active").removeClass("active");
    container.find("a[href=#" + key + "]").addClass("active");
};
```

What just happened?

In this second section of code, we define a function that we'll call after an animation ends. This is used for some housekeeping to do various things that may need doing repeatedly, so it is more efficient to bundle them up into a single function instead of defining them separately within event handlers. This is the postAnim() function and it may accept a single parameter which refers to the direction that the slider has moved in.

The first thing we do in this function is use the regular expression /\d+$/ with JavaScript's match() function to parse the panel number from the end of the string saved in the key variable which we initialized in the first section of code, and which will always refer to the currently visible panel.

Our postAnim() function may be called either when a panel is selected using the numeric links, or when the previous/next links are used. However, when the previous/next links are used we need the key to know which panel is currently being displayed in order to move to the next or previous panel.

We then check whether the first panel is currently being displayed by checking the left CSS style property of the #slide element. If the #slide element is at 0, we know the first panel is visible so we hide the previous link. If the left property is less than 0, we show the previous link. We do a similar test to check whether the last panel is visible, and if so, we hide the next link. The previous and next links will only be shown if they are currently hidden.

We then check whether the dir (direction) argument has been supplied to the function. If it has, we have to work out which panel is now being displayed by reading the keyMatch variable that we created earlier and then either subtracting 1 from it if the dir argument is equal to back, or adding 1 to it if not.

The result is saved back to the key variable, which is then used to update the <h2> title element. The title text for the current panel is obtained from our details object using the key variable. Lastly we add the class name active to the numeric link corresponding to the visible panel.

Although not essential, this is something we will want to use when we come to add a skin to the widget. We select the right link using an attribute selector that matches the `href` of the current link. Note that we don't create any new jQuery objects in this function; we use our cached `container` object and the `find()` method to obtain the elements we require.

Time for action – adding event handlers for the UI elements

Now that the slider has been created, we can add the event handlers that will drive the functionality:

```
$("#ui li a").not(prevChild).not(nextChild).click(function(e){
  e.preventDefault();

  key = $(this).attr("href").split("#")[1];

  slide.animate({
    left: details[key].position
  }, "slow", "easeOutBack", postAnim);
});

nextChild.add(prevChild).click(function(e){
  e.preventDefault();

  var arrow = $(this).parent();

  if (!slide.is(":animated")) {
    slide.animate({
      left: (arrow.attr("id") === "prev") ? "+=400" : "-=400"
    }, "slow", "easeOutBack", function(){

      (arrow.attr("id") === "prev") ? postAnim("back") :
        postAnim("forward")
    });
  }
});
```

What just happened?

The first handler is bound to the main links used to display the different panels, excluding the previous and next links with the jQuery `not()` method. We first stop the browser following the link with the `preventDefault()` method.

We then update the `key` variable with the panel that is being displayed by extracting the panel name from the link's `href` attribute. We use JavaScript's `split()` method to obtain just the panel `id` and not the # symbol.

Finally, we animate the slide element by setting its `left` CSS style property to the value extracted from the `details` object. We use the `key` variable to access the value of the `position` property.

As part of the animation, we configure the duration as `slow` and the easing as `easeOutBack`, and specify our `postAnim` function as the callback function to execute when the animation ends.

Finally, we need to add a click handler for the previous/next links used to navigate to the next or previous image. These two links can both share a single click handler. We can select both of these two links using our cached selectors from earlier, along with jQuery's `add()` method to add them both to a single jQuery object in order to attach the handler functions to both links.

We again stop the browser from following the link using `preventDefault()`. We then cache a reference to the parent of the link that was clicked, using the `arrow` variable, so that we can easily refer to it later on in the function. This is needed because within the callback function for the `animate()` method, the `$(this)` keyword will be scoped to the `#slide` element instead of the link that was clicked.

We then check that the `#slide` element is not already being animated using the `:animated` filter. This check is important because it prevents the viewer breaking if one of the links is clicked repeatedly.

If it is not already being animated, we perform the animation and move the slide element either `400` pixels (the `width` of a single content panel) backwards or forwards. We can check which arrow was clicked by looking at the `id` attribute of the element referenced by the `arrow` variable.

We specify the same duration and easing values as before in the animation method, but instead of passing a reference to the `postAnim` function as the callback parameter we pass an anonymous function instead. Within this anonymous function, we determine which link was clicked and then call the `postAnim` function with the appropriate argument. Remember, this is necessary to obtain the correct key for the `details` object because neither the previous nor the next links have `href` attributes pointing to an image.

Try the page out in a browser at this point and you should find that an image can be viewed by clicking on any of the links, including the previous and next links. This is how the widget should appear at this stage:

The previous screenshot shows the widget in its un-skinned state, with only the CSS required for it to function included.

Skinning the widget

'There's more than one way to skin a cat' was once proclaimed, and this applies to widgets as well as cats. Lastly, let's add some custom styling to the widget to see how easy it is to make the widget attractive as well as functional.

Time for action – adding a new skin

At the bottom of the `animate-position.css` file, add the following code:

```
a { outline:0 none; }
#slider {
  border:1px solid #999; -moz-border-radius:8px;
  -webkit-border-radius:8px; border-radius:8px;
  background-color:#ededed; -moz-box-shadow:0px 2px 7px #aaa;
  -webkit-box-shadow:0px 2px 7px #aaa; box-shadow:0px 2px 7px #aaa;
}
#title, #slider ul { margin-top:10px; margin-bottom:12px; }
#title {
  font:normal 22px "Nimbus Sans L", "Helvetica Neue", "Franklin
    Gothic Medium", Sans-serif;
```

```
    color:#444;
}
#viewer { border:1px solid #999; background-color:#fff; }
#slider ul { width:120px; }
#slider ul li a {
   display:block; width:10px; height:10px; text-indent:-5000px;
   text-decoration:none; border:2px solid #666;
   -moz-border-radius:17px; -webkit-border-radius:17px;
   border-radius:17px; background-color:#fff; text-align:center;
}
#slider #prev, #slider #next { margin:0; text-align:center; }
#slider #prev { left:10px; }
#slider #prev a, #slider #next a {
   display:block; height:28px; width:28px; line-height:22px;
   text-indent:0; border:1px solid #666; -moz-border-radius:17px;
   -webkit-border-radius:17px; border-radius:17px;
   background-color:#fff;
}
#prev a, #next a { font:bold 40px "Trebuchet MS"; color:#666; }
#slider ul li a.active { background-color:#F93; }
```

What just happened?

With this code we style all of the visual aspects of the widget without interfering with
anything that controls how it works. We give it some nice rounded corners and add a
drop-shadow to the widget, turn the numeric links into little clickable icons, and style
the previous and next links. Colors and fonts are also set in this section as they too are
obviously highly dependent on the theme.

These styles add a basic, neutral theme to the widget, as shown in the following screenshot:

The styles we used to create the theme are purely arbitrary and simply for the purpose of the example. They can be changed to whatever we need in any given implementation to suit other elements on the page, or the overall theme of the site.

Pop quiz – creating an animated content-viewer

1. What arguments may the `animate()` method be passed?

    a. An array where the array items are the element to animate, the duration, the easing, and a callback function

    b. The first argument is an object containing the style properties to animate, optionally followed by the duration, an easing type, and a callback function

    c. An object where each property refers to the style properties to animate, the duration, easing, and a callback function

    d. A function which must return the style properties to animate, the duration, easing, and a callback function

2. What does the `animate()` method return?

    a. An array containing the style properties that were animated

    b. A array containing the elements that were animated

    c. A jQuery object for chaining purposes

    d. A Boolean indicating whether the animation completed successfully

Have a go hero – making the image viewer more scalable

In our animated content viewer, we had a fixed number of images and a hardcoded navigation structure to access them. Extend the content viewer so that it will work with an indeterminate number of images. To do this, you will need to complete the following tasks:

◆ Determine the number of images in the content viewer at run time and set the `width` of the `#slide` wrapper element based on the number of images

◆ Build the navigation links dynamically based on the number of images

◆ Create the `details` object dynamically based on the number of images and set the correct `left` properties to show each image

Animating an element's size

As I mentioned at the start of the chapter, almost any style property that contains a purely numeric value may be animated with the `animate()` method.

We looked at animating an element's position by manipulating its `left` style property, so let's move on to look at animating an element's size by manipulating its `height` and `width` style properties.

In this example, we'll create image wrappers that can be used to display larger versions of any images on the page by manipulating the element's size.

Time for action – creating the underlying page and basic styling

First, we'll create the underlying page on which the example will run.

1. Add the following HTML to the `<body>` of our template file:

```
<article>
  <h1>The Article Title</h1>
  <p><img id="image1-thumb" class="expander" alt="An ASCII Zebra"
    src="img/ascii.gif" width="150" height="100">Lorem ipsum
    dolor...</p>
  <p><img id="image2-thumb" class="expander" alt="An ASCII Zebra"
    src="img/ascii2.gif" width="100" height="100">Lorem ipsum
    dolor...</p>
</article>
```

2. Save the example page as `animate-size.html`. We'll keep the styling light in this example; in a new file in your text editor, add the following code:

```
article {
  display:block; width:800px; margin:auto; z-index:0;
  font:normal 18px "Nimbus Sans L", "Helvetica Neue", "Franklin
    Gothic Medium", sans-serif;
}
article p {
  margin:0 0 20px; width:800px; font:15px Verdana, sans-serif;
  line-height:20px;
}
article p #image2-thumb { float:right; margin:6px 0 0 30px; }
img.expander { margin:6px 30px 1px 0; float:left; }
.expander-wrapper { position:absolute; z-index:999; }
.expander-wrapper img {
  cursor:pointer; margin:0; position:absolute;
}
.expander-wrapper .expanded { z-index:9999; }
```

3. Save this file as `animate-size.css` in the `css` folder.

What just happened?

The HTML could be any simple blog post consisting of some text and a couple of images. The points to note are that each image is given an id attribute so that it can be easily referenced, and that each image is actually the full-sized version of the image, scaled down with width and height attributes.

The styles used are purely to lay out the example; very little of the code is actually required to make the example work. The expander-wrapper styles are needed to position the overlaid images correctly, but other than that the styling is purely arbitrary.

We're floating the second image to the right. Again this isn't strictly necessary; it's used just to make the example a little more interesting.

Time for action – defining the full and small sizes of the images

First we need to specify the full and small sizes of each image:

```
var dims = {
  image1: {
    small: { width: 150, height: 100 },
    big: { width: 600, height: 400 }
  },
  image2: {
    small: { width: 100, height: 100 },
    big: { width: 400, height: 400 }
  }
},
webkit = ($("body").css("-webkit-appearance") !== "" && $("body").
css("-webkit-appearance") !== undefined) ? true : false;
```

What just happened?

We create an object which itself contains properties matching each image's filename. Each property contains another nested object which has small and big properties and the relevant integers as values. This is a convenient way to store structured information that can easily be accessed at different points in our script.

We also create a variable called webkit. There is a slight bug in how images floated to the right are treated in Webkit-based browsers such as Safari or Chrome. This variable will hold a Boolean that will indicate whether Webkit is in use.

A test is performed which tries to read the -webkit-appearance CSS property. In Webkit browsers, the test will return none as the property is not set, but other browsers will either return an empty string or the value undefined.

Time for action – creating the overlay images

Next we should create an almost exact copy of each image on the page to use as an overlay:

```
$(".expander").each(function(i) {

   var expander = $(this),
      coords = expander.offset(),
      copy = $("<img>", {
         id: expander.attr("id").split("-")[0],
         src: expander.attr("src"),
         width: expander.width(),
         height: expander.height()
      });
```

What just happened?

In this part of the `<script>`, we select each image on the page and process them using jQuery's `each()` method. We set some variables, caching a reference to the current image and storing its coordinates on the page relative to the document using the jQuery `offset()` method.

We then create a new image for each existing image on the page, giving it an `id` attribute that pairs it with the image it is overlaying, the `src` of the original image, and the `width` and `height` of the original image. We use the JavaScript `split()` function to remove the part of the string that says `thumb` when we set the `id` of the new image.

Note that the previous code does not represent an entire snippet of fully-functional code. The outer function passed to the `each()` method has not yet been closed as we need to add some additional code after these variables.

Time for action – creating the overlay wrappers

We now need to create the wrappers for each of the overlay images (note that this code is still within the `each()` method and so will be executed for each of the images that have the expanded class name):

```
$("<div></div>", {
   "class": "expander-wrapper",
   css: {
      top: coords.top,
      left: (webkit === true && expander.css("float") === "right") ?
         (coords.left + expander.width()) : coords.left,
         direction: (expander.css("float") === "right") ? "rtl" :
         "ltr"
```

```
  },
  html: copy,
  width: expander.width(),
  height: expander.height(),
  click: function() {

    var img = $(this).find("img"),
      id = img.attr("id");

    if (!img.hasClass("expanded")) {
      img.addClass("expanded").animate({
        width: dims[id].big.width,
        height: dims[id].big.height
      }, {
        queue: false
      });
    } else {
      img.animate({
        width: dims[id].small.width,
        height: dims[id].small.height
      }, {
        queue: false,
        complete: function() {
          $(this).removeClass("expanded");
        }
      });
    }
  }
})).appendTo("body");
```

What just happened?

In this section of code, we create the wrapper element for the new image. We give it a new class name so that it can be positioned correctly.

Quoting the class property

We need to use quotes around the property name `class` so that it works correctly in Internet Explorer. If we fail to quote it, IE will throw a script error stating that it **expected an identifier, string, or number**.

We set the position of the wrapper element using the `css` property in conjunction with the coordinates we obtained from the `offset()` method earlier.

When setting the `left` position of the wrapper element, we need to check our `webkit` variable to see if Safari is in use. If this variable is set to `true`, and if the image is floated to the right, we position the overlay according to the `cords.left` value in addition to the `width` of the original image. If the `webkit` variable is `false`, or if the original image is floated `left`, we just set the `left` position of the wrapper to the value stored in `coords.left`.

We also need to set the `direction` property of any images that are floated right. We check the `float` style property and set the `direction` to `rtl` if the image is floated right, or `ltr` if not. This is done using JavaScript's ternary conditional.

This check is done so that the wrapper expands from right-to-left when the image is floated `right`. If we didn't set this, the wrapper would open up from left-to-right, which could make the full-sized image overflow the viewport or the content container resulting in scroll bars.

We add the new image to the wrapper by passing a reference to it into the jQuery `html()` method, and set the `width` of the wrapper to the `width` of the original (and new) image. This is necessary for the overlay to be positioned correctly over any images that are floated right.

Next we add a click handler to the wrapper. Within the anonymous function passed as the value of the `click()` method, we first cache a reference to the image within the wrapper that was clicked, and get the `id` of the image for convenience. Remember, the `id` of the overlay image will be the same as the original image it is covering minus the text string `-thumb`.

We then check whether the image has the class name `expanded`. If it doesn't, we add the class name and then animate the image to its full size using the second format of the `animate()` method. We pass two objects into the method as arguments; the first contains the CSS properties we wish to animate, in this case the `width` and `height` of the image.

The correct `width` and `height` to increase the image to are retrieved from the `dims` object using the `id` of the image that was clicked as the key. In the second object passed to the `animate()` method, we set the `queue` property to `false`. This has the same effect as using the `stop()` method directly before the `animate()` method and ensures that nothing bad happens if the overlay wrapper is repeatedly clicked.

If the image already has the class name expanded, we animate the image back to its small size. Again we use the two-object format of the animate() method, supplying false as the value of the queue property, and removing the class name expanded in an anonymous callback function passed to the complete property. Once the wrapper has been created, we append it to the <body> of the page.

At this point the code we've written will work as intended—clicking an image will result in the expanded version being animated to its full size. However, if the page is resized at all, the overlays will no longer be overlaying their images.

Time for action – maintaining the overlay positions

Because the overlays are positioned absolutely, we need to prevent them from becoming misaligned if the window is resized:

```
$(window).resize(function() {

  $("div.expander-wrapper").each(function(i) {

    var newCoords = $("#image" + (i + 1) + "-thumb").offset();

    $(this).css({
      top: newCoords.top,
      left: newCoords.left
    });
  });
});
```

What just happened?

All we need to do is make sure the overlay images stay directly on top of the original images when the page resizes, which we can achieve by binding a handler for the resize event to the window object. In the handler function, we just get the new coordinates of the underlying image, and set the top and left properties of the wrapper accordingly. Note that we don't animate the repositioning of the overlays.

Save the file and preview it in your browser. We should find that we can click on either image and it will expand to show a full-sized version of the image, with the first image expanding to the right, and the second expanding to the left:

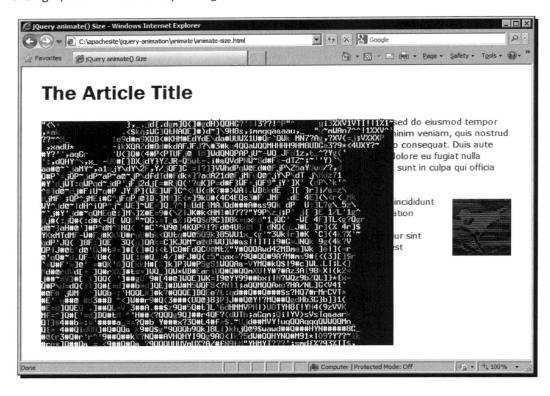

In the previous screenshot we see the first image as it expands to its full size.

Pop quiz – creating expanding images

1. In this example, we used a different format for the arguments passed to the `animate()` method, what format did the arguments take?

    a. Two arrays where the first array contains selectors for the elements to animate, and the second contains the duration, easing, and `specialEasing` strings, and a callback function

    b. A single object containing the style properties to animate, duration, easing, and `specialEasing` strings, and `step` and `complete` callback functions

    c. A function which must return the style properties to animate, the duration and easing strings, and a callback function

d. Two objects where the first object contains the style properties to animate, and the second object contains the duration, easing and `specialEasing` strings, a Boolean indicating whether to queue repeated `animate()` calls, and the step and complete callback functions

2. What is the keyword `this` scoped to in an animation's callback function?

a. The element that was animated

b. The current window

c. The container of the element that was animated

d. The event object

Have a go hero – doing away with the hardcoded dims object

In the previous example, we hardcoded an image into the top of our script that was used to tell the `animate()` method what size the image should be animated to. While this was fine for the purpose of the example, it doesn't really scale well as a long-term solution as we would have to remember to set this every time we used the script (or otherwise ensure our images are always a fixed size).

The problem is that we have no way to programmatically get both the full size and thumb size from a single image. The good news is that any data that can be stored in a JavaScript object can also be passed across a network for consumption as a JSON object. Extend this example so that when the page loads, it passes the `src` attributes of the images on the page to the server, which returns a JSON object containing the small and large image sizes. An image manipulation library, like GD or ImageMagick, for PHP, or the `System.Drawing.Image` type in .Net, will be your friend here.

Creating a jQuery animation plugin

Plugins are an excellent way of packaging up functionality into an easy to deploy and share module of code that serves a specific purpose. jQuery provides the `fn.extend()` method precisely for this purpose, making it easy to create powerful and effective plugins that can be easily distributed and used.

There are a few guidelines that should be adhered to when creating jQuery plugins; these are as follows:

◆ New methods, which are called like other jQuery methods, for example `$(elements).newMethod()` should be attached to the `fn` object, and new functions, which are used by the plugin, for example `$.myFunction()`, should be attached to the `jQuery` object

- New methods and functions should always end in a semi-colon (;) to preserve functionality when the plugin is compressed

- Inside methods, the `this` keyword always refers to the current selection of elements, and methods should always return `this` to preserve chaining

- Always attach new methods and functions to the `jQuery` object as opposed to the `$` alias, unless using an anonymous function with an aliased `$` object

In this section, we'll create a plugin which can be used to create advanced transition effects when showing a series of images. The finished widget will be similar in some respects to the image viewer we created earlier, but will not animate the images themselves. Instead, it will apply transition effects between showing them.

Time for action – creating a test page and adding some styling

Once again we'll create the example page and basic styling first and add the script last.

1. The underlying HTML for this example is very light. All we need in the `<body>` of our template file are the following elements:

```
<div id="frame">
    <img class="visible" src="img/F-35_Lightning.jpg" alt="F-35
      Lightning">
    <img src="img/A-12_Blackbird.jpg" alt="A-12 Blackbird">
    <img src="img/B-2_Spirit.jpg" alt="B-2 Spirit">
    <img src="img/SR-71_Blackbird.jpg" alt="SR-71 Blackbird">
    <img src="img/F-117_Nighthawk.jpg" alt="F-117 Nighthawk">
</div>
```

2. Save this page as `advanced-transitions.html`.

3. Like the markup, the CSS we rely on for a plugin should also be as minimal as possible. Luckily not much CSS is required for our small collection of elements.

4. Add the following code to a new file in your text editor:

```
#frame { position:relative; width:520px; height:400px; z-index:0;
}
#frame img { position:absolute; top:0; left:0; z-index:1; }
#frame img.visible { z-index:2; }
#frame a {
  display:block; width:50%; height:100%; position:absolute; top:0;
  z-index:10; color:transparent;
  background-image:url(transparent.gif); filter:alpha(
    opacity = 0);
```

```
    text-align:center; text-decoration:none;
    font:90px "Palatino Linotype", "Book Antiqua", Palatino, serif;
    line-height:400%;
}
#frame a:hover {
    color:#fff; text-shadow:0 0 5px #000; filter:alpha(
      opacity = 100);
    filter: Shadow(Color=#000, Direction=0);
}
#frame a:focus { outline:none; }
#prev { left:0; }
#next { right:0; }
#overlay {
    width:100%; height:100%; position:absolute; left:0; top:0;
    z-index:3;
}
#overlay div { position:absolute; }
```

5. Save this in the css folder as advanced-transitions.css.

What just happened?

All we have on the underlying page are the images we wish to transition between within a container. It's best to keep the markup requirements for plugins as simple as possible so that they are easy for others to use and don't place undue restrictions on the elements or structure they want to use.

The images are positioned absolutely within the container using CSS so that they stack up on top of one another, and we set our visible class on the first element to ensure one image is above the rest in the stack.

Most of the styling goes towards the previous and next anchors, which we'll create with the plugin. These are set so that each one will take up exactly half of the container and are positioned to appear side-by-side. We set the z-index of these links so that they appear above all of the images. The font-size is ramped up considerably, and an excessive line-height means we don't need to middle-align the text with padding.

In most browsers, we simply set the color of the anchors to transparent, which hides them. Then we set the color to white in the hover state. This won't work too well in IE however, so instead we set the link initially to transparent with the Microsoft opacity filter and then set it to fully opaque in the hover, which serves the same purpose.

Another IE-specific fix

IE also presents us with another problem in that the clickable area of our links will only extend the height of the text within them because of their absolute positioning. We can overcome this by setting a reference to a background-image.

The best part is that the image doesn't even need to exist for the fix to work (so you'll find no corresponding `transparent.gif` file in the book's companion code bundle). The fix has no detrimental effects on normal browsers.

Creating the plugin

Now let's create the plugin itself. Unlike most of the other example code we've looked at, the code for our plugin will go into its own separate file.

Time for action – adding a license and defining configurable options

In a new file create the following outer structure for the plugin:

```
/*
  Plugin name jQuery plugin version 1.0

  Copyright (c) date copyright holder

  License(s)

*/

;(function($) {

  $.tranzify = {

    defaults: {
      transitionWidth: 40,
      transitionHeight: "100%",
      containerID: "overlay",
      transitionType: "venetian",
      prevID: "prev",
      nextID: "next",
      visibleClass: "visible"
    }
  };

})(jQuery);
```

What just happened?

All plugins should contain information on the plugin name and version number, the copyright owner (usually the author of the code) and the terms, or links to the terms, of the license or licenses it is released under.

The plugin is encapsulated within an anonymous function so that its variables are protected from other code which may be in use on the page it is deployed on, and has a semicolon placed before it to ensure it remains a discrete block of code after potential minification, and in case it is used with other, less scrupulously written code than our own.

We also alias the $ character for safe use within our function, to ensure it is not hijacked by any other libraries running on the page and to preserve the functionality of jQuery's `noConflict()` method.

It is good practice to make plugins as configurable as possible so that end users can adjust it to suit their own requirements. To facilitate this, we should provide a set of default values for any configurable options. When deciding what to make configurable, a good rule of thumb is to hardcode nothing other than pure logic into the plugin. Hence, IDs, class names, anything like that, should be made configurable.

The defaults we set for the plugin are stored in an object that is itself stored as a property of the `jQuery` object that is passed into the function. The property added to the `jQuery` object is called `tranzify`, the name of our plugin, and will be used to store the properties, functions, and methods we create so that all of our code is within a single namespace.

Our default properties are contained in a separate object called `defaults` within the `tranzify` object. We set the `width` and `height` of the transition elements, the `id` of the container that gets created, the default transition, the `ids` for the previous and next links, and the class name we give to the currently-showing image.

As I mentioned, it's best not to hardcode any `id` values or class names into a plugin if possible. The person implementing the plugin may already have an element on the page with an `id` of `overlay` for example, so we should give them the option to change it if need be.

Time for action – adding our plugin method to the jQuery namespace

Next we can add the code that will insert our plugin into the jQuery namespace so that it can be called like other jQuery methods:

```
$.fn.extend({
  tranzify: function(userConfig) {

    var config = (userConfig) ? $.extend({}, $.tranzify.defaults,
```

```
        userConfig) : $.tranzify.defaults;

    config.selector = "#" + this.attr("id");

    config.multi = parseInt(this.width()) / config.transitionWidth;

    $.tranzify.createUI(config);

    return this;
    }
});
```

What just happened?

jQuery provides the `fn.extend()` method specifically for adding new methods into jQuery, which is how most plugins are created. We define a function as the value of the sole property of an object passed to the `extend()` method. We also specify that the method may take one argument, which may be a configuration object passed into the method by whoever is using the plugin to change the default properties we have set.

The first thing our method does is check whether or not a configuration object has been passed into the method. If it has, we use the `extend()` method (not `fn.extend()` however) to merge the user's configuration object with our own `defaults` object.

The resulting object, created by the merging of these two objects, is stored in the variable `config` for easy access by our functions. Any properties that are in the `userConfig` object will overwrite the properties stored in our `defaults` object. Properties found in the `defaults` object but not the `userConfig` object will be preserved. If no `userConfig` object is passed into the method, we simply assign the `defaults` object to the `config` variable.

Next we build an `id` selector that matches the element that the method was called on and add this as an extra property to the `config` object, making it convenient to use throughout the plugin. We can't store this as a default property because it is likely to be different on every page that the plugin is used on, and we also can't expect users of the plugin to have to define this in a configuration object each time the plugin is used.

The number of transition elements we need to create will depend on the size of the images, and the width of the transition elements (defined as a configurable property), so we work out a quick multiplier based on the width of the image and the configured transition width for use later on.

Following this we call the function that will create the prev/next links (we define this shortly) and pass the function the `config` object so that it can read any properties that the user has configured.

Finally, we return the jQuery object (which is automatically assigned to the value of the `this` keyword within our plugin method). This is to preserve chaining so that the user can call additional jQuery methods after calling our plugin.

Time for action – creating the UI

Next we need to create the previous and next links that are overlaid above the images and allow the visitor to cycle through the images:

```
$.tranzify.createUI = function(config) {
  var imgLength = $(config.selector).find("img").length,
    prevA = $("<a></a>", {
    id: config.prevID,
    href: "#",
    html: "&laquo;",
    click: function(e) {
      e.preventDefault();

      $(config.selector).find("a").css("display", "none");

      $.tranzify.createOverlay(config);

      var currImg = $("." + config.visibleClass, $(config.selector));
      if(currImg.prev().filter("img").length > 0) {
        currImg.removeClass(config.visibleClass).prev().addClass
          (config.visibleClass);
      } else {
        currImg.removeClass(config.visibleClass);
        $(config.selector).find("img").eq(imgLength -
          1).addClass(config.visibleClass);
      }

      $.tranzify.runTransition(config);

    }
  }).appendTo(config.selector),

  nextA = $("<a></a>", {
    id: config.nextID,
    href: "#",
    html: "&raquo;",
    click: function(e) {
      e.preventDefault();
```

```
            $(config.selector).find("a").css("display", "none");

            $.tranzify.createOverlay(config);

            var currImg = $("." + config.visibleClass, $(config.selector));

            if(currImg.next().filter("img").length > 0) {
              currImg.removeClass(config.visibleClass).next().addClass(
                config.visibleClass);
            } else {
              currImg.removeClass(config.visibleClass);
              $(config.selector).find("img").eq(0).addClass(
                config.visibleClass);
            }

            $.tranzify.runTransition(config);
          }
      }).appendTo(config.selector);
    };
```

What just happened?

This is by far our largest function and deals with creating the previous and next links, as well as defining their click handlers during creation using the jQuery 1.4 syntax. The first thing we do is obtain the number of images in the container as the click handlers we add will need to know this.

We create the anchor for the previous link and in the object passed as the second argument we define the id (using the value from the config object), a dummy href, an HTML entity as its innerHTML, and a click handler.

Within the click handler, we use the preventDefault() method to stop the browser following the link, then hide the previous and next links in order to protect the widget against multiple clicks, as this will break the transitions.

Next we call our createOverlay() function, passing it the config object, to create the overlay container and the transition elements. We also cache a reference to the currently selected image using the class name stored in the config object.

We then test whether there is another image element before the visible image. If there is, we remove the class from the element that currently has it and give it to the previous image in order to bring it to the top of the stack. If there aren't any more images before the current image, we remove the visible class from the current image and move to the last image in the container to show that instead.

Once we've defined everything we need, we can append the new anchor to the specified container. We also create the next link within the current function as well, giving it a very similar set of attributes and a click handler too. All that differs in this click handler is that we test for an image after the current one, and move to the first image in the container if there isn't one.

Time for action – creating the transition overlay

Our next function will deal with creating the overlay and transition elements:

```
$.tranzify.createOverlay = function(config) {

  var posLeftMarker = 0,
    bgHorizMarker = 0

  overlay = $("<div></div>", {
    id: config.containerID
  });

  for (var x = 0; x < multiX; x++) {

    $("<div></div>", {
      width: config.transitionWidth,
      height: config.transitionHeight,
      css: {
        backgroundImage: "url(" + $("." + config.visibleClass,
          $(config.selector)).attr("src") + ")",
        backgroundPosition: bgHorizMarker + "px 0",
        left: posLeftMarker,
        top: 0
      }
    }).appendTo(overlay);
      bgHorizMarker -=config.transitionWidth;
    posLeftMarker +=config.transitionWidth;

  }
  overlay.insertBefore("#" + config.prevID);
};
```

What just happened?

Our next function deals with creating the overlay container and the transition elements that will provide the transition animations. The plugin will need to set the `position` and `background-position` of each transition element differently in order to stack the elements up horizontally. We'll need a couple of counter variables to do this, so we initialize them at the start of the function.

We then create the overlay container `<div>` and give it just an `id` attribute so that we can easily select it when we run the transitions.

Next we create the transition elements. To do this, we use a standard JavaScript `for` loop, which is executed a number of times depending on the multiplier we set earlier in the script. On each iteration of the loop, we create a new `<div>` which has its `width` and `height` set according to the properties stored in the configuration object.

We use the `css()` method to set the `backgroundImage` of the overlay to the currently visible image, and the `backgroundPosition` according to the current value of the `bgHorizMarker` counter variable. We also set the `left` property to position the new element correctly according to the `posLeftMarker` variable, and the `top` property to `0` to ensure correct positioning.

Once created, we append the new element to the container and increment our counter variables. Once the loop exits and we have created and appended all of the transition elements to the container, we can then append the container to the element on the page that the method was called on.

Time for action – defining the transitions

The final function will perform the actual transitions:

```
$.tranzify.runTransition = function(config) {
  var transOverlay = $("#" + config.containerID),
    transEls = transOverlay.children(),
    len = transEls.length - 1;

    switch(config.transitionType) {
      case "venetian":
      transEls.each(function(i) {
        transEls.eq(i).animate({
          width: 0
        }, "slow", function() {

          if (i === len) {
            transOverlay.remove();
```

```
        $(config.selector).find("a").css("display", "block");
      }
    });
  });
  break;
  case "strip":
  var counter = 0;

function strip() {
  transEls.eq(counter).animate({
    height: 0
  }, 150, function() {

    if (counter === len) {
      transOverlay.remove();
      $(config.selector).find("a").css("display", "block");
    } else {
      counter++;
      strip();
    }
  });
}
strip();
  }
};
```

What just happened?

Our last function deals with actually running the transitions. In this example, there are just two different types of transitions, but we could easily extend this to add more transition effects.

This function also requires some variables, so we set these at the start of the function for later use. We cache a reference to the overlay container as we'll be referring to it several times. We also store the collection of transition elements, and the number of transition elements. We subtract 1 from the number of children because the figure will be used with jQuery's eq() method, which is zero-based.

To determine which of our transitions to run, we use a JavaScript switch statement and check the value of the config.transitionType property. The first transition is a kind of venetian-blind effect. To run this transition, we just animate the width of each element to 0 using the jQuery each() method. The function we specify as the argument to this method automatically receives the index of the current element, which we access using i.

In the callback function for each animation, we check whether i is equal to the `length` of the collection of transition elements, and if it is we remove the overlay and show the previous and next links once more.

The second transition removes the old image one strip at a time. To do this, we use a simple `counter` variable and a standard JavaScript function. We can't use the `each()` method this time, or all of the transition elements will slide down together, but we want each one to slide down on its own.

Within the function, we animate the current transition element's height to 0 and set a rather low duration so that it happens fairly quickly. If the animation is too slow it spoils the effect. In the callback function, we check whether our `counter` variable is equal to the number of transition elements, and if so remove the overlay and show the links again. If the `counter` hasn't reached the last element at this point, we increment the `counter` variable and call the function once more.

Save this file as `jquery.tranzify.js` in the `js` folder. This is the standard naming convention for jQuery plugins and should be adhered to.

Using the plugin

To use the plugin, we just call it like we would call any other jQuery method, like this:

```
$("#frame").tranzify();
```

In this form, the default properties will be used. If we wanted to change one of the properties, we just supply a configuration object, such as this:

```
$("#frame").tranzify({
  transitionType: "strip"
});
```

The default animation should run something like this:

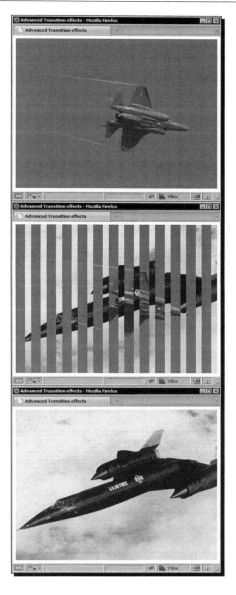

In the previous screenshot, we see the transition elements all simultaneously shrinking to 0 `width`, creating an effect like Venetian blinds being opened to reveal the new image.

Using the plugin is simple; there is just one point to remember. The images should all be the same size, and the `width` of each image should be exactly divisible by the `transitionWidth` property. As we've exposed the `transitionWidth` as a configurable property, we should be able to use any size image we wish and set this accordingly.

For reference, the second transition effect runs like this, with strips of the old image sliding away to reveal the new image:

In the previous screenshot, we can see the effects of the second transition type, with the old image being stripped away to reveal the new image.

Pop quiz – creating a plugin

1. What is the difference between a plugin method and a function?

   a. There is no difference, conceptually and in practice they are the same

   b. Methods are able to accept arguments, functions are not

   c. Methods execute faster

   d. Methods are attached to the `fn` object and are used like existing jQuery methods, while functions are attached directly to the jQuery object and called like any normal function

2. What must each new method return?

   a. A string containing the `id` attribute of the selected element

   b. An array containing the `id` attributes of selected elements

   c. The `this` object, which points to the currently selected element

   d. Nothing should be returned

Have a go hero – extending the plugin

Our plugin currently contains just two transition effects (venetian and strip). Extend the plugin to include more transition effects of your own devising. The plugin currently creates a number of transition elements that are the full height of each image.

By wrapping our existing `for` loop within another `for` loop and adding some new counter variables for `top` position and vertical `background-position`, it is relatively easy to add square transition elements in a checker-board style, which opens up the possibility of more complex, and attractive, transition effects. Do this.

Summary

In this chapter, we looked at some common usages of the `animate()` method, which is the means for us to create custom animations in jQuery when the built-in effects are not enough for our requirements. The method is robust, easy to use, and makes complex animations trivial.

When simple sliding or fading does not meet our requirements, we can fall back onto the `animate()` method in order to craft our own high-quality custom animations. We learnt the following points about the method:

- The `animate()` method can be used to animate any numeric CSS property (except colors, for which a separate plugin is required).
- The arguments passed into the method may take one of two formats. The first allows us to pass in an object containing the CSS properties to animate, as well as separate duration, easing, and callback arguments. The second format allows us to pass in two objects, the first allowing us to specify the CSS properties to animate as before, and the second allowing us to specify additional options such as the duration, easing, and callback. The second option gives us access to some special arguments not accessible in the first format such as `specialEasing` and the `step` callback.
- All CSS properties specified in the first object will be executed simultaneously.
- How to achieve animations involving an element's position, or its dimensions

We also looked at how we can extend the jQuery library with brand new functions and methods in the form of plugins. Plugins are a great way of wrapping up code for easy deployment and sharing.

Now that we've looked at all of jQuery's animation methods, we're going to move on and take a look at the additional animation functionality provided by the excellent jQuery UI library. The next chapter will cover all of the additional effects added by the UI library, as well as look at class transitioning and smooth color animating.

6

Extended Animations with jQuery UI

jQuery UI is the official user interface library for jQuery and adds a suite of interactive widgets such as tabs and accordions, a series of interaction helpers such as drag and drop, and a comprehensive set of effects that extend those provided natively by jQuery.

Over the course of this chapter, we'll be looking at the additional effects added by jQuery UI. Topics we'll cover include:

- ◆ Obtaining and setting up jQuery UI
- ◆ The new effects added by jQuery UI
- ◆ Using the `effect()` method
- ◆ Extending the `show()`, `hide()`, and `toggle()` methods
- ◆ Using easing with jQuery UI
- ◆ Animating an element's color
- ◆ Animated class transitions

jQuery UI adds several new animation methods, as well as modifying several jQuery methods. The methods we'll be looking at in this chapter are:

- ◆ `animate()`
- ◆ `addClass()`
- ◆ `effect()`
- ◆ `hide()`
- ◆ `switchClass()`
- ◆ `show()`
- ◆ `toggle()`

Obtaining and setting up jQuery UI

jQuery UI is very easy to obtain and set up. There is an online tool that will build a custom download package for us containing just the parts of jQuery UI that we'll need. Due to the modular nature of jQuery UI it makes sense to minimize the code payload we use on any given web project and so the ability to include only the modules of code we intend to use helps us to minimize any impact on the visitor our code may have.

The jQuery UI download builder can be found at `http://jqueryui.com/download`. The page is split into two sections with the components of the library listed at the left and the theme details at the right. The download builder has a certain amount of intelligence, and will ensure that any dependencies are automatically selected when we choose the components we require.

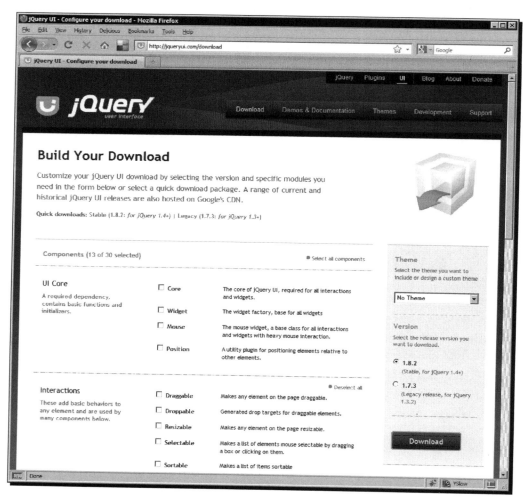

The download builder shown in the previous screenshot gives us everything we need to run any subset of the library components.

All we'll be using in this chapter are the effects, so when we download a package we should only select the components found in the effects subsection at the left. We don't need to include a theme, and we don't even need to include the library core. The effects can be used completely independently of the rest of the library; all we need is the effects Core file and the individual effects we require. Make sure all of them are selected and download the package.

The package will give us everything we need to use the components we've selected, including a copy of the latest stable release of jQuery, so when using jQuery UI, jQuery itself does not need to be downloaded separately.

All of the JavaScript for each selected component is combined and compressed into a single file by the download builder, and any functional CSS or theme files will be combined into a single stylesheet. We don't need any of the theme files for working with the effects, but ensure the `.js` file from the archive provided by the download builder goes into our `js` folder.

A new template file

The examples in the remainder of this chapter will be short, mostly image-based examples that illustrate each effect in turn, so it makes sense to use a slightly different template file for them. Create a new template file by adding a reference to the jQuery UI source file directly after the jQuery one just before the closing `</body>` tag. We won't be using any HTML5 elements in this chapter so we can safely remove the link to `shiv.js` in our new template file.

The new effects added by jQuery UI

jQuery UI gives us 14 new predefined animations to use in our pages; these are listed, together with a brief description of their usage, as follows:

Animations	Description
blind	The target element is shown or hidden by rolling it down or up like a window blind.
bounce	The target element is bounced horizontally or vertically for a specified number of times.
clip	The target element is shown or hidden by moving opposing edges in towards the center of the element, or out to its full width or height.
drop	The element appears to drop onto or off of the page in order to show or hide it respectively.

Animations	Description
explode	The explode effect causes the target element to separate into a specified number of pieces before fading away, or to fade into view in several pieces before coming together to form the complete element.
fold	The element appears to fold closed or open.
highlight	The background-color of the target element is set (to yellow by default, although this is configurable), and then fades away after a short interval.
puff	The target element increases in size slightly and then fades away.
pulsate	The target element's opacity is adjusted a specified number of times, making the element appear to flicker on and off.
scale	The dimensions of the target element are adjusted to increase or decrease its size.
shake	The target element is shaken a specified number of times. This effect is similar to the bounce effect with the key difference that the distance of the shake remains the same on each iteration of the animation.
size	The dimensions of the target element are adjusted to increase or decrease its size. This effect is almost identical to scale.
slide	The target element is made to slide in or out of view, horizontally or vertically.
transfer	The outline of the specified element is transferred to another element on the page.

Using the effect API

jQuery UI introduces the effect() method which can be used to trigger any of the effects listed in the previous table. The effect() method's usage pattern is as follows:

```
jQuery(elements).effect(effect name, [configuration], [duration],
[callback]);
```

The name of the effect that we would like to use is always the first argument of the effect() method. It is supplied in string format.

Each effect has custom configuration options that can be set to control how the effect displays. These options are set in a configuration object which is passed to the effect() method as the second argument, following the name of the effect.

We can also supply a duration for the effect as an argument. As with standard jQuery animations, we can supply either an integer representing the duration of the effect in milliseconds, or one of the strings slow or fast.

If no configuration is required, the duration may be passed to the effect() method as the second argument. If no duration is supplied, the default duration of 400 milliseconds will be used.

Optionally, a callback function may be provided as the final argument. The supplied function will be executed once for each selected element when the effect ends.

Let's look at a few examples of how the `effect()` method can be used.

The bounce effect

The bounce effect is similar to, but much more controllable than, the `easeOutBounce` easing function. It can be used with either the effect API or show/hide logic depending on your requirements.

Configuration options

The following configuration options are available for the bounce effect:

Option	Default	Usage
direction	"up"	The direction of bounce. The other possible option is the string down.
distance	20	The initial distance of bounce (successive bounces reduce in distance) in pixels.
mode	"effect"	Whether to run the effect normally or use show/hide logic. Other values accepted may be the strings show, hide, or toggle.
times	5	The number of bounces.

Time for action – using the bounce effect

In this example we'll see how the jQuery UI effect can be combined to create a bouncing ball that travels across the page:

1. Use the following simple elements in the `<body>` of the template file:

```
<div id="travel">
  <div id="ball"><!-- --></div>
</div>
```

2. All we need is a simple container `<div>` and an inner `<div>`. In the empty function at the end of the `<body>`, add the following script:

```
$("#ball").click(function() {
  $("#travel").animate({
    left: "+=300px"
  }, 2000).find("div").effect("bounce");
});
```

3. Save the file as bounce.html. We also need a few simple styles. Add the following CSS to a new file:

```
#travel { position:absolute; top:100px; }
#ball {
  width:150px; height:150px; cursor:pointer;
  background:url(../img/ball.jpg) no-repeat 0 0;
}
```

4. Save this as bounce.css in the css folder. When we run the page and click on the ball we should find that it bounces along the page, gradually coming to a halt:

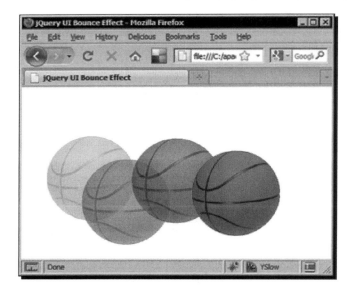

The previous composition shows the ball traveling across the page, bouncing up and down as it goes from left to right.

What just happened?

When the ball is clicked, we first use jQuery's animate() method to animate the left style property of the container by 300 pixels, over a duration of 2 seconds. We slow this animation down to improve the appearance of the overall animation, but it is not strictly required. We then navigate down to the inner <div> element and use the effect() method, specifying the bounce effect.

We need to use both elements because if we use the animate() and effect() methods on the same element, the bounce effect will go into the element's animation queue and the two animations will execute one after the other instead of running simultaneously.

The highlight effect

The highlight effect is a simple but effective way to draw the visitor's attention to new items that have been added to the page, and is used for this purpose in many of today's leading web-based interfaces.

Configuration options

There are only two configuration options for the highlight effect; these are listed as follows:

Options	Default	Usage
color	"#ffff99"	Sets the `background-color` of the element being highlighted.
mode	"show"	Sets whether the effect will be hidden or shown when used with the `effect()` method. Other possible values include `hide`, `toggle`, or `effect`.

Time for action – highlighting elements

In this example we'll create a simple todo list, with a series of default items that can be checked off. We can also allow new items to be added to the list and will apply the highlight effect to new items as they are added.

1. Add the following HTML to the `<body>` of the template file:

```
<div id="todo">
  <h2>Todo List</h2>
  <ul>
    <li><label><input type="checkbox">Item 1</label></li>
    <li><label><input type="checkbox">Item 2</label></li>
    <li><label><input type="checkbox">Item 3</label></li>
  </ul>
  <input type="text" id="new"><button id="add">Add</button>
</div>
```

2. Add the behavior for our todo list using the following code:

```
$("#add").click(function() {
  var newItem = $("#new"),
    text = newItem.val();

  if (text) {
    var li = $("<li>"),
      label = $("<label>").html(
        "<input type=\"checkbox\">" + text).appendTo(li);
```

```
        li.appendTo("#todo ul").effect("highlight", 2000);
        newItem.val("");
    }
});
```

3. Save this page as `highlight.html`. We also need some CSS for this example. In a new file in your text editor add the following code:

```
#todo {
  width:208px;
  font:normal 13px "Nimbus Sans L", "Helvetica Neue", "Franklin
    Gothic Medium", Sans-serif;
}
#todo ul { padding:0; margin-bottom:30px; }
#todo li { list-style-type:none; }
#todo label { display:block; border-bottom:1px dotted #000; }
li input { position:relative; top:2px; }
input { margin-right:10px; }
```

4. Save this page as `highlight.css`.

5. When we run the page in a browser, we can add a new item and it will be highlighted briefly as the new item is added to the list:

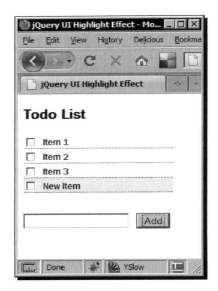

In the previous screenshot we see the fade effect before it fades away from the newly added item.

What just happened?

We add a click handler to the `<button>` at the bottom of the list which drives the functionality of the rest of the behavior. When the `<button>` is clicked, we cache the selector for the `<input>` field and obtain the text that was entered into it.

If the variable holding the text is not empty, we then create a new `<label>` and `<input>`. We add the text to the `<label>` as well and then append the new item to the list. Finally, we apply the highlight effect and empty the `<input>` field.

The pulsate effect

The pulsate effect fades the element in and out of view a specified number of times so that the target element appears to pulsate. Like most of the effects we have looked at so far, it is easy to use and requires little or no configuration.

Configuration options

The pulsate effect also has just two configurable options; these are shown in the following table:

Option	Default	Usage
mode	"show"	Sets whether the target element is shown or hidden when used with the `effect()` method. Other possible values include `hide`, `toggle`, and `effect`.
times	5	Sets the number of times the target element is pulsated.

Time for action – making an element pulsate

In this example, we'll show a simple time sheet in which rows can be deleted by clicking a link. If a link is clicked, the corresponding row will be pulsated before it is removed.

1. Use the following markup in the template file:

```
<table>
  <tr><th>Job Number</th><th>Start Time</th><th>End Time</th>
    <th colspan="2">Total</th></tr>
  <tr><td>05432</td><td>8:00</td><td>8:43</td><td>43
    minutes</td><td><a class="delete" href="#" title="Delete this
    item">Delete</a></td></tr>
  <tr><td>05684</td><td>8:43</td><td>10:21</td><td>1 hour 38
    minutes</td><td><a class="delete" href="#" title="Delete this
    item">Delete</a></td></tr>
```

```
<tr><td>05684</td><td>10:21</td><td>13:30</td><td>3 hour 9
   minutes</td><td><a class="delete" href="#" title="Delete this
   item">Delete</a></td></tr>
</table>
```

2. Add the code to apply the effect to the closure at the bottom of the page:

```
$(".delete").click(function(e) {
  e.preventDefault();

  var row = $(this).closest("tr");

  row.closest("tr").children().css("backgroundColor",
    "red").effect("pulsate", function() {
    row.remove();
  });
});
```

3. Save this file as `pulsate.html`. Only a couple of styles are required for this example. These should go into a new file:

```
table {
  border-spacing:0;
  font:normal 13px "Nimbus Sans L", "Helvetica Neue", "Franklin
    Gothic Medium", Sans-serif;
}
th, td { text-align:left; padding-right:20px; }
```

4. Save this file in the `css` folder as `pulsate.css`.

5. Clicking the delete link in any row will apply the pulsate effect and then remove the table row:

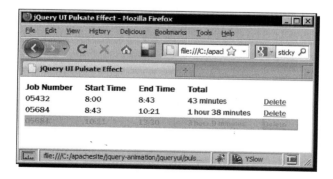

The previous screenshot shows a single pulsate iteration as it fades out.

What just happened?

When a **Delete** link is clicked, our handler function first sets the `background-color` of the `<tr>` that the link is within. This is not mandatory for the effect, but it does help bring it to life.

We then apply the pulsate effect to all `<td>` elements within the row using the `effect()` method. We need to apply the effect to the `<td>` elements instead of the `<tr>` element so that the effect works as intended in IE.

When the effect ends, our inline callback function will be executed which removes the `<tr>`. Obviously the `<tr>` can only be removed once, but once it has been removed, subsequent attempts to remove it will just fail silently.

The shake effect

The shake effect shakes the element that it is applied to back and forth a specified number of times.

Configuration options

The shake effect exposes three configuration options that allow us to customize its behavior. These are listed in the following table:

Option	Default	Usage
direction	"left"	Sets the direction that the element moves in
distance	20	Sets the number of pixels the element travels when it is shaken
times	3	Sets the number of times the element shakes

Time for action – shaking an element

The open source .Net CMS Umbraco uses the shake effect when incorrect login details are entered in the sign-in form for its back-office administration area. In this example we can see how easy it is to implement this behavior using the shake effect.

1. Add the following markup to the template file as the basis of the log in form:

```
<form>
  <h2>Login</h2>
  <label>Username:<input id="name" type="text"></label>
  <label>Password:<input id="pass" type="text"></label>
  <button id="submit">Login</button>
</form>
```

2. Now add the following code to the empty closure at the bottom of the template file:

```
$("#submit").click(function(e) {
  e.preventDefault();

  $("input").each(function(i, val) {
    if (!$(this).val()) {
      $(this).css("border", "1px solid red").effect("shake", {
        distance: 5 }, 100);
    }
  });
});
```

3. Save this file as `shake.html`. We also need a basic stylesheet for this example. Add the following CSS to a new file:

```
form {
  width:145px; padding:20px; margin:auto; border:1px solid #000;
  font:normal 13px "Nimbus Sans L", "Helvetica Neue", "Franklin
    Gothic Medium", Sans-serif;
}
h2 { font-size:14px; margin-top:0; }
input { display:block; margin-bottom:10px; border:1px solid #000;
}
```

4. Save this file as `shake.css`.

5. If we run the page in a browser and click the `<button>` without completing either of the `<input>` fields, both fields will have their borders set to red and will shake from side to side:

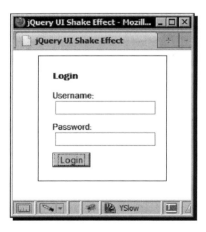

In the previous screenshot, we see the text fields being shaken when they are left empty and the `<button>` is clicked.

What just happened?

When the `<button>` is clicked we simply check to see if each `<input>` has a value and if not, we apply a red border and then call the `effect()` method specifying shake as the effect. We use a configuration object to reduce the distance the element moves, as well as specifying a relatively short duration.

The size effect

The size effect is used to resize an element, making it grow or shrink depending on its configuration. Unlike most of the other effects, the size effect must be configured for it to be used successfully.

The size effect is also one of the only effects that has the base core file as well as another effect as dependencies. Most components rely only on the core file. As we downloaded the entire effect suite from the jQuery UI download builder, we don't need to worry about including the additional effect. It's already in the single file that the download builder created when we downloaded it at the start of the chapter.

Configuration options

The size effect gives us four configurable options, which are listed as follows:

Option	Default	Usage
from	none	Sets the size of the target element at the beginning of the animation. This option accepts an object with `height` and `width` keys which are used to set the starting size of the target element. This option is not mandatory.
to	none	Sets the size of the target element at the end of the animation. This option accepts an object with `height` and `width` keys which are used to set the ending size of the target element. This option must be supplied.
origin	['middle ', 'center']	Sets the vanishing point for hiding animations, or the point from which it grows when used with show logic.
scale	"both "	This option sets whether the whole `box` of the element (including border and padding CSS values) is scaled, just the `content`, or as in the default, `both`.

Time for action – resizing elements

A popular use of growing and shrinking elements is the Fisheye menu, where elements grow when the mouse pointer hovers over them, and shrink back down when the pointer moves off them. This effect is also used by the icons on the dock in Apple's OSX.

Using the size effect, we can implement our own basic Fisheye menu with just a few lines of code.

1. Add the following markup to the <body> of the template file:

```
<div id="dock">
  <a href="#" class="icon" id="finder">
    <img src="img/finder.png"></a>
  <a href="#" class="icon" id="mail">
    <img src="img/mail.png"></a>
  <a href="#" class="icon" id="safari">
    <img src="img/safari.png"></a>
  <a href="#" class="icon" id="firefox">
    <img src="img/firefox_small.png"></a>
  <a href="#" class="icon" id="itunes">
    <img src="img/itunes.png"></a>
</div>
```

2. Add the following JavaScript to the third <script> element at the bottom of the <body>:

```
$(".icon", "#dock").hover(function() {
  $(this).stop().animate({
    top: -31
  }).find("img").stop().effect("size", {
    to: { width: 64, height: 64 }
  });
}, function() {
  $(this).stop().animate({
    top: -15
  }).find("img").stop().effect("size", {
    to: { width: 48, height: 48 }
  });
});
```

3. Save this file as `size.html`. We also need some styling. In a new file add the following code:

```
#dock {
  width:380px; height:90px; position:fixed; bottom:0;
```

```
    background:url(../img/dock.png) no-repeat 0 0;
}
.icon { position:absolute; top:-15px; left:44px; }
.icon img { border:none; }
#mail { left:108px; }
#safari { left:170px; }
#firefox { left:229px; }
#itunes { left:289px; }
```

4. Save this file as `size.css` in the `css` folder.

5. When we run the file in a browser, we should see that the individual items in the menu grow and shrink as the mouse pointer moves over them:

In the previous screenshot we see the menu as the pointer hovers over one of the items in the menu.

What just happened?

We attach `mouseenter` and `mouseleave` event handlers to each item within the dock using jQuery's `hover()` method, which accepts two functions, the first being executed on the `mouseenter` event, the second being executed on `mouseleave`.

In the first function we use the `stop()` method to manage the queue and then animate the element's position by changing its `top` CSS value. Using `stop()` here prevents an unsightly jarring of the element's position on screen.

We then navigate down the image inside the link and call the `stop()` method on this element too before applying the size effect. We provide integer values for the `width` and `height` keys in a configuration object and as these values are larger than the dimensions of the image, the image will be increased in size.

Note that when we use the `stop()` method with the image, it is to prevent a build-up of effects if the mouse pointer is repeatedly moved on and off one of the links. The second function is really the reverse of the first function, which simply resizes the element back to its original position and size.

The transfer effect

The transfer effect simply transfers the outline of one element to another element. Like the size effect that we looked at a moment ago, the transfer effect will not work if it is not configured.

Configuration options

The transfer effect has only two configuration options, although only one is mandatory. These options are listed in the following table:

Option	Default	Usage
className	none	The value of this option, if set, is added to the transfer element when the effect runs
to	none	A jQuery selector that specifies the target element that the transfer element is sent to

Time for action – transferring the outline of one element to another

In this example we'll recreate a popular application installation dialog from OSX, and use the transfer effect to help show visitors where to drag the icon (the icon won't actually be draggable, all we're doing is looking at the transfer effect).

1. Add the following elements to the `<body>` of the template file to create the install dialog:

```
<div id="install">
  <div id="firefox"><!-- --></div>
  <div id="apps"><!-- --></div>
</div>
<p>To install the application, drag its icon over to the apps
folder icon.</p>
<button id="show">Show me</button>
```

2. Add the following script to the empty function at the bottom of the template file:

```
$("#show").click(function() {
  $("#firefox").effect("transfer", {
    to: "#apps",
    className: "ui-effect-transfer"
  }, 1000);
});
```

3. Save the page as `transfer.html`. For the stylesheet add the following code to a new file:

```
body {
  font:normal 14px "Nimbus Sans L", "Helvetica Neue", "Franklin
    Gothic Medium", Sans-serif;
}
#install {
  width:417px; height:339px; position:relative;
  background:url(../img/install.jpg) no-repeat 0 0;
}
#firefox {
  width:124px; height:121px; position:absolute; left:34px;
  top:132px; background:url(../img/firefox.png) no-repeat 0 0;
}
#apps {
  width:54px; height:52px; position:absolute; right:58px;
  top:172px; background:url(../img/apps.png) no-repeat 0 0;
}
.ui-effect-transfer { border:2px solid #7bee76; }
```

4. Save this file as `transfer.css` in the `css` folder.

5. When the `<button>` is clicked, an outline is transferred from the Firefox icon to the App folder icon to direct the visitor:

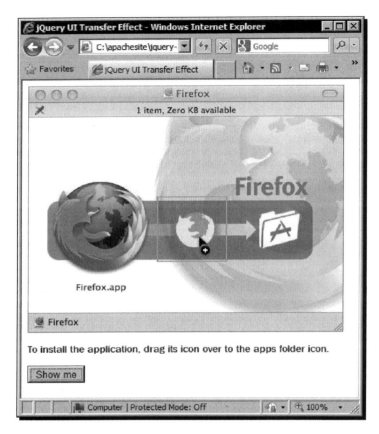

The transfer element is resized as it moves from the starting element across to the target element. The animation is approximately 50 % complete in the previous screenshot.

What just happened?

In the underlying HTML we have a container `<div>` which is given the background image of the application install dialog box. Within this we have a `<div>` which is given the Firefox icon background, and a second `<div>` which is given the App folder icon. Both inner `<div>` elements are given `id` attributes for styling purposes and for easy selection with jQuery.

In the script we add a click-handler to the `<button>` which applies the effect every time the `<button>` is clicked. The handler function calls the transfer effect on the `#firefox` element, which sets the icon as the starting element.

In the configuration object, we set the `to` option to a selector for the apps element, and the `className` option to the string `ui-effect-transfer`. This string is applied to the element as a class name and is used to add a green border to the transfer element while it is visible.

Each time the `<button>` is clicked, the transfer element will be shown and will animate from the starting element (the Firefox icon) to the ending element (the Apps folder icon).

Pop quiz – using the effect API

1. How many new effects does jQuery UI give us?

    a. 2

    b. 18

    c. 9

    d. 14

2. How is the effect we wish to use specified?

    a. By calling the effect as a function, for example `bounce()`

    b. The name of the effect is passed in string format to the `effect()` method as the first argument, for example `effect("bounce")`

    c. The name of the effect is provided as the value of the `effect` key in an object passed to the `animate()` method, for example `animate({ effect: "bounce" })`

    d. The name of the effect is passed as a string to an event helper, for example `click("bounce")`

Using effects with show and hide logic

Some of the jQuery UI effects can also be used in conjunction with jQuery's `show()`, `hide()`, and `toggle()` methods when showing or hiding logic is required. In fact, some of the effects are better suited to this method of execution.

The blind effect

The blind effect is the perfect example of an effect that is usually best used with show/hide logic as opposed to the standard effect API. Although the blind effect will work with the standard effect API, what will happen is that the effect will run according to its default mode, but then the element will be put back into its original state. This is true for all effects that have a `mode` configuration option.

Configuration options

The blind effect has the following configuration options:

Option	Default	Usage
direction	"vertical"	Sets the axis along which the target element is shown or hidden.
mode	"hide"	Sets whether the element is shown or hidden when used with the effect() method. Other possible values include show, toggle, and effect.

Time for action – using the blind effect

I mentioned earlier that the effect is reminiscent of a window blind rolling up or down, so let's base our next example on that:

1. In the `<body>` of the template file add the following code:

```
<div id="window">
  <div id="blind"><!-- --></div>
</div>
```

2. Implement the effect with the following script:

```
$("#window").click(function() {
  $("#blind").toggle("blind");
});
```

3. Save this file as blind.html. The stylesheet for this example is as follows:

```
#window {
  width:464px; height:429px; position:relative; cursor:pointer;
  background:url(../img/window.jpg) no-repeat 0 0;
}
#blind {
  display:none; width:332px; height:245px; position:absolute;
  left:64px; top:113px;
  background:url(../img/blind.png) no-repeat 0 100%;
}
```

4. Save this as blind.css in the css folder.

5. When we run the page in a browser, the blind should alternately roll down and up each time the window is clicked:

The previous screenshot shows the blind in its fully-open state.

What just happened?

We set a click handler on the outer container which calls the `toggle()` method on the inner element. In the CSS we set the inner element to be hidden initially, so the first time the container element is clicked, the inner element will be shown.

The clip effect

The clip effect causes the element it is called upon to reduce in size vertically or horizontally until it disappears.

Configuration options

The configuration options we have at our disposal when using the clip effect allow us to control the direction in which the animation proceeds, and whether the element is shown or hidden:

Option	Default	Usage
direction	"vertical"	Sets the axis along which the element animates.
mode	"hide"	Configures whether the element is hidden or shown. Other possible values are show, toggle, and effect .

Time for action – clipping an element in and out

This effect is billed as being similar to what happens to the picture when an old television set is turned off, so let's work that into our example.

1. Add the following elements to the `<body>` of the template file:

```
<div id="tv">
  <div id="bg"><!-- --></div>
  <div id="static"><!-- --></div>
</div>
```

2. Then use the following simple script at the bottom of the page:

```
$("#tv").click(function() {
  $("#static").effect("clip");
});
```

3. Save this file as `clip.html`. The stylesheet for this example is as follows:

```
#tv {
  width:300px; height:269px; position:relative; cursor:pointer;
  background:url(../img/tv.png) no-repeat 0 0;
}
#bg {
  width:220px; height:180px; position:absolute; left:42px;
  top:30px;
  z-index:-2; background-color:#000;
}
#static {
  width:216px; height:178px; position:absolute; left:44px;
  top:31px;
  z-index:-1; background:url(../img/static.gif) no-repeat 0 0;
}
```

4. Save this file in the `css` folder as `clip.css`.

5. When the page is run, we should be able to click anywhere on the television and see the effect run:

The previous screenshot shows the static element as it is being clipped.

What just happened?

The underlying page has a collection of elements on it with the outer container being styled to look like the television and a couple of inner elements, one of which is a simple background which sits behind the static element. Both inner containers use CSS z-index to sit behind the outer container.

When any part of the television is clicked, the static element has the effect applied to it without any additional configuration, and because the default mode of the effect is hide, the element will be hidden automatically when the effect ends. To see the reverse of the effect, we could hide the static by default and set the mode to show, or we could set the mode to toggle and have the static alternately show and hide.

The drop effect

The drop effect is used to show an element while sliding it open, or hide it while sliding it closed. This effect works on both the position and opacity of the element it is applied to.

Configuration options

The drop effect allows us to control the direction that the element drops, and whether it is shown or hidden:

Option	Default	Usage
direction	"left"	Sets the direction that the element drops in or out of the page. The other option is the string right .
mode	"hide"	Sets whether the element is shown or hidden when using the effect() method. Other possible values include show, toggle, and effect .

Time for action – using the effect

The social networking site Twitter introduced a novel effect whereby the system reports actions to the visitor by displaying a message that drops down at the top of the page. We can easily replicate this behavior using the drop effect.

1. Add the following markup to the `<body>` of our template page:

```
<div id="confirmation">
  <p>Your request has been completed!</p>
</div>
```

2. Now at the bottom of the page add the following code:

```
$("#confirmation").effect("drop", {
  mode: "show",
  direction: "up"
}, function() {
  var timer = function() {
    $("#confirmation").effect("drop", { mode: "hide", direction:
      "up"});
  }

  setTimeout(function() { timer() }, 3000);
});
```

3. Save the page as `drop.html`. We only need a few styles for this example. Create the following very basic stylesheet:

```
body { background-color:#3cf; }
#confirmation {
  display:none width:100%; height:60px; position:absolute; top:0;
  left:0; z-index:999; background-color:#fff; text-align:center;
  font:normal 18px "Nimbus Sans L", "Helvetica Neue", "Franklin
```

```
    Gothic Medium", Sans-serif;
}
#confirmation p { margin:0; position:relative; top:18px; }
```

4. Save the CSS as `drop.css`.

5. When the page loads, the message should initially be displayed before fading away after a short interval:

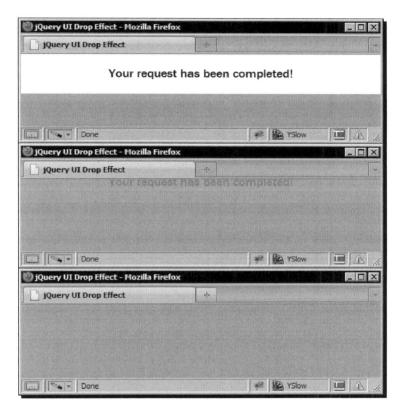

The previous screenshot shows the message slowly being hidden. It will appear to slide up and fade out at the same time when being hidden after the timer interval has passed.

What just happened?

The underlying markup of the message itself is extremely simple; we just need a container and the actual message. In our example the message is hardcoded into the page, but we could easily set this dynamically depending on the action being reported.

The CSS is equally as simple, supplying a background color for the page to better highlight the message, and providing some basic styles for the container and the message itself. The most important rule (in this implementation) is that the container is initially hidden from view.

Our script shows the message as soon as the page has loaded, but normally it would be triggered by the completion of some system action. We use the `effect()` method to initiate the effect and configure the `mode` to `show` and the `direction` to up (the element will still appear to drop downwards because it is positioned absolutely) using a configuration object passed as the second argument to the `effect()` method.

Within the callback function passed to the effect method, we create an inline function stored in the `timer` variable. Within this function we just hide the confirmation message, using the `effect()` method and setting the `mode` configuration option to `hide` and the `direction` option to up once again.

After this function definition we use JavaScript's `setTimeout` function to execute the timer function after three seconds have elapsed. We use a closure to call our `timer` function in keeping with the current best-practice.

The explode effect

The explode effect provides a great visual show by literally exploding the selected element into a specified number of pieces before fading them away. This effect can be used with both the effect API as well as show, hide, or toggle logic.

Configuration options

When using the explode effect we can control how many pieces the element is exploded into, and whether the element is shown or hidden:

Option	Default	Usage
mode	"hide"	Sets whether the element is shown or hidden when used with the `effect()` method. Other values are `show`, `effect`, and `toggle`.
pieces	9	Sets the number of pieces the element is exploded into.

Time for action – exploding an element

In this example we will make an image explode.

1. Just add the following simple image to the `<body>` of the template file:

```
<img src="img/grenade.jpg" alt="Grenade">
```

2. Then add the following equally simple code to the empty function at the bottom of the template file:

```
$("img").click(function() {
  $(this).effect("explode");
});
```

3. Save this page as `explode.html`.

4. This example is so simple we don't even need a stylesheet. Once we click on the grenade, it is exploded into the default number of pieces:

The exploded element fades away as the individual pieces of the element move apart.

What just happened?

In the example, all we need to do is attach a click handler directly to the image which applies the explode effect using the `effect()` method. No configuration in this instance is required because the default `mode` of the effect is `hide`.

Note that we can also run this effect in reverse by setting the `mode` option to `show`, or using the `show()` logic instead. In this scenario, we will see the target element constructed from a series of pieces that fade in and fly together—an explosion in reverse.

The fold effect

The fold effect simulates something being folded in half along one axis and then folded in half along the other axis. Of course, the element isn't actually folded in the 3D sense, first one side of the element moves up a specified amount, then another side is moved in and the element disappears.

By default the effect uses the `hide` mode so it will automatically be hidden at the end of the animation. The element being folded is not scaled; it is clipped instead so images and text will not squash up as the effect runs.

Configuration options

The fold effect exposes three configurable options which are shown in the following table:

Option	Default	Usage
`horizFirst`	`false`	Sets whether the element is clipped along the horizontal axis first or not.
`mode`	`"hide"`	Sets whether the element is shown or hidden when used with the `effect()` method. Other values may include `show`, `effect`, or `toggle`.
`Size`	`15`	This sets the distance of the first fold in pixels and can take either an integer, or a string specifying a value, such as a percentage.

Time for action – folding an element away

In this example, we'll apply the effect to a simple image of a piece of paper.

1. All we need is an image; add the following code to the `<body>` of the template file:

```
<img src="img/paper.jpg" alt="A piece of paper">
```

2. Next add the following simple script to the bottom of the page, in the empty function as with previous examples:

```
$("img").click(function() {
  $(this).effect("fold", { size: "50%" }, 1000);
});
```

3. Save this file as `fold.html`.

4. This is another example that we don't need a stylesheet for. When the image is clicked, it should fold up and disappear:

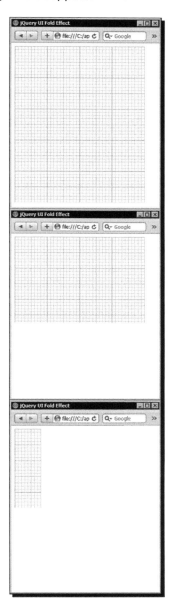

In the previous screenshot we see the image first as it starts out, then when the effect has hidden the bottom half of the image, and finally as the top half of the image is being hidden. Notice that the target element is clipped and not resized.

What just happened?

We simply set a click handler on the `<img>` element, which will apply the fold effect. We specify the `size` option as `50%` so that the amount of fold along each axis is equal, and slow the effect down slightly by specifying a longer than default duration of 1000 milliseconds.

The puff effect

The puff effect expands the element it is applied to by a specified amount while fading it away to nothing, or fades it in and then shrinks it slightly, depending on how it is used.

Configuration options

The puff effect gives us control over the size that the element is increased to, and whether it is shown or hidden:

Option	Default	Usage
mode	"hide"	Sets whether the element is displayed or hidden when used with the `effect()` method. Other possible values include `show`, `effect`, and `toggle`.
percent	150	Sets the size the element is scaled to in percent.

Time for action – making an element disappear in a puff

In this example, we'll have a dialog box displayed in the center of the browser window and apply the puff effect to it when either the **Ok** or **Cancel** buttons are clicked.

1. In the `<body>` of our template file, add the following elements for the dialog:

```
<div id="confirm">
  <img src="img/help.png" alt="Help Icon">
    <p>Are you sure you want to do that?</p>
  <button>Ok</button><button>Cancel</button>
</div>
```

2. Add the accompanying script to the empty function as follows:

```
$("#confirm").css({
  left: $(window).width() / 2 - $("#confirm").width() / 2,
  top: $(window).height() / 2 - $("#confirm").height() / 2
});

$("#confirm, button").click(function() {
  $("#confirm").effect("puff");
});
```

3. Save this page as `puff.html`. Add the following styles for the dialog box to a new file in your text editor:

```
#confirm {
  display:block; width:400px; height:120px; position:absolute;
  border:1px solid #ccc;
  background-image:-moz-linear-gradient(0% 5px 90deg, #eee, #666);
  background-image:-webkit-gradient(linear, 0% 0%, 0% 5%,
    from(#333), to(#eee));
  font:normal 13px "Nimbus Sans L", "Helvetica Neue", "Franklin
    Gothic Medium", Sans-serif;
}
#confirm img { margin:20px 20px 0 20px; float:left; }
#confirm p { margin:40px 0 0 0; }
#confirm button { width:68px; margin:20px 10px 0 0; float:right; }
```

4. Save this new file as `puff.css` in the `css` directory.

5. When we run the page in a browser, we should find that the dialog is initially centered in the window, and that clicking either of the `<button>` elements closes it using the puff effect:

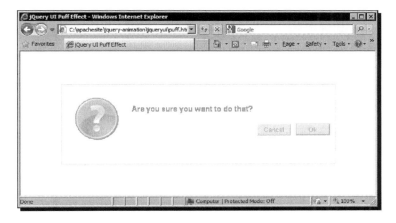

The previous screenshot shows the dialog expanding while it is faded away.

What just happened?

The first part of our script centers the dialog in the window both vertically and horizontally. One point to note is that we cannot use `margin:auto` to center the dialog because it will lose these margins when the effect is applied.

The second part of the script simply adds click handlers to each of the `<button>` elements which apply the puff effect when they are clicked.

The slide effect

The slide effect is very similar to the drop effect. The only difference is that with slide the opacity of the target element is not adjusted at all. It's also very similar to the slide family of effects exposed by jQuery itself, although with the jQuery UI slide effect, we're not restricted to the vertical axis—we can slide horizontally too.

Configuration options

The slide effect has three configuration options which let us specify the direction and distance of the slide, and whether it is shown or hidden:

Option	Default	Usage
direction	`"left"`	Sets the direction the animation proceeds in.
distance	The width of the target element, including padding	Sets the distance that the target element slides to.
mode	`"show"`	Sets whether the element is displayed or hidden when used with the `effect()` method. Other acceptable values are `hide`, `effect`, and `toggle`.

Time for action – sliding elements in and out of view

Displaying captions when a visitor hovers over an image is an interactive and interesting way of displaying additional information about the image without making your design appear cluttered. With the slide effect we can easily animate the showing and hiding of the caption, which is what we'll do in this example.

1. Add the following code to `<body>` of the template file:

```
<div id="image">
  <img src="img/mantis.jpg" alt="Praying Mantis">
  <div>Praying Mantis: Mantis religiosa</div>
</div>
```

2. Then at the bottom of the page, in the empty function, add the following short script:

```
$("#image").hover(function() {
  $(this).find("div").stop(true, true).show("slide");
}, function() {
  $(this).find("div").stop(true, true).hide("slide");
});
```

3. Save this as `slide.html`. Next create the following stylesheet:

```
#image { position:relative; float:left; }
#image img { margin-bottom:-5px; }
#image div {
   display:none; width:100%; padding:10px 0; position:absolute;
   left:0; bottom:0; top:auto !important; text-align:center;
   font-style:italic; background-color:#000; color:#fff;
}
```

4. Save this file as `slide.css`.

5. When we view the page we should find that the caption is displayed as soon as we move the mouse over the image, and then removed when we move the mouse off it:

In the previous screenshot we see the caption sliding out from the left edge of the container.

What just happened?

The image and caption are held in a container so that the caption can be positioned accurately. We use jQuery's `hover()` method, which allows us to attach event handlers for both the `mouseover` and `mouseout` events, to show the caption by sliding it in, or hide it by sliding it out.

We don't need any additional configuration in this simple example, but we do need to manage the queue effectively to stop a build up of animations if the mouse pointer is moved on and off the image repeatedly, which we handle with the `stop()` method.

The scale effect

The scale effect is very similar to the size effect that we looked at earlier, and as we saw, several effects actually require this effect as a dependency. The main difference between this effect and the size effect is that with scale, we can only specify a percentage that the target element should be scaled to, not supply exact pixel sizes.

Configuration options

The scale effect has more configuration options than any other effect added by jQuery UI. These options are listed in the following table:

Option	Default	Usage
direction	"both"	Sets which axis the element is scaled along.
from	none	Sets the starting dimensions of the element.
origin	['middle', 'center']	Sets the vanishing point of the element if it is being hidden, or the point from which it grows if it is being shown.
percent	0	Sets the percentage by which the element will grow or shrink.
scale	"both"	This option sets whether the whole `box` of the element (including border and padding CSS values) is scaled, just the `content`, or as in the default, `both`.

Time for action – scaling an element

It's common practice on an image-heavy site to show a set of thumbnail images which link to a full-sized image which is displayed when the image is clicked, either inline in a modal pop up, or in a separate window. In this example we'll create a thumbnail image that scales to a full-sized version when clicked.

1. Add the following few elements to the `<body>` of the template file:

```
<div id="container">
  <img src="img/mantis.jpg">
</div>
```

2. The script we need is a little longer, but is still pretty simple. In the empty function at the end of the page add the following code:

```
$("img").click(function() {
  var img = $(this);

  if(!img.hasClass("full")) {
    img.addClass("full").effect("scale", { percent: 400 },
      function() {
      $("<a>", {
        href: "#",
        text: "x",
        click: function(e) {
          e.preventDefault;

          var a = $(this);

    a.parent().find("img").removeClass("full").effect("scale", {
      percent: 25 });
          a.remove();
        }
      }).appendTo("#container");
    });
  };
});
```

3. Save the page as `scale.html`. In the stylesheet for this example, we'll need the following code:

```
#container { position:relative; float:left; cursor:pointer; }
#container img { width:150px; height:150px; }
#container a {
  position:absolute; top:0; right:10px; color:#f21515;
  text-decoration:none; font:bold 22px "Nimbus Sans L", "Helvetica
    Neue", "Franklin Gothic Medium", Sans-serif;
}
#container a:hover { color:#fb5e5e; }
```

4. Save this file as `scale.css`.

5. When we run the page we should find that clicking on the image causes it to be scaled up to 400 percent of its initial size:

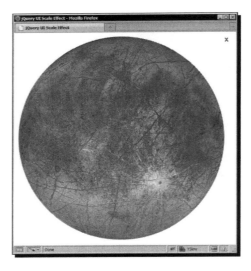

The previous screenshot shows the image in its "scaled-up" size, with the red close icon in the top-right of the image.

What just happened?

On the page our image is held in a simple container `<div>`. The image is scaled down from its original size using CSS, so when we scale the image up we will actually be returning it to full size, so it won't look blocky or fuzzy at all.

In the script we first set a click handler on the image and then we cache a reference to it so that we don't have to keep creating jQuery objects referring to `this`. If the image doesn't have a class name of `full`, we know the image has not been scaled up already, so we add the class `full` and then scale it up by 400 percent using the `percent` option.

Once the image has been scaled, we then create a new anchor element which will be appended to the container element and used as a close button. We set the link's inner text and `href` attribute, and then assign a click handler to it. Within this handler we prevent the browser following the link and then cache the selector once more, which this time points to the anchor.

We then reduce the image to a quarter of its size, retuning it back to its original dimensions. Once this is done we remove the close link.

Pop quiz – using show/hide logic

1. How are supported arguments passed to an effect?

   a. In string format as the second argument, for example `show("blind", "vertical")`

   b. As values in a configuration object passed directly to the `animate()` method, for example `animate({ effect: "blind", configuration: { direction: "vertical" })`

   c. As values in a configuration object passed as the second argument, for example `show("blind", { direction: "vertical" })`

   d. By setting the `effect.config` global property, for example `$.effect.config = { direction: "vertical" })`

2. What else can be passed to the method?

   a. An integer or string representing the duration, and a callback function or function reference

   b. Nothing

   c. A Boolean that controls whether the animation should repeat indefinitely

   d. A Boolean indicating whether further effects should be queued or executed in parallel

Have a go hero – experimenting with the effect API

I would strongly recommend that you experiment with the effects that we have looked at in this section to see which ones work well with the `effect()` method and which ones work best with show/hide logic, and so you can see exactly what happens when the ones that don't work so well are used. This should improve your ability to quickly decide exactly when and where each method is appropriate.

Easing functions

To use the full set of easing functions with jQuery, we needed to use an extra plugin, but with jQuery UI all of the functions are included directly in the core effects file, so we can use them natively with any of our jQuery UI effects.

Easing can be used with all of the jQuery UI effects with the exception of explode, although it can look a little strange in a few of the effects, such as bounce or pulsate. Easing can also be used if jQuery UI is present with standard jQuery.

For a full list of the easing functions available with jQuery (either via the easing plugin, or jQuery UI) see the table in the easing section in *Chapter 4, Sliding Animations*.

Time for action – adding easing to effects

To use easing, all we need to do is include the easing function name as a configuration option. For example, to add easing to the blind.html example that we looked at earlier, we could change the JavaScript so that it appeared as follows:

```
$("#window").click(function() {
  $("#blind").toggle("blind", { easing: "easeOutBounce" });
});
```

What just happened?

We use the configuration option easing, with the name of the easing function as a string supplied as the value of the option. Any of the easing functions can be used by referencing their name in this way.

Color animations

As well as the complete range of easing functions, the effects core file also gives us the ability to attractively and smoothly animate between different colors. Several CSS properties can be animated including the color, background-color, border-color, and outline-color.

jQuery UI extends jQuery's animate() method to achieve color animations, so the syntax to implement it is the same as using animate(). For any other purpose, we just need to target one of the above CSS properties and supply the new color value as a string, hexadecimal (#xxxxxx), or RGB (rgb(xxx, xxx, xxx)) value. Let's look at a basic example.

Time for action – animating between colors

In this example, we'll use color animations to show that a form field has been left empty.

1. In a fresh copy of the template file, use the following elements in the <body> of the page:

```
<input><button id="search">Search</button>
```

2. To invoke the color changes when the `<button>` is clicked, we can use the following JavaScript in the empty function near the bottom of the document:

```
$("#search").click(function (e) {
  e.preventDefault();

  var input = $(this).prev();

  if (input.val() == "") {
    input.animate({
      backgroundColor: "#f78080",
      borderTopColor: "#a72b2e",
      borderRightColor: "#a72b2e",
      borderBottomColor: "#a72b2e",
      borderLeftColor: "#a72b2e"
    }, 1200);
  };
});
```

3. Save this page as `color-animations.html`. We literally only need a couple of styles for this example. We could probably get away with defining them in a `<style>` block in the `<head>` of the page. We just use the following CSS:

```
input { width:200px; border:2px solid #27659f; }
```

4. When we run the page, we see that the text field changes color if the `<button>` is clicked while it is empty.

What just happened?

The CSS, while extremely small, is required in this example because the `<input>` will lose any attractive styling provided by modern browsers when the colors are animated. Setting the CSS properties we are animating helps prevent this ugly switch.

In the script we simply cache a selector that points to the `<input>`, and then test whether the field is empty. If it is we call the `animate()` method, specifying the aspects of the target element we'd like to animate. Notice that we must specify each border-color independently for the animation to work correctly.

Class transitions

As well as extending jQuery's `animate()` method in order to provide color animations, jQuery UI also extends some of jQuery's element manipulation methods. The following methods are extended to provide class transitions:

◆ `addClass()`

◆ `removeClass()`

◆ `toggleClass()`

jQuery UI also exposes a new method for transitioning between two classes—the `switchClass()` method, which accepts the current class and new class, as well as duration, easing, and callback arguments.

Time for action – transitioning between classes

We can rework our previous example so that it uses some of the class transition methods.

1. Add the class name `default` to the `<input>` element and then change the JavaScript so that it appears as follows:

```
$("#search").click(function(e) {
  e.preventDefault();

  var input = $(this).prev();

  if (input.val() == "") {
    input.switchClass("default", "error", 1200);
  } else if (input.val() && input.hasClass("error")) {
    input.removeClass("error", 1200);
  }
});
```

2. Save the new page as `class-animation.html`. We'll need to make some changes to the stylesheet as well. Create a new stylesheet and add the following rules to it (or change the styles in the `<head>` of the page):

```
input { width:200px; }
.default, input { border:2px solid #27659f; }
.error { border:2px solid #a72b2e; background-color:#f78080; }
```

3. Save the new file as `class-animation.css`.

4. Run the page in a browser and again, click the `<button>` without entering anything into the text field. The `<input>` should transition to the error class and appear the same as it did in the last example. This time however enter some text in the `<input>` and click the `<button>` again. The error should then transition back to default.

What just happened?

This time if the `<input>` has no value we just call the `switchClass()` method specifying the current class of `default`, the new class of `error`, and a duration of 1.2 seconds. Note that you must supply both the current and new classes for the example to work correctly.

In the next branch of the conditional, we check that the `<input>` has both a value and a class name of `error`. If it does we call the `removeClass()` method specifying just the class to remove and a duration. The duration is required in order to trigger the transition.

In the CSS we provide the default styling using the class name `default` as well as generally for all `input` elements. We need to do this because otherwise the element loses its styles while the `error` class is in the process of being removed, causing it to revert to a standard un-styled `<input>` element.

Performance

When using jQuery, we are always advised that changing the class name of an element is more efficient than manipulating an element's `style` attribute directly, so it's natural to assume that using `switchClass()` would be more efficient than using `animate()`.

This however is not the case, as Firebug's profile tool will show. In the previous example, if the second branch of the conditional is removed and the page and both `color-animation.html` and `class-animation.html` are profiled, it is `color-animation.html` that wins by a margin of around 20 milliseconds.

Pop quiz – easing, color, and class animations

1. How are easing functions specified?

   a. In string format as the third argument to the `effect()` method, for example `effect("blind", {}, "easeOutBounce")`

   b. As Boolean in a callback function, for example `effect("blind", function() { easeOutBounce = true })`

   c. Easing cannot be used

   d. In string format as the value of the easing configuration option, for example `effect("blind", { easing: "easeOutBounce" })`

2. Which method is extended to produce color animations?

    a. The `effect()` method

    b. The `show()` method

    c. The `animate()` method

    d. The `switchClass()` method

Summary

In this chapter we looked at the complete range of new effects which are added by the jQuery UI library. We looked at how they can be used with the `effect()` method, or the `show()`, `hide()`, and `toggle()` methods when necessary. We saw the configuration arguments that each effect takes, and their default values when used out of the box.

We also covered how jQuery UI extends the `animation()`, `addClass()`, and `removeClass()` methods, and the `switchClass()` method that it adds in order to add the ability to animate between colors and classes.

The key points to take from this chapter include:

- jQuery UI together with jQuery can be downloaded using the jQuery UI download builder, which builds a custom package, complete with a theme if required for you to download.

- jQuery UI adds a total of 14 new predefined effects to our animation toolkit. The effects are easy to use but highly configurable.

- The `effect()` method is the basic means of specifying an effect, its configuration options, a duration, and a callback function.

- Some of the effects work much better with the `show()`, `hide()`, or `toggle()` methods and are equally as easy to use with this aspect of the API.

- The easing functions are built directly into jQuery UI and can be used by specifying them as values for the `easing` configuration option.

- jQuery UI also gives us the ability to transition an element's color or class name by extending some of jQuery's methods and adding the new `switchClass()` method.

In the next chapter, we'll switch back to jQuery and look at full page animations including how to animate the page's background image, animating page scroll, and feature animations that are the main focus of the page.

7
Full Page Animations

So far the examples that we've looked at are animations that have formed a single part of the user interface of the page, or formed part of a specific widget. In this chapter, we'll look at animations that take up the whole page, such as background-image *animations, or "feature" animations where the thing being animated is the main focus of the page.*

In this chapter, we'll cover the following subjects:

◆ Animating page scroll

◆ Animating background-position to create a parallax effect

◆ Combining page scroll with page navigation

◆ Creating stop-motion animation

All of the examples that we'll look at in this chapter will be based on the animate() method that was introduced earlier in the book. As we've already learnt how the method is used, we can jump straight into the action and start on the examples.

Animated page scroll

We can animate the scroll of the entire page very easily using a combination of some built-in jQuery functionality and some plain vanilla JavaScript. Long blog pages are often split into smaller, more readable sections with sub-headings, and a secondary navigation structure, separate from the main site navigation, which links to the different sections. Optionally, there may also be **back to top** links that take the reader back up to the top of the page.

Can we animate the scroll using jQuery's `animate()` method so that the document scrolls smoothly instead of jumping to the desired location when any of these links are clicked? Not exactly—the `scrollTop()` method that jQuery exposes cannot be used directly in conjunction with the `animate()` method.

But we can spoof the animation effect ourselves manually and make it appear as if the scroll is animated very easily, which is what we'll do in the first example of this chapter.

Time for action – creating the page that will scroll and its styling

The example page needs to be quite long for the scroll effect to work. The underlying HTML used could be any modern blog post.

1. Add the following code to the `<body>` of the template file:

```html
<article id="post">
  <header id="top">
    <h1>A long article with lots of sections</h1>
    <nav>
      <ul>
        <li><a href="#section1" title="Section 1">
        Section 1</a></li>
        <li><a href="#section2" title="Section 2">
        Section 2</a></li>
        <li><a href="#section3" title="Section 3">
        Section 3</a></li>
        <li><a href="#section4" title="Section 4">
        Section 4</a></li>
        <li><a href="#section5" title="Section 5">
        Section 5</a></li>
      </ul>
    </nav>
    <p>Posted on <time datetime="2010-11-13">
    13 November 2010</time> by Dan Wellman</p>
  </header>
  <section id="section1">
    <h1>Section 1</h1>
    <p>Lorem ipsum dolor...</p>
    <p>Lorem ipsum dolor...</p>
      <a href="#top" title="Back to top" class="top">
      Back to top</a>
  </section>
  <section id="section2">
```

```
    <h1>Section 2</h1>
    <p>Lorem ipsum dolor...</p>
    <p>Lorem ipsum dolor...</p>
    <a href="#top" title="Back to top" class="top">
    Back to top</a>
  </section>
  <section id="section3">
    <h1>Section 3</h1>
    <p>Lorem ipsum dolor...</p>
    <p>Lorem ipsum dolor...</p>
    <a href="#top" title="Back to top" class="top">
    Back to top</a>
  </section>
  <section id="section4">
    <h1>Section 4</h1>
    <p>Lorem ipsum dolor...</p>
    <p>Lorem ipsum dolor...</p>
    <a href="#top" title="Back to top" class="top">
    Back to top</a>
  </section>
  <section id="section5">
    <h1>Section 5</h1>
    <p>Lorem ipsum dolor...</p>
    <p>Lorem ipsum dolor...</p>
    <a href="#top" title="Back to top" class="top">
    Back to top</a>
  </section>
</article>
```

2. Save this file as scroll.html. We'll also need a little CSS to lay out the example page. Add the following selectors and rules to a new page in your text editor:

```
#post {
  display:block; width:960px; margin:auto;
  font:22px "Nimbus Sans L", "Helvetica Neue",
    "Franklin Gothic Medium", sans-serif;
  color:#444;
}
#post header p, #post section .top {
  margin-bottom:0;
  font:italic 14px "Palatino Linotype", "Times New Roman",
    "Nimbus Roman No9 L", serif;
  color:#aaa; text-align:right;
}
#post section .top {
```

```
    display:block; text-decoration:none;
    border-bottom:1px dotted #aaa;
    float:right;
}
#post section .top:hover { border-bottom-style:solid; }
#post ul { margin:0; padding:0; }
#post li { list-style-type:none; }
#post section h1, #post section p {
    margin:0 0 6px; clear:right; font-size:24px;
}
#post section p { font-size:20px; }
```

3. Save this in the `css` folder as `scroll.css`. Don't forget to link to this stylesheet from the `<head>` of the HTML file. Here's a screenshot to show how the page should appear:

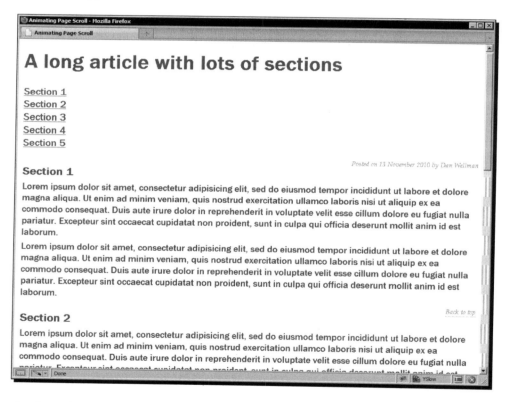

Showing how the screen is scrolled in a simple screenshot could be problematic so the previous image is just to show you how the page should appear at this point for reference purposes.

What just happened?

The HTML is very simple. There's just more of it than there has been in previous examples. It represents a single article that is divided into different sections, with each section having a sub-heading and some layout text.

A table of contents style navigation menu at the top of the article (this would be considered a secondary nav) links to each of the different sections. The styling is also very basic and simply sets some rules to lay out the page in a clean format.

Time for action – animating the scroll

The script itself is relatively straight-forward too. Add the following code to the empty function at the bottom of the HTML file:

```
var parent = document.getElementById("post"),
  speed = 7,
  win = $(window);

$("nav a", parent).click(function(e) {

  e.preventDefault();

  var target = $(this).attr("href"),
    offset = $(target).offset(),
    newScroll = 0,
    maxScroll = document.body.scrollHeight;

    while (newScroll < offset.top && win.scrollTop() < maxScroll) {

      win.scrollTop(newScroll);
      newScroll = newScroll + speed;
    }
  });

$(".top", parent).click(function(e) {

  e.preventDefault;

  var newScroll = win.scrollTop();

  while (newScroll > 0 && win.scrollTop() > 0) {

    win.scrollTop(newScroll);
    newScroll = newScroll - speed;
  }
});
```

Save the HTML file again and run it in a browser. You should find that the document smoothly scrolls to the desired location when any of the top links on the page are clicked.

What just happened?

First we set some variables including a reference to the DOM node of the parent container (the `<article>`). We obtain this with the raw JavaScript `getElementById()` function so that we can pass it into a jQuery selector as a context for the selector.

Doing this is great for performance and means that we don't have to give multiple elements `id` attributes for the sole purpose of jQuery element selection. Everything is selected by starting at the parent that is originally selected from the document.

We also set a variable called `speed` which we'll use when we create the simulated animation. This is the figure that the current scroll amount is incremented by, so lower values will mean a longer "animation" time and higher values will mean a shorter time, completely the opposite of jQuery's `duration` argument.

We also cache a selector for the `window` object as we'll need to refer to this several times, often from within `for` or `while` conditional branches, so again this is purely for performance reasons.

We then set a click handler on the table of contents links. Within this function we first stop the browser from following the link using the `preventDefault()` method, which jQuery normalizes across all common browsers.

We then set some more variables, first getting the target element of the link that was clicked, then storing its current offset, and the maximum scroll amount of the document. We also initialize a `newScroll` variable so that we can calculate what the new scroll amount should be.

We then use a JavaScript `while` loop to incrementally scroll the document, using the `speed` variable that we set earlier. The condition of the loop is that it should continue while the `newScroll` variable is less than the `top` offset of the target element and while the current scroll is less than the maximum scroll.

The offset of the target element is obtained using jQuery's `offset()` method, which returns an object with `top` and `left` properties that correspond to the element's position relative to the document. The maximum scroll is obtained using standard JavaScript to query the `scrollHeight` property of the document body.

The current scroll is normalized by jQuery so that the `scrollTop()` method returns the current position of the vertical scroll bar. This is useful because it means that we don't have to feature-detect the browser and obtain the value using either `document.body.scrollTop` or `window.pageYOffset` depending on the browser in use.

Within the `while` loop, we use jQuery's `scrollTop()` method in setter mode to set the scroll to the value of the `newScroll` variable, and then increment the `newScroll` value using our `speed` variable. This is what I meant by spoofing the animated scroll—the document just scrolls sequentially in a series of jumps; it isn't actually animated, but because it happens fairly rapidly it gives the `impression` of being animated.

After the click handler for the table of contents links, we also set a click handler on the **back to top** links. Because we're just going straight back to the top of the page, we don't need to do any complex calculations, so this function is really just a simplified version of the first function.

There is already a jQuery plugin that can be used to animate scroll: the scrollTo plugin. This plugin allows us to easily animate both vertical and horizontal scroll on any element whose contents overflows the dimensions set on it.

However, as an exercise in how to fake animation without using any of jQuery's animation methods, I thought it would be of value to do it ourselves manually here. We'll use the plugin later in the chapter. For reference it was created by Ariel Flesler and can be downloaded from `http://flesler.blogspot.com/2007/10/jqueryscrollto.html`.

Pop quiz – animating page scroll

1. In this example we used old-school JavaScript to obtain a reference to the `<article>` DOM node instead of using jQuery. Why?

    a. Because it's easier

    b. Because it's fun to mix things up a little

    c. Because it's faster to give jQuery selectors a DOM node context so that the entire document doesn't need to be searched when selecting elements from the page

    d. Because it makes the byte count of the page smaller

2. Why can we not use jQuery to animate the page scroll?

    a. Because `scrollTop` (or `window.pageYOffset`) are properties of the document or window and not CSS style properties

    b. Because the values for these properties are not true integers

    c. Because jQuery does not want us to animate scroll

    d. We can, we just chose to do it this way instead

Have a go hero – extending animated page scroll

In this example we just animated the vertical scroll of the document. Have a go at changing the example so that the horizontal scroll can also be animated. This will entail making the page not just longer than the viewport, but also wider too.

The illusion of depth with parallax

The term parallax, when used in the context of computer graphics, especially in video games, refers to the technique of using multiple background layers that scroll at slightly different speeds to create the illusion of depth. Although not as widely deployed in modern gaming, thanks to the advent of richer 3D graphics engines, parallax is still seen frequently in portable gaming devices, and increasingly, on the Web.

A parallax effect is achievable using pure CSS, as demonstrated nicely by the Silverback site (see `http://silverbackapp.com/` for the effect, and `http://thinkvitamin.com/design/how-to-recreate-silverbacks-parallax-effect/` for the details on how it was implemented). This application of parallax will only become apparent when the window is resized, which is a fantastic effect when the window *is* resized, but doesn't help us if we want the effect to take more of a center stage.

A little help from the new cssHooks functionality

jQuery 1.4.3 introduced a new mechanism for easily extending the `css()` and `animate()` methods of jQuery. The new cssHooks feature allows us to easily extend the `css()` method to allow the getting and setting of CSS style properties not natively supported by jQuery. As the `animate()` method makes use of the `css()` method internally, we can use the cssHooks to add animation support for certain style properties that previously were unsupported.

This is great, but even better is the fact that some of the jQuery core contributors, most notably Mr Brandon Aaron, have already begun building a suite of pre-built cssHooks for certain style properties, including `background-position`. We can use one of these brand new, pre-built cssHooks in our next example.

 The file containing the cssHook for background-position is included in the code download accompanying this book, but for reference, the complete suite can be found at `https://github.com/brandonaaron/jquery-cssHooks`.

Time for action – creating the stage and adding the styling

The underlying page requires just five elements (for this simple example), which sit in the `<body>` of the page.

1. Add the elements in the following structure to a fresh copy of the template file:

```
<div id="background"><!-- --></div>
<div id="midground"><!-- --></div>
<div id="foreground"><!-- --></div>
<div id="ground"><!-- --></div>
```

2. This page can be saved as `parallax.html`. Don't forget to link to the cssHooks file that we'll be using in this example after the link to jQuery at the bottom of the `<body>`:

```
<script src="js/jquery.js"></script>
<script src="js/bgpos.js"></script>
<script>
```

3. The CSS in this example is equally as simple as the underlying HTML. Add the following code to a new file in your text editor:

```
div { width:100%; height:1000px; position:absolute; left:0; top:0;
}
#background { background:url(../img/background.png) repeat-x 0 0;
}
#midground { background:url(../img/midground.png) repeat-x 0 0; }
#foreground { background:url(../img/foreground.png) repeat-x 0 0;
}
#stage { background:url(../img/ground.png) repeat-x 0 100%; }
```

4. Save this file as `parallax.css` in the `css` directory. At this point the page should appear like this:

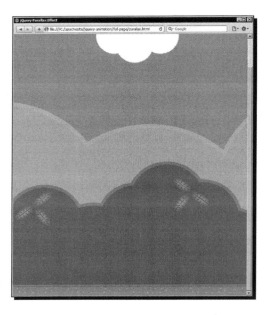

The stage area is the ground, the foreground layer is the dark green bushes, the midground is the light green bushes, and the background slice is the sky and clouds.

What just happened?

You'll also find the images for this example in the `img` folder of the code download accompanying this book. We have a separate image for each element that we wish to be part of the parallax effect, three in this example, one for the background, one for the midground, and one for the foreground.

The underlying HTML is also very simple. We just have a separate `<div>` for each layer of the background. In the CSS, each image layer is positioned absolutely so that they overlay each other.

Time for action – animating the background position

Now for the `<script>` itself. At the bottom of the HTML file, in the empty function as usual, add the following code:

```
var bg = $("#background"),
  mg = $("#midground"),
  fg = $("#foreground");
```

```
$(document).keydown(function(e) {

  if (e.which === 39) {
    bg.animate({ "backgroundPosition": "-=1px" }, 0, "linear");
    mg.animate({ "backgroundPosition": "-=10px" }, 0, "linear" );
    fg.animate({ "backgroundPosition": "-=20px" }, 0, "linear" );
  }
});
```

If we run this page in a browser now, we should find that as we hold down the right arrow key, the different background slices move at progressively slower speeds with the foreground almost rushing past, and the background moving along leisurely.

What just happened?

In the script we first cache the selectors we'll be using so that we don't have to create a new jQuery object and select the elements from the DOM each time the background-position changes, which will be very frequently indeed. We then set a keydown event listener on the document object. Within the anonymous function we use as the event handler, we check whether the key code supplied by the which property of the event object (this is normalized by jQuery so it will be accessible cross-browser) is equal to 39, which is the key code returned by the right arrow key.

We then call the animate() method, which is extended by the cssHooks bgpos.js file to allow us to specify backgroundPosition as the style property to animate. We supply relative values of +=1px, +=10px, and +=20px to move each layer at progressively faster speeds which gives us the parallax effect. These animations are called simultaneously and also have very short durations and linear easing. This is the last thing our keydown handler needs to do.

Pop quiz – implementing the parallax effect

1. Why is it necessary to use linear easing in the previous example?

    a. To prevent a flickering effect

    b. It's not necessary, we just used it for fun

    c. To prevent the animation using the default easing type of swing, which causes a slowing down at the start and end as this would stop the animation from running smoothly

    d. To slow the animation down slightly

2. The `bgpos` cssHooks file extends the jQuery `css()` method and allows us to animate the `background-position` of an element. What format does the value we provide to the `backgroundPosition` key need to take?

   a. An integer

   b. An array of integers

   c. A string

   d. An array of strings

Have a go hero – extending parallax

In this example the backgrounds animate only from right to left. Extend the example so that both left to right and right to left motion is available.

Animated single-page navigation

Instead of navigating to separate pages when links in a navigation menu are clicked, we can navigate to different areas of the current page. While it would be SEO-suicide to build your entire site on a single page, and could potentially hide a lot of content from users without JavaScript enabled, we can progressively enhance the site to take this format, while still leaving the site overall as a normal collection of separate HTML documents.

Time fr action – creating individual pages and adding the styles

In this example we'll start with a collection of separate pages. These are pretty much just carbon copies of each other with the numbers in the headings changed.

1. Add the following markup to the `<body>` of our template file:

```
<div id="outer-container">
  <header>
    <h1>A Whole Site on a Single Page</h1>
    <nav class="clear-float">
      <ul>
        <li><a class="on" href="single-page-site-1.html"
        title="Page 1">Page 1</a></li>
        <li><a href="single-page-site-2.html" title="Page 2">
        Page 2</a></li>
        <li><a href="single-page-site-3.html" title="Page 3">
        Page 3</a></li>
        <li><a href="single-page-site-4.html" title="Page 4">
        Page 4</a></li>
        <li><a href="single-page-site-5.html" title="Page 5">
```

```
      Page 5</a></li>
    </ul>
  </nav>
</header>
<div id="content">
  <h1>Single Page Site Page 1</h1>
  <p>This is the first page of the site</p>
  <p>Lorem ipsum dolor...</p>
</div>
<footer>
  <small>Copyright &copy; Dan Wellman 2010</small>
  <nav class="clear-float">
    <ul>
      <li><a href="single-page-site-1.html" title="Page 1">
      Page 1</a></li>
      <li><a href="single-page-site-2.html" title="Page 2">
      Page 2</a></li>
      <li><a href="single-page-site-3.html" title="Page 3">
      Page 3</a></li>
      <li><a href="single-page-site-4.html" title="Page 4">
      Page 4</a></li>
      <li><a href="single-page-site-5.html" title="Page 5">
      Page 5</a></li>
    </ul>
  </nav>
</footer>
</div>
```

2. Save five copies of this page, calling them `single-page-site-[1-5].html`. The CSS used in this example is almost purely to get a feel for the page; it isn't decorative at all. Add the following code to a new file in your text editor:

```
body { margin:0; overflow:hidden; }
#outer-container { width:960px; margin:auto; }
header {
  display:block; border:1px solid #000; border-top:none;
  -moz-border-radius-bottomright:8px;
  -moz-border-radius-bottomleft:8px;
  -webkit-border-bottom-right-radius:8px;
  -webkit-border-bottom-left-radius:8px;
  border-bottom-right-radius:8px; border-bottom-right-radius:8px;
  background-color:#fff;
}
header h1 { margin:0 0 0 20px; float:left; line-height:2em; }
header nav { display:block; margin-top:23px; }
```

```
nav ul { margin:0; padding:0; float:right; }
nav li {
  border-left:1px solid #000; padding:0 20px; float:left;
  list-style-type:none;
}
nav li:first-child { border:none; }
#content { padding-left:20px; }
footer {
  display:block; width:960px; padding:10px 0;
  border:1px solid #000;
  border-bottom:none;
  -moz-border-radius-topright:8px;
  -moz-border-radius-topleft:8px;
  -webkit-border-top-right-radius:8px;
  -webkit-border-top-left-radius:8px;
  border-top-right-radius:8px;
  border-top-right-radius:8px; clear:both; background-color:#fff;
}
footer small { display:block; float:left; margin-left:20px; }
footer nav { font-size:12px; }
.clear-float:after {
  display:block; content:"."; clear:both; visibility:hidden;
  height:0;
}

.fixed { width:960px; position:fixed; z-index:1; }
header.fixed { top:0; }
footer.fixed { bottom:0; }
#pages { position:relative; }
.page { width:920px; position:absolute; }
```

3. Save this file as `single-page-site.css` in the `css` directory. Note that each of the five HTML pages link to this stylesheet.

4. The page will appear like this with no JS functionality added, which is how it would appear were JavaScript disabled on the client:

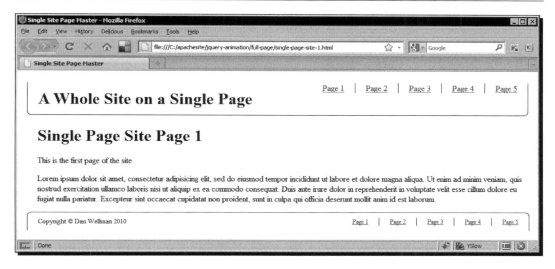

As the screenshot shows, the page still works and the site can be navigated with JavaScript disabled. Some of our styling is added with JavaScript (via class name additions), so the final page will appear slightly differently.

What just happened?

The underlying HTML is fairly straight-forward and just represents a simple collection of example elements including header and footer navigation. The styles are also very light and are there mostly just to lay out the example pages. The rules at the bottom of the file are for elements or classes that are added dynamically by the script.

The previous screenshot shows how the page will appear to those with scripting disabled, although it is very similar to how the page will appear once we've added the script, which we'll do next.

Time for action – adding the scroll navigation

In this section we will add the code that will enable animated scrolling.

1. In another new file in your text editor, add the following code (it should go into an empty function which aliases the $ character, the same as in the other examples):

```
$("#content").empty();

var win = $(window),
  links = $("header nav a"),
  content = $("#content"),
  positions = {},
```

```
screensize = {
  width: win.width(),
    height: win.height()
  },

  pages = $("<div></div>", {
    id: "pages"
  }).bind("contentLoaded", function() {

    var multiplier = Math.ceil(links.length / 2);

    $(this).appendTo(content).parent().addClass("full");

    content.width(screensize.width * multiplier +
      screensize.width);
    content.height(screensize.height * multiplier);
    content.parent().find("header, footer").addClass(
      "fixed").closest("body").css(
      "padding-top", $("header").outerHeight());

    links.add("footer nav a").click(function(e) {

      e.preventDefault();

        var id = (this.href.indexOf("#") != -1) ?
        this.href.split("#")[1] : "page-" +
        this.title.split(" ")[1];
        navs = $("header").add("footer");

      navs.fadeOut("fast");

      $.scrollTo({ top: positions[id].top,
        left: positions[id].left }, 800, function() {
        navs.slideDown("fast");
      });
    });
  });

links.each(function(i) {

  var id = "page-" + (i + 1);

    positions[id] = {};
    positions[id].left = (i === links.length - 1) ?
```

```
        screensize.width * i - (screensize.width / 2) -
        (960 / 2) + parseInt(content.css("paddingLeft")) :
        screensize.width * i;
      positions[id].top = (i % 2) ? screensize.height : 0;

    $("<div></div>", {
      "class": "page",

      load: this.href + " #content > *"
    }).css({

      left: positions[id].left,
      top: positions[id].top
    }).appendTo(pages);

    this.href = "#" + id;

  if(i == links.length - 1) {

    pages.trigger("contentLoaded");
  }
});
```

2. Save this file as `single-page-site.js` in the `js` folder. You'll need to link to this new file, as well as the scrollTo plugin, which we'll make use of in this example, from each individual page. Add the script references at the end of the `<body>` element:

```
<script src="js/jquery.scrollTo-min.js"></script>
<script src="js/single-page-site.js"></script>
```

3. Run the page in a browser now. You should be able to navigate smoothly around the page to each of the external pages that have been pulled in.

We can't run this page successfully on a local machine (that is using a `file:///` URL) in Google Chrome without changing the **--allow-file-access-from-files** option due to a bug in the browser (see issue 4197 documented at `http://code.google.com/p/chromium/issues/detail?id=4197`).

The example will however work as intended if we run it through a web server (this can even be a test/development web server running on the local machine) using an `http://` URL.

What just happened?

The script can be roughly broken into two sections. We have a series of variables first, followed by an `each()` method that processes the navigation in the header. The very first thing we do however is to empty the contents of the current page. This helps make our script cleaner, because we don't have to avoid processing the first navigation link in our `each()` function.

It also ensures the page continues to work if someone visits, say, `page-3.html` instead of the first page by typing the URL of that page directly into the browser's address bar. It resets the site so that the content of the first page is always shown first.

So we first define a series of variables. We cache references to the window object, the top set of navigation links, and the content container, and create a new object that we'll populate later in the script to determine where each page is positioned. We also create an object containing the `width` and `height` of the window, again so that we can reference these properties easily from different points in the script.

We then create a new `div` element and give it an `id` attribute for styling purposes. We then bind an event handler to it which listens for a custom `contentLoaded` event. jQuery easily allows us to create custom events which can be triggered programmatically by our script when appropriate.

Within the anonymous handler function, we first define a multiplier that will be used to work out how big the container for the collection of pages should be.

We then append the pages element, which will contain the content of each external page, to the content container on the page, and then add a class name to the content container, again for styling, but this time for styles that only need to be applied with JavaScript enabled.

Next we set the size of the content container so that it can accommodate all of the external page content. We use our `screensize` object and `multiplier` to determine its size. The container needs to be one screen-width wider due to how the external page content is laid out.

We cater for a little more dynamic styling to the header and footer elements by adding a class name to them. This allows us to give these two elements `fixed` positioning so that they always appear at the top and bottom of the viewport and hence remain usable while we (or our visitors) are navigating around the page. We also add some padding equal to the `height` of the header so that the content does not slide below it at any point.

Next we can add a click handler to each of the top and footer navigation links. Within the handler function, we first prevent the browser from following the link and then get the region of the page that we need to scroll to from the `href` property of the link that was clicked. When we process the header links in a moment, we add some code that will change the `href` of these links so that they no longer point to the individual pages, but to the page regions on the single page.

The footer links aren't processed like the header links will be, so we can't just use whatever value the `href` is because it may still point to a separate page. Instead we use the JavaScript ternary conditional to see whether the `href` contains a # sign. If it does, we just `split` the string on the # and keep everything after.

If it doesn't we get the number of the page that it points to and add this to a string. We also cache a reference to a jQuery object containing both the header and footer.

The this object versus a jQuery object

Note that when we read the `href` attribute, we're interacting with the `this` object directly, without wrapping the object in jQuery functionality. We can read the `href` property of the `this` object without any special JavaScript magic, so there is no point creating a new jQuery object, and paying for the performance hit when we do, just to read this attribute.

Next we hide the header and footer with a fast fade-out and then invoke the `scrollTo()` method added by the `scrollTo` plugin.

This method accepts an object with `top` and `left` properties, to which we pass references to the relevant properties from our `positions` object, using the string we saved in the `id` variable. We populate the `positions` object in the next section of code, but for reference the object will end up with a property and value pair for each external page linked to in the navigation, where each key will be `page-1...page-n`, and each value will contain the precise coordinates that need to be scrolled to.

Once the scroll animation has completed, we then show the header and footer again using the `slideDown()` method. As these elements have fixed positioning, we can apply the slide animation to them together and they will both slide in the intended direction.

Using the `scrollTo()` method is very similar to using the `animate()` method. We can supply a duration, as well as a callback function, as we do in this example. Calling the `scrollTo()` method directly on the jQuery object is a shortcut to calling it on the window object. The plugin handles this internally for us.

Don't forget, most of the functionality we've just added won't be executed straight away—it's mostly all stored in the page's variable. The variable will be created and the pages `<div>` will exist in memory, but it won't actually be appended to the page until the `contentLoaded` custom event is triggered by the next section of code.

The second section of code is encompassed within an anonymous function passed to jQuery's `each()` method which we use to process each of the links in the header. The function we define is automatically passed an index (`i`) as an argument representing the current iteration which we use to build an ID string ready for populating the `positions` object.

This object will contain a set of nested objects where each nested object represents one of the external pages and has a left and a top property which correspond to where on the single page the content is positioned.

Working out where to place the content section on the vertical axis is easy; we just use the JavaScript modulus operator (`%`) to see if there is a remainder left after dividing the index by two, in conjunction with a ternary conditional.

If the index can be divided by two without a remainder, we position the content from the external page one window's `height` from the top of the page. If there is a remainder, we just position it at the top of the page. This means that the content sections will be laid out in a zig-zag pattern along two rows, where each row is equal to the height of the window.

Working out where to place each content section along the page horizontally is a little more challenging, but it's only the very last section that proves to be tricky. We use the ternary here as well, this time checking whether we are processing the last link or not.

If we aren't, we simply position the content by multiplying the `width` of the window by the index, moving each successive section along the page by one window's `width`.

If we are processing the last link however, we need to position the content by multiplying the `width` by the window `width`, but then subtracting one window's `width` dived by two, minus the `width` of the content's container dived by two. This ensures that the content section is aligned with the header and footer correctly.

Once the location for the page that the current link points to has been added to the position's object, we then create the new container for the page content and give it a class name for styling purposes.

We also use the `load()` method to load the external pages asynchronously. This method accepts the URL of the page to load, which we can get from the `href` property of the current link and a selector that matches all child elements within the content element in the page that is loaded. When a selector is passed to the `load()` method, only that portion of the external page will be retrieved.

Once the container has been created, we position it using the `css()` method, setting its `left` and `top` properties to the corresponding properties in our positions object for convenience. Finally we append the new `<div>` to the page's `<div>` (which still only exists in memory at this point).

We then set the `href` of the current link to a document fragment identifier pointing to the name of the corresponding content section. This wouldn't have any effect if we weren't intercepting clicks on the `nav` links because the content sections don't have matching `id` attributes, but it is necessary to store the fragment here so that we can read it back when the link is clicked.

Lastly, we check again whether we're processing the last link or not, and if we are, we trigger our custom `contentLoaded` event, which results in the page's element being appended to the page, and the click handlers bound to the navigation links.

Building a site like this which pulls all of its content into a single page won't suit every type of site. Most clients would probably pay the cancellation fees and swiftly withdraw if this idea was presented to them. However, on highly stylized sites, where the design and behavior of the site is of special importance, this kind of effect can work well. Sites with little content on each page are especially suited to it.

The following screenshot shows the functionality in action:

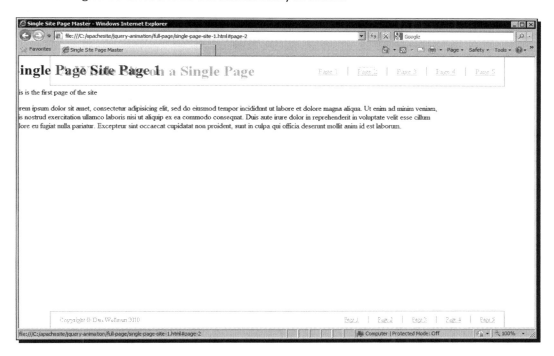

In the previous screenshot, we can see the header and footer partly faded out, and the page content being scrolled diagonally downwards to the right.

Pop quiz – creating a single-page website

1. We interact with the `this` object directly in this example instead of the jQuery equivalent `$(this)`, why?

   a. Because it uses fewer characters

   b. Its faster and more efficient because an entirely new jQuery object is not created

   c. Because it looks better

   d. Because it contains more information

2. We create and use a custom event in this example, why?

   a. Because custom events execute faster than standard browser events

   b. Because the `each()` method does not allow us to update the `scrollTop` property of the window

   c. Because it is more efficient for the code executed by the handler to be called once than on every iteration of the `each()` method

   d. Because the scrollTo plugin can only be used in conjunction with custom events

Have a go hero – extending single-page navigation

There are several things you could do to expand on this example. One thing you could do is add functionality that checks which page is requested by looking at the `href` property of the document. If a page other than the first page is requested, you could scroll to the corresponding page section so that the page they link to is actually shown instead of resetting to the first page.

Another thing you could do would be to extend the example so that the pages don't have to be numbered `page-2.html`, and so on, and instead could have any file name. In the first section of code, we read the `href` of the link if one of the footer links is clicked instead of looking for a document fragment identifier. This same technique could be applied to the header links as well, so that any page that is linked to can be included in the single page.

Or, to really appreciate the visual effect of our site-on-a-page, you could add some additional content and a theme to the site. Each page need not have the same skin, and scrolling between different colors and imagery can really bring the page to life.

Stop-motion animation

Stop-motion animation is a technique whereby a scene is laid out (either in 2 or 3 dimensions) and a picture or snap-shot is taken (typically referred to as a frame), then that scene, or certain characters within it are manipulated, moved, or otherwise changed, before another picture or snapshot is taken. This process continues, creating a series of frames that when replayed sequentially produce the effect of motion.

It is generally quite easy to produce animations in this way and we can do the same thing on a web page trivially. We won't be using any of jQuery's built-in animation methods, or the `animate()` method. jQuery is used to help us select elements from the page, and build the frames, but is not essential in this application.

Imagery

The hard part of any stop-motion animation is the number of frames that need to be generated. Too few frames and the animation will become jerky or overly rapid. But the smoothness that is generally required takes many, many frames. In this example, we'll use a series of separate images. One image is equal to one frame and there are 75 images in total—not a huge number, but enough to make their creation somewhat labor-intensive and time-consuming.

Our animation will consist of a stick man that runs across the page, does a flying kick, and then bows to an unseen opponent. You will find all of these images in a folder called `stickman` in the `img` folder of the downloadable code archive that accompanies the book.

There are many available software products that animators can use to simplify the process of frame creation. I used an application called Pivot Stickfigure Animator, created by Peter Bone, which was specially created to make animating stick figures easier.

Technique

As well as creating all the individual frames of our animation, hardcoding 75 images into a page, as well as defining a unique style for each one, would also be quite tedious, and our example animation is relatively short. This type of animation can easily run into hundreds of frames for even quite short animations.

Instead, we'll create the 75 images and set their attributes and styles programmatically, which makes the process much easier for us to complete, and still happens quite quickly when the page loads.

Time for action – adding the markup and styling

1. Add the following markup to the template file:

```
<div id="cartoon">
  <img class="loading" src="img/stickman/ajax-loader.gif"
    alt="Loading Frames">
</div>
```

2. Save the template file as `stickman.html`. Now add the following styles to a new file:

```
#cartoon { width:500px; height:500px; position:relative; }
img { position:absolute; top:0; left:0; }
img.loading { z-index:0; left:50%; top:50%; }
```

3. Save this stylesheet as `stickman.css` in the `css` folder.

What just happened?

All we have on the page is a container to load the frames into and a loading icon so that it appears as if something is happening when the page initially loads and the frames are being created. While running this example locally, the frames should be loaded pretty much instantly, but in the wild there would certainly be some delay.

The CSS sets the container to the width of a single frame, and the frames are positioned absolutely so that they stack up on top of each other. We'll set the z-index for each element manually in the script. We can also position the loader so that it is roughly in the centre of the container.

Time for action – creating the frames and running the animation

Next, add the following code to the empty function at the end of the `<body>` in `stickman.html`:

```
var counter = 1,
  srcStr1 = "img/stickman/stick-kick",
  srcStr2 = ".jpg",
  frames = $("<div id=\"frames\"></div>"),
  removeFrame = function() {
    if (frames.children().length > 1) {
      frames.children(":first").remove();
    } else {
      clearInterval(timer);
    }
```

```
    },
    timer = setInterval(function() { removeFrame() }, 50);

    for(var x = 75; x--;) {
      $("<img />", {
        src:  srcStr1 + counter + srcStr2
      }).css("zIndex", x).appendTo(frames);
      counter++;
    }

    frames.appendTo("#cartoon");
```

When we run the page, the animation should proceed as we expect, much like the type of sketch we perhaps may have idly created in a notepad in our youth and "watched" by flicking through the pages quickly. The following screenshot shows a single frame of the stickman animation:

Clearly, the best way to view the animation is in a browser.

What just happened?

We start out by initializing some variables. We set a counter variable and a series of strings representing the common strings that we'll need to use repeatedly. These will be used inside a for loop so we don't want to define them within the loop as JavaScript will create the same string objects repeatedly, whereas by defining them outside of the loop will ensure they only get created once.

We also create a new container <div> which we'll append each of the new frames to, and assign a function to the setInterval JavaScript function.

Next we define the `removeFrame()` function which will be executed by `setInterval`. All this function does is check whether there is more than one element within the `frames` container and if so, remove the first one. Every 50 milliseconds, the top image will be removed, which is fast enough for the repeated showing of still images to be perceived as an animation. If there is only one image left, we clear the timeout as the animation has completed.

Next we define the `for` loop, specifying the maximum number of frames, and decrementing on each iteration of the loop. We don't need to specify a comparison condition in this form of loop however, because the loop will naturally end when $x = 0$ (because 0 is a `falsey` value). Using decrementing `for` loops is a proven strategy for faster JavaScript.

On each iteration of the loop we create a new `<img>` element and set its `src` to point to the correct image file using a combination of the strings we created earlier and the `counter` variable. We set the z-index of each image as it is created using the `css()` method and the x variable used to control the loop. On each iteration, x will decrease, so each image added to the page will be lower down in stacking order than the previous one, which is exactly the order we require. We then append the image to our new container `<div>`.

At the end of each iteration, we increment the counter variable by 1. After the loop has completed, we append our container element, which now contains all of the necessary images, to the container hardcoded into the page. This will overlay the loading spinner. In a full implementation, we'd probably remove the spinner at this point.

Pop quiz – implementing stop-motion animation with jQuery

1. In this example, we used a decrementing `for` loop, why?

    a. We need to in order to set a descending `z-index` on the images.

    b. The decrementing format of the loop is required when creating inline elements with jQuery.

    c. Because the code is easier to read.

    d. For performance reasons. Because the loop isn't checking a condition on every iteration. It's simply removing one from the value of x, so it runs faster.

Have a go hero – extending stop-motion animation

Simple two dimensional stickmen aren't the only images that can be used to create a stop-motion animation. Pretty much any series of sequential images can be used, so experiment with color images or photographs. Time-lapse photography offers an excellent source of the right kind of photos to use.

Summary

In this chapter, we looked at some examples of full page animation, where the animation itself is one of the key elements of the page, not just an attractive but short-lived feature of the interface.

In this example-based chapter, we looked at the following animation techniques:

◆ Scroll animations where the page is automatically scrolled vertically to different parts of the page when table of contents links are clicked.

◆ Parallax animations where several background layers are animated at different speeds to create the illusion of depth. In this example, we utilized the brand new cssHooks `bgpos.js` file to animate the `background-position` of the different layers.

◆ Scroll animations where individual pages making up a site are pulled into a single page and the window scrolls both horizontally and vertically to different areas of the page. In this example, we didn't scroll the page manually but relied on the scrollTo plugin.

◆ Stop motion animation where a series of images are shown so rapidly that it creates an animation.

The next chapter will also be a series of examples looking at other popular animations that may be used on websites.

8

Other Popular Animations

This chapter will follow a similar format to the previous one and will consist of a series of recipe-style examples that show real-world implementations of animations in action. We won't restrain ourselves to full-page animations this time however—anything goes!

We'll look at the following examples in this chapter:

◆ Proximity animations, where the animation is a reaction to the proximity of the mouse pointer to a target element or area of the page

◆ An animated header element

◆ A text-scrolling marquee widget

Proximity animations

Proximity animations, which are usually driven by the position of the mouse pointer relative to an element or series of elements on the page, are an awesome effect. While not suitable on all sites and in all contexts, it can add real flair when used in certain situations.

The effect isn't often very accessible, and pretty much shuts the door on non-mouse users, but it can be implemented as an additional bonus to visitors that are able to make use of it, while at the same time providing other, more accessible forms of interaction.

In this example, we'll create an image scroller that is triggered when the mouse pointer enters its container. The speed that the images will scroll will be determined by the distance of the mouse pointer from the center of the container. Moving the pointer will slow down or speed up the animation accordingly.

Time for action – creating and styling the page

In this part of the example we'll create the underlying page that the animation will run on and add the styling.

1. First we'll create the default page and add the CSS for the example. Add the following elements to the `<body>` of our template file:

```
<div id="proximity">
  <img src="img/proximity1.jpg" alt="CH-47 Chinook">
  <img src="img/proximity2.jpg" alt="Mi-24W">
  <img src="img/proximity3.jpg" alt="Mil Mi-24A">
  <img src="img/proximity4.jpg" alt="AH-1J Cobra">
  <img src="img/proximity5.jpg" alt="Mi-24P">
  <img src="img/proximity6.jpg" alt="AH-1Z Viper">
  <img src="img/proximity7.jpg" alt="AH-1W Cobra">
  <img src="img/proximity8.jpg" alt="UH-1Y Huey">
  <img src="img/proximity9.jpg" alt="AH-64 Apache">
  <img src="img/proximity10.jpg" alt="AH-1W Super Cobra">
  <img src="img/proximity11.jpg" alt="MI-28 Havoc">
  <img src="img/proximity12.jpg" alt="AH-1W Super Cobra">
  <img src="img/proximity13.jpg" alt="AH-1W Cobra">
  <img src="img/proximity14.jpg" alt="Mi-24 HIND E">
  <img src="img/proximity15.jpg" alt="AH-1W Super Cobra">
  <img src="img/proximity16.jpg" alt="UH-1N Huey">
  <img src="img/proximity17.jpg" alt="AH-64D Apache">
  <img src="img/proximity18.jpg" alt="UH-1N Huey">
  <img src="img/proximity19.jpg" alt=" Lempira Bell 412">
  <img src="img/proximity20.jpg" alt="UH-60L Blackhawk">
</div>
```

2. Save this file as `proximity.html`. Next we'll add some CSS. In a new file, add the following code:

```
/* base classes (scripting disabled) */
#proximity {
  width:960px; margin:auto; border:1px solid #000;
  -moz-border-radius:8px; -webkit-border-radius:8px;
  border-radius:8px;
}
#proximity img { border:1px solid #000; }

/* scripting enabled classes */
#proximity.slider {
  width:550px; height:250px; position:relative; overflow:hidden;
```

```
}
.slider #scroller { position:absolute; left:0; top:0; }
.slider #scroller img {
  display:block; width:150px; height:150px; margin:50px 0 0 50px;
    float:left; color:#fff; background-color:#000;
}
.slider #scroller img:first-child { margin-left:0; }
#message {
  width:100%; height:30px; padding-top:10px; margin:0;
  -moz-border-radius:0 0 8px 8px;
  -webkit-border-bottom-radius:8px;
  -webkit-border-bottom-right-radius:8px;
  border-radius:0 0 8px 8px; position:absolute; bottom:0;
  left:0;
  background-color:#000; color:#fff; text-align:center;
  font:18px "Nimbus Sans L", "Helvetica Neue",
    "Franklin Gothic Medium", Sans-serif;
}
```

3. Save this in the css folder as proximity.css and don't forget to link to it from the
<head> of the HTML page.

What just happened?

Keeping the HTML as simple and as light as possible, we simply add the images that we want
to show to a container element. Any extra elements that we need can be added dynamically
in the nature of progressive enhancement.

There are two sections in the CSS file. The first section is a collection of base styles which
are used if the page is loaded by a visitor that has JavaScript disabled. This ensures that
all of the images are visible and therefore accessible—none of them are hidden or
otherwise obscured.

The second section changes the appearance of the container element and adds styling to
elements or classes that are added dynamically, transforming the appearance of the slider,
provided JavaScript is enabled.

We set the height and width of the container so that only three images are visible at any
one time and set its overflow style property to hidden so that all of the other images are
hidden, ready to be scrolled into view.

We also add positioning for an element with an id of scroller. This element doesn't yet
exist and will be added by the script, which we'll look at shortly. This element will also need
a width, but we can assign this dynamically based on the number of images in the container.

We also change the styling of the images themselves, setting them to block-level elements and floating them to the left so that they stack up horizontally in a long line without wrapping onto two lines as this would destroy the functionality of the scroller. It is the combination of floating the images, and setting the `width` of the container to accommodate them all that allows them to stack up as horizontally as required. We'll add a message that tells the visitor how to use the scroller so we also include some styling for this as well.

The following screenshot shows how the page will appear with scripting disabled:

In the previous image we can see that the images are all visible. It's not pretty, but it's highly accessible and doesn't hide the content when scripting is disabled on the client.

Time for action – prepping the page for sliding functionality

When scripting is enabled we can enhance the page to add the additional elements that the proximity slider requires. Add the following code to the empty function at the bottom of the HTML page:

```
var prox = $("#proximity"),
    scroller = $("<div></div>", {
        id: "scroller"
```

```
    }),

    pointerText = "Use your pointer to scroll, moving to the edge
       scrolls faster!",
    keyboardMessage = "Use your arrow keys to scroll the images!",
    message = $("<p></p>", {
       id: "message",
       text: keyboardMessage
    });

prox.addClass("slider").wrapInner(scroller).append(message);

var middle = prox.width() / 2;

scroller = $("#scroller");

scroller.width(function() {
  var total = 0;
  scroller.children().each(function(i, val) {
    var el = $(this);
    total = total + (el.outerWidth() +
      parseInt(el.css("marginLeft")));
});
return total;

}).css("left", "-" + (scroller.width() / 2 - middle) + "px");
```

What just happened?

First we cache the selector for the proximity container, which we'll use a couple of times in this chunk of code, and a couple of times a little later on in the script. Next we create a new `<div>` element and give it an `id` attribute so that we can easily select it again when necessary. We also use this `id` for styling purposes.

Next we store a couple of text strings in variables for convenience. These will be used as messages to display to the visitor at different points. We also create a new paragraph element as a container for the message text, give the element an `id` (again for selecting purposes), and use the jQuery `text()` method to set its `innerText` to one of the text strings. Using jQuery 1.4 syntax we can use the property `text` on the object passed as the second argument to the element creation jQuery method format, which automatically maps to the `text()` method.

Next we add a class name to the outer proximity container. Remember, this class name is used to differentiate between scripting being disabled and enabled so that we can add the required styling. We also wrap the contents of the proximity container (the 20 images) in our newly created scroller element, and append the message to the proximity container.

Next we set a variable which is equal to the `width` of the proximity container divided by two, which gives us the horizontal middle of the element, which we'll need to use in some calculations to position the scroller element, and work out where the mouse pointer is relative to the proximity container.

We could just as easily have set the number that the `middle` variable needs to contain, instead of calculating it in this way. The `width` of the proximity container (with scripting enabled) is set in our CSS file and is highly arbitrary to this particular example. If we changed its `width` however, the script would break if we set the figure directly in the variable instead of working it out programmatically. It is always best to avoid hardcoding 'magic' numbers into scripts whenever possible.

At this point we also need to cache a reference to the scroller element now that it has been appended to the page. We can't use the contents of the `scroller` variable that we created at the start of the script, so we overwrite it with a fresh reference to the element by selecting it from the page again.

We now need to set the `width` of the scroller element so that it is wide enough to accommodate all of the images in a single row. To do this we pass a function to jQuery's `width()` method which returns the `width` to set.

The function calculates this figure by iterating over each image and adding both its `width` and horizontal `margin` to the `total` variable. This means that an indeterminate number of images can be used without changing the script, and that images with different widths and spacing can be used.

Once we've set the `width` of the scroller element, we then need to position it so that the center of the scroller is at the center of the proximity container. This is so that when the page loads, the visitor can move it to the left or right depending on where they move their pointer or which arrow key is pressed.

If we load the page in a browser at this point, we should find that the appearance of the elements on the page has changed:

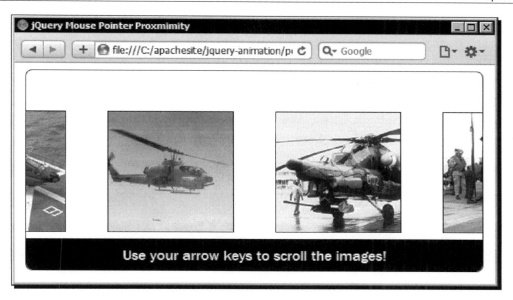

In the previous screenshot, we can see that the proximity container is resized and the scroller element is centered within it. We can also see the default message at the bottom of the proximity container.

Time for action – animating the scroller

The next section of code deals with actually animating the scroller element based on where the mouse pointer is relative to the outer proximity container:

```
function goAnim(e) {

  var offset = prox.offset(),
    resetOffset = e.pageX - offset.left - middle,

    normalizedDuration = (resetOffset > 0) ? resetOffset :
      -resetOffset,

    duration = (middle - normalizedDuration) * 50;

    scroller.stop().animate({
      left: (resetOffset < 0) ? 0 : "-" + (parseInt(scroller.width())
        - parseInt(prox.width())))
    }, duration, "linear");
}
```

What just happened?

Within the `goAnim()` function, we first get the `offset` of the proximity container so that we know its position relative to the document. We then work out where the mouse pointer is relative to the middle of the proximity container. This means that numerically, the pointer offset will be 0 when it is in the center.

If the mouse pointer is in the left half of the proximity container, the number in the `resetOffset` variable will be negative. This would cause our calculations later in the function to be incorrect, so we need to check whether the `resetOffset` variable is greater than 0, and if it isn't we invert the number using its minus value.

Ultimately, what we want to happen is for the speed of the scroller to increase as the pointer moves towards either end of the proximity container, and slow down as it moves into the center. In other words, the speed of the animation needs to be inversely proportionate to the distance of the pointer from the middle of the proximity container.

The problem that we have at this point is that the figure representing the distance of the pointer from the middle of the proximity container gets larger as it moves towards the edge, so the animation would slow down instead of speeding up if we were to use this figure as the duration of the animation.

To invert the value stored in the `normalizedDuration` variable, we subtract it from the value representing the middle of the proximity container, and then multiply the resulting figure by 50. The duration argument is in milliseconds, so if we don't use a multiplier (50 was arrived at by trial and error) to increase our value, the animations will occur too quickly.

We can now initiate the animation. We use the JavaScript ternary statement to test whether the `resetOffset` figure is less than 0 and if it is, we know that to get the scroller to slide to the right we just need to set the `left` style property of the scroller element to 0.

If the variable is greater than 0, we have to move the scroller element negatively (to the left) in order to show the images hidden at the right. To align the right edge of the scroller `<div>` to the right edge of the proximity container, we set the end point of the animation to the `width` of the scroller `<div>` minus the `width` of the proximity container.

Time for action – adding the mouse events

Now we need to add the mouse events that will trigger the animations:

```
prox.mouseenter(function(e) {

    message.text(pointerText).delay(1000).fadeOut("slow");

    goAnim(e);
```

```
    prox.mousemove(function(ev) {

      goAnim(ev);
    });
  });

  prox.mouseleave(function() {
    scroller.stop();
    prox.unbind("mousemove");
  });
```

What just happened?

First we set a mouseeenter event handler so that we can detect when the pointer initially enters the proximity container. When this occurs we change the message text so that it shows what to do with the mouse pointer and then fade out the message slowly after a delay of one second.

We then call our goAnim() function to start the animation. At this point, we set a mousemove event so that we can increase or decrease the speed of the animation as the pointer moves within the proximity container. Each time the pointer moves, we call the goAnim() function once more. Each time this function is called we pass in the event object.

We also set a mouseleave event handler on the proximity container so that we can detect when the pointer leaves this element altogether. When this occurs we stop the currently running animation and unbind the mousemove event handler.

At this point we should have a fully working proximity slider. Earlier we discussed how the proximity effect is only useful to mouse users, so let's add a keyboard event handler to our script that will let keyboard users navigate the scroller as well.

Time for action – adding keyboard events

The following code enables keyboard driven animations:

```
$(document).keydown(function(e) {

  if (e.keyCode === 37 || e.keyCode === 39) {

    message.fadeOut("slow");

    if (!scroller.is(":animated")) {
      scroller.stop().animate({
        left: (e.keyCode === 37) ? 0 : -(scroller.width() -
```

```
            prox.width()
      }, 6000, "linear");
    }
  }
}).keyup(function() {
  scroller.stop();
});
```

What just happened?

We attach the keydown event handler to the document object so that the visitor doesn't have to focus the proximity container somehow. Within the anonymous function, we first check whether the left or right arrow keys were pressed.

The key code 37 refers to the left arrow key and the code 39 refers to the right arrow key. The keyCode property, normalized by jQuery so that it is accessible to all browsers, will contain the code for whichever key was pressed, but we only want to react to either of the specified keys being pressed.

When either of these keys are pressed, we first fade out the message and then check that the scroller is not already being animated using jQuery's is() method in conjunction with the :animated filter.

As long as the scroller element is not already being animated (denoted by the ! at the start of the condition), we then animate it. We check the keyCode once again with a ternary so that we can move the scroller in the correct direction depending on which key is pressed.

Finally we add a keyup event handler that stops the scroller animation once the key is released. This improves the interactivity of animation as it allows the visitor to intuitively stop the scroller whenever they wish.

Have a go hero – extending proximity animations

The obvious way to extend our example would be to trigger animations on the vertical axis as well. We could have a grid of images instead of a single row and animate the grid up and down as well as left and right.

One thing to do to extend the example would be to add additional keyboard functionality. Check for additional keys such as the home and end keys for example, which could navigate to the start or end of the scroller element accordingly.

Pop quiz – implementing proximity animations

1. We provided additional functionality by adding keyboard navigability in the previous example, why?

    a. For fun

    b. To look good

    c. To provide an alternate way for the content to be explored by non-mouse users

    d. Keyboard events must be bound whenever mouse events are used

2. Why should we avoid hardcoding 'magic' numbers into our scripts?

    a. To make our code more readable

    b. So that our scripts are less reliant on the content that they act upon

    c. hardcoded integers take longer to process

    d. Because jQuery prefers working with strings

Animated page headers

Another quite fashionable technique at the moment is to have an animation that runs in the header of the page when the home page loads. Sometimes the animations run continually on every page of the site; others run once on the home page only.

This technique is an easy and effective way to make your site stand out, and they needn't be complex or heavily apparent animations; a short, subtle animation can be enough to add the wow factor.

Earlier in the book we looked at using the new cssHooks functionality in conjunction with a pre-written file that makes use of cssHooks, which extends jQuery's `css()` method to allow an element's `background-position` style property to be animated. In this example, we'll look at how we can do this manually without the use of the plugin.

Well-written plugins can be an effective and easy solution, but there are times when a plugin adds much more functionality than we actually need and therefore increase a page's script overhead. It's not often that reinventing the wheel is necessary or advised, but there can be times when it's beneficial to write a custom script that does only what we require.

Time for action – creating an animated header

The underlying page for this example will be relatively straight-forward, with just a `<header>` element whose `background-position` we'll animate manually:

1. The header of the example page will consist of just an empty `<header>` element:

```
<header>
</header>
```

2. Save this as `animated-header.html`. The CSS is even simpler, with just a single selector and a few rules:

```css
header {
    display:block; width:960px; height:200px; margin:auto;
    background:url(../img/header.jpg) repeat 0 0;
}
```

3. Save this as `animated-header.css`. We'll need to link to the file from the `<head>` of the page we just created.

4. The script itself is also surprisingly simple. Add the following code to the function at the end of the `<body>`:

```javascript
var header = $("header");

header.css("backgroundPosition", "0 0");

var bgscroll = function() {

    var current = parseInt(header.css("
      backgroundPosition").split(" ")[1]),
      newBgPos = "0 " + (current - 1) + "px";

    header.css("backgroundPosition", newBgPos);
};

setInterval(function() { bgscroll() }, 75);
```

5. When we run the file in a browser, we should find that the background image used for the `<header>` slowly scrolls.

What just happened?

In the script we cache the `header` selector outside of our main function for efficiency, so that we aren't creating a new jQuery object every time the function is executed. Even though the `header` is cached in a variable outside of the function, the variable is still accessible by the function.

Within the function we first get the current vertical `background-position` of the `header` element, extracting just the part of the returned string we require using the JavaScript `split()` function. We also use `parseInt` to convert the string into an integer.

We then decrement the integer by one. This means that the background image will scroll up. This is not important. There's no reason why the image couldn't scroll down, I just happen to prefer motion in the upwards direction for some reason. Finally we set the new `background-position` using jQuery's `css()` method.

After the function definition, we use the JavaScript `setInterval()` method to repeatedly call the function every 75 milliseconds. This is relatively quick, but is quite smooth—much higher than this and the animation begins to get a bit jerky. There's no reason however that different background images might not need to run as quickly.

Have a go hero – extending the animated header

As the example is so small, there is a lot that could be done to build on it. Depending on the background image in use, it could be extended to move along the horizontal axis instead, or even both, perhaps moving diagonally in a north-westerly direction.

Marquee text

The use of the `<marquee>` element died out many years ago, but a similar effect, created with JavaScript is resurfacing in recent years thanks to its use on high-profile sites such as the typed headlines on the BBC News site, and the animated trending topics on the twitter home page.

This is an effective and attractive way to present potentially relevant content to the visitor without taking up too much content space. It won't suit all sites of course, but used sparingly, and in as non-intrusive a way as possible, it can be a great effect.

Time for action – creating and styling the underlying page

In this example, we can see how easy it is to grab a series of text strings and display them in a smoothly scrolling marquee style. We'll use jQuery's built-in AJAX capabilities to grab a JSON file of the latest posts on my blog. Let's get started.

1. Add the following markup to the `<body>` of the template file:

```
<div id="outer">
  <header>
    <hgroup>
      <h1>Site Title</h1>
      <h2>Site Description</h2>
    </hgroup>
    <nav>Main site navigation along here</nav>
  </header>
  <article>
    <h1>A Blog Post Title</h1>
    <p>The post copy</p>
  </article>
  <aside>
    <div>
    <h2>Ads</h2>
      <p>Probably a bunch of ads here that take up a reasonable
        section of this aside vertically</p>
    </div>
    <div>
    <h2>Popular Posts</h2>
      <p>Some links here to other posts, which may or may not
        be related to the current post, but are deemed popular
        based on the number of comments</p>
    </div>
    <div>
    <h2>Related Posts</h2>
      <p>Some links here to other posts that are definitely
        related to this post, based on post tags</p>
    </div>
    <div>
    <h2>Twitter Feed</h2>
      <p>Maybe a twitter feed here that displays recent tweets
        or something. Aside could be quite long by now</p>
    </div>
  </aside>
</div>
```

2. Save the new page as `marquee.html`.

3. We can also add some basic CSS at this point to layout the example in an acceptable, generic manner. In a new file in your text editor, add the following code:

```
#outer {
  width:960px; margin:auto; color:#3c3c3c;
  font:normal 17px "Palatino Linotype", "Book Antiqua",
    Palatino, serif;
}
header {
  display:block; padding:0 20px 0; margin-bottom:40px;
  border:3px solid #d3d1d1; background-color:#e5e5e5;
}
hgroup { float:left; }
h1, h2 { margin-bottom:10px; }
nav {
  display:block; width:100%; height:40px; clear:both;
  text-align:right;
}
article {
  width:700px; height:900px; border:3px solid #d3d1d1;
  background-color:#e5e5e5; float:left;
}
article h1, article p { margin:20px; }
p , nav{
  font:normal 17px "Nimbus Sans L", "Helvetica Neue",
    "Franklin Gothic Medium", Sans-serif;
}
p { margin-top:0; }
aside {
  width:220px; height:900px; border:3px solid #d3d1d1;
  background-color:#e5e5e5; float:right;
}
aside div { padding:0 20px 20px; }
```

4. Save this file as `marquee.css` in the `css` directory. Link to this stylesheet from the `<head>` of the page we just created.

What just happened?

The underlying HTML represents a typical blog. We've added a series of elements for two reasons, primarily so that we have somewhere to insert the marquee, but also so that we can see why this approach can be necessary.

Having the latest posts scrolling across the page near the top of the site ensures that this content is seen straight away, and the fact that it's animated also helps to draw the visitor's attention to it.

The CSS used so far is purely to layout the example elements in a precise and mildly aesthetic way, giving us a generic layout and a light skinning. We'll add some more CSS a little later in the example for our dynamically created marquee. At this point, the page should appear like this:

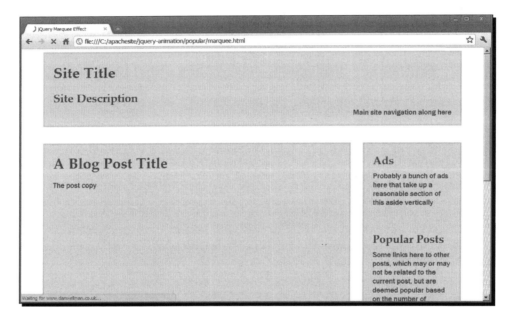

Remember, all of the elements in the previous screenshot are there for the marquee to be inserted between. They are not specifically required, and are there for this example.

Time for action – retrieving and processing the post list

Now we're ready to retrieve the list of latest posts and process them, making them ready to be displayed as items in the marquee. In order to access this data across the Internet from another domain, we need to use JSONP, which stands for JSON with Padding, and involves dynamically creating and injecting a `<script>` element to the page, although jQuery actually handles this aspect of it for us.

1. jQuery provides native support for JSONP and allows us to bypass the same-origin security policy of the browser. In order to output JSON in the correct format, I'm using the JSON API plugin on a WordPress-powered blog, which outputs JSON in the following format:

```
{
  "status": "ok",
  "count": 1,
  "count_total": 1,
  "pages": 1,
  "posts": [
    {
      "id": 1,
      etc...
    },
  {
      "id": 2,
      Etc...
  }
  ]
}
```

2. There are more properties in the posts array shown in the previous code block, as well as other arrays and properties in the outer object, but the previous snippet should give you an idea of the structure of the data we'll be working with.

3. Add the following code to the bottom of the HTML page:

```
$.getJSON("http://danwellman.co.uk?json=1&count=10&callback=?",
function(data) {

  var marquee = $("<div></div>", {
      id: "marquee"
  }),
    h2 = $("<h2></h2>", {
    text: "Recent Posts:"
    }),
    fadeLeft = $("<div></div>", {
    id: "fadeLeft"
    }),
    fadeRight = $("<div></div>", {
    id: "fadeRight"
    });

    for(var x = 0, y = data.count; x < y; x++) {
```

```
      $("<a></a>", {
        href: data.posts[x].url,
        title: data.posts[x].title,
        html: data.posts[x].title
      }).appendTo(marquee);
    }

  marquee.wrapInner("<div></div>").prepend(h2).append(fadeLeft)
    .append(fadeRight).insertAfter("header").slideDown("slow");

  $("#marquee").find("div").eq(0).width(function() {

    var width = 0;

    $(this).children().each(function() {
      var el = $(this);
      width += el.width() + parseInt(el.css("marginRight"));

    });

    return width;
  });

  marquee.trigger("marquee-ready");
});
```

4. We can also add some more CSS, this time for the newly-created elements. Add the
    following code to the bottom of `marquee.css`:

```
#marquee {
  display:none; height:58px; margin:-20px 0 20px;
  border:3px solid #d3d1d1; position:relative;
  overflow:hidden;
  background-color:#e5e5e5;
}
#marquee h2 { margin:0; position:absolute; top:10px; left:20px; }
#marquee a {
  display:block; margin-right:20px; float:left;
  font:normal 15px "Nimbus Sans L", "Helvetica Neue",
    "Franklin Gothic Medium", Sans-serif;
}
#marquee div { margin:20px 0 0 210px; overflow:hidden; }
#marquee div:after {
  content:""; display:block; height:0; visibility:hidden;
```

```
    clear:both;
  }
  div#fadeLeft, div#fadeRight {
    width:48px; height:21px; margin:0; position:absolute;
    top:17px;
    left:210px; background:url(../img/fadeLeft.png) no-repeat;
  }
  div#fadeRight {
    left:906px; background:url(../img/fadeRight.png) no-repeat;
  }
```

5. When we run the page now, we should see that the new marquee element, along with its links, is inserted into the page:

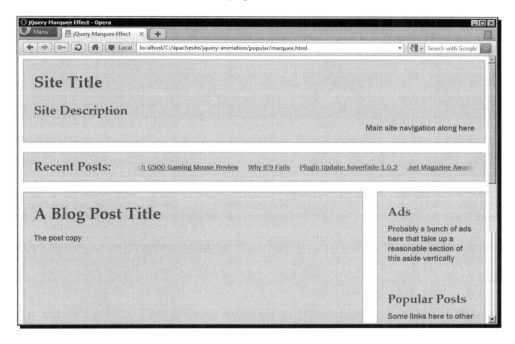

The previous screenshot shows the elements in the new marquee section including the heading, the links themselves, and the fade elements which are added purely for aesthetics.

What just happened?

All of our JavaScript is wrapped up in jQuery's `getJSON()` method, which uses jQuery's AJAX functionality to make a request to the URL specified as the first argument to the method. The second argument is an anonymous function that is executed if the request is successful. The returned JSON data is passed to this function automatically.

Within the function we first create some of the elements that make up our marquee including the outer container, the heading and two purely aesthetic `<div>` elements used to add the left and right fade effect at the start and end of the row of links. All of these elements are stored in variables so that we can access them easily when required.

Next we process the JSON object passed into the function. Remember, this object contains a series of properties where the values of some of these properties are arrays, such as the `posts` array, which contains each of the returned posts as objects within each of its array items.

We use a `for` loop to iterate over each object in the `posts` array that is returned with the JSON object. This object contains a property called `count`, where the number of posts that are returned is stored as an integer, so we can use this to tell the `for` loop how many times to execute, which is marginally easier than counting the objects in the `posts` array.

For each post that has been returned, we create a new `<a>` element, setting its `href` to point to the `url` property of the current object, and the `title` and `text` of the element set to the `title` property of the current object, and then append the new `<a>` to the `marquee` element that we created a minute ago.

Once we've created and appended a link for each post, we then wrap the contents of the marquee element (the links) in a new `<div>`, prepend the `<h2>` to the start of the `marquee`, and append the `<div>` elements for the fades to the end of the `marquee` element. We then append the `marquee` to the page before sliding it into view with the `slideDown()` method.

At this point we need to set a `width` on the container `<div>` that we wrapped the links in a moment ago. This is so that the links can all line up in a single row. We need to take into account the `width` of each link, plus any `margin` it has (which we set in the CSS).

We use a function as the value of jQuery's `width()` method to iterate over each link and add its `width` and `margin` to a running total. We can't do this until the marquee has been appended to the page because it is not until this point that each element actually has a `width` or `margin` that we can retrieve.

The last thing we do in the callback function for our `getSJON()` method is fire off a custom event with the `trigger()` jQuery method. The custom event is called `marquee-ready` and is used to tell our script when the `marquee` has been added to the page. We'll use this custom event shortly to animate the post links.

We also added some new CSS to our stylesheet. Some of this code is to give our marquee elements the same light skin as the rest of the page. But other parts of it, such as floating the links, and setting the marquee's `overflow` property to `hidden` is so that the links line up in a single row, and so that the majority of the links are hidden, ready to be scrolled into view. We also add the fade images to the last two `<div>` elements inside the `marquee` element.

Time for action – animating the post links

We're now ready to begin scrolling the post links within the marquee. We can do this using our custom event.

1. After the `getJSON()` method, add the following code to the page:

```
$("body").delegate("#marquee", "marquee-ready", function() {

  var marquee = $(this),
    postLink = marquee.find("a").eq(0);
    width = postLink.width() +
      parseInt(postLink.css("marginRight")),
    time = 15 * width;

  postLink.animate({
    marginLeft: "-=" + width
  }, time, "linear", function() {
    $(this).css({
      marginLeft: 0
    }).appendTo(marquee.find("div").eq(0));
    marquee.trigger("marquee-ready");
  });
});
```

2. Our example is now complete. When we run the page at this point, the posts should begin scrolling from left to right.

What just happened?

We use the jQuery `delegate()` method to bind an event handler to our custom `marquee-ready` event. We need to use event delegation to achieve this because when this part of the code is executed, the JSON response is unlikely to have returned so the `marquee` element won't even exist. Attaching the event handler to the `body` of the page is an easy way to prepare the page for when the `marquee` element does exist.

Within the anonymous event-handling function, we first cache a reference to the marquee element using the `this` object, which is scoped to our `marquee` element. We then select the first link in the `marquee`, and determine its total `width` including `margin`.

We also work out what is effectively the speed of the animation. jQuery animations use a duration to determine how quickly an animation should run, but the problem this causes us is that posts with longer titles will move faster, because they have a greater distance to animate in the same amount of time.

To fix this, we work out a duration to pass to the animation method based on an arbitrary "speed" of 15 multiplied by the `width` of the current `<a>`. This ensures that each post will scroll at the same speed regardless of how long it is.

Once we have obtained the total `width` and `duration`, we can then run the animation on the first link in the `marquee`, using our `width` and `time` variables to configure the animation. We animate the post link by setting a negative `margin` of the first link, which drags all of the other links along with it.

Once the animation is complete, we remove the `margin-left` from the link, re-append it to the end of the `<div>` within the `marquee` element, and fire the `marquee-ready` event once more to repeat the process. This occurs repeatedly, creating the ongoing animation and bringing us to the end of this example.

Have a go hero – extending the marquee scroller

One feature that would certainly be beneficial to your users would be if the post titles stopped being animated when the mouse pointer hovered over them. The animation could then be restarted when the pointer moves off them again. Have a go at adding this functionality yourself. It shouldn't be too tricky at all and should involve adding `mouseenter` and `mouseleave` event handlers.

You'll need to work out how much of any given link is already outside of the visible area of the marquee in order to ensure the animation restarts at the same speed that it stopped at, but this should be quite similar to how we worked out the duration in this version of the example. See how you get on.

Pop Quiz – creating a marquee scroller

1. Why did we create a dynamic-duration variable (`time`) instead of using one of jQuery's predefined durations?

   a. Because its quicker using an integer, even if that integer has to be calculated, than using one of the duration strings

   b. Because it's more fun

   c. To make sure the links are appended to the correct element after being animated

   d. To ensure that the links all animate at the same speed regardless of how long they are

2. In this example we used the `delegate()` method, why?

   a. Because the `delegate()` method executes faster than the `bind()` or `live()` methods

   b. Because the `delegate()` method must be used when binding to custom events

   c. Because the element we need to bind to doesn't exist when the handler for it is added, and therefore the `delegate()` or `live()` methods are our only options, with `delegate()` being the more efficient

   d. Because we don't need to use the event object

Summary

In this chapter, the second of our heavily example-based as opposed to theory-based chapters, we looked at some more common animations that are increasingly found on the Web. Specifically we looked at the following types of animations:

◆ A proximity driven image scroller where the images scrolled in a certain direction, and at a certain speed, depending on the movements of the mouse pointer

◆ Background-position animations, in which we created a continuous header animation manually with just a few lines of code

◆ A text marquee, where a series of headlines were grabbed from a live Internet feed and displayed in a scrolling marquee-style banner

In the next chapter, we'll move to look at some of the new pure CSS animations that have been introduced with CSS3, and how jQuery can be used to enhance them and generally make working with them easier.

9
CSS3 Animations

CSS3 brings many impressive new styles to the web-development arena, and even though the specification is far from complete, many aspects of it are being used in the latest browsers. Pure-CSS animation may even make it into the specification at some point, and although at the time of writing few browsers support this, with a little help from jQuery we can create our own CSS3 animations that work with varying degrees of success, across most common browsers.

In this chapter, we'll be covering the following topics:

- The different CSS3 transforms available
- Animating an element's rotation
- Using the CSS3 transforms matrix
- Animating an element's skew with jQuery

 For further information on CSS3 2D transforms, see the W3C Working Draft specification at http://www.w3.org/TR/css3-2d-transforms/.

CSS3 2D transforms

CSS3 defines a style property called `transform` which allows us to transform targeted elements in a two-dimensional space along x and y axes. A range of transform functions can be supplied as the value of the `transform` property, which dictates how the transformation should be applied.

The following `transform` functions are defined:

Function	Example usage	Description of the transform
`matrix`	`matrix(a, b, c, d, e, f)`	Rotates, scales, skews, or translates the element according to the combination of supplied parameters.
`rotate`	`rotate(x)`	Rotates the element the specified number of degrees around the transform-origin. By default, the origin should be the center of the element.
`scale`	`scale(x, y)`	Scales the element the specified number of units along the x and y axes. If y is not supplied, it is assumed to be the same as x.
`scaleX`	`scale(x)`	Scales the element the specified number of units along the x axis.
`scaleY`	`scale(y)`	Scales the element the specified number of units along the y axis.
`skew`	`skew(x, y)`	Skews the element the specified number of degrees along the x and y axes. If y is not supplied it is assumed to be 0.
`skewX`	`skew(x)`	Skews the element the specified number of degrees along the x axis.
`skewY`	`skew(y)`	Skews the element the specified number of degrees along the y axis.
`translate`	`translate(x, y)`	Repositions the element the specified number of pixels along the x and y axes. If y is not provided it is assumed to be 0.
`translateX`	`translate(x)`	Repositions the element the specified number of pixels along the x axis.
`translateY`	`translate(y)`	Repositions the element the specified number of pixels along the y axis.

Understanding the matrix

All of the individual transform functions (`rotate()`, `skew()`, among others) can be thought of as shortcuts for specific matrix transforms. Indeed, most browsers will apply a matrix behind-the-scenes even when a transform function is provided.

The matrix takes six parameters, and each of the above transforms can be performed by providing different combinations of values for these parameters. Sometimes we can apply several transforms simultaneously by using the matrix. Let's look at some quick examples to illustrate how the matrix can be used.

Translate

Translating an element causes it to move from its original location. Positive values translate to the right or down the page (depending on the axis), and negative values move it to the left or up the page. For example, an element could be moved 100 pixels right along the x axis and 100 pixels down along the y axis using the following transformation matrix:

```
transform: matrix(1, 0, 0, 1, 100px, 100px);
```

This matrix function, equivalent to using the transform function: `translate(100px, 100px)`, would cause the targeted element to appear like this:

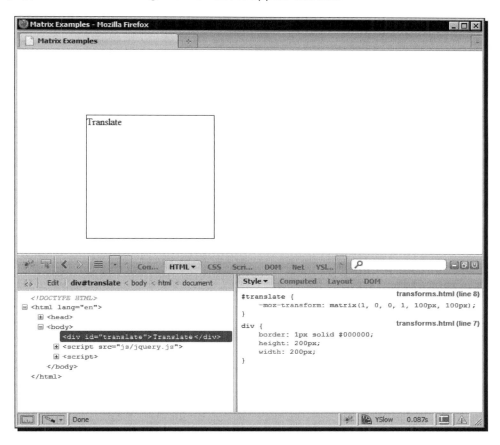

As we can see in the previous screenshot, the element has moved from its original location even though it has not been positioned, which we can see is the case in Firebug.

The fifth parameter of the matrix in this example corresponds to the x axis, and the sixth parameter to the y axis. Don't worry too much about the first four parameters as we will cover these in more detail shortly.

Units

It is of critical importance to note that some browsers, such as Firefox, expect these values with the units specified (as in the previous picture), while other browsers, such as Opera, or those based on the Webkit rendering engine, will expect these values without units.

An element does not need to be positioned in order for it to be translated, and the transform does not affect the flow of the document, or other elements around it. Adjacent elements will position themselves according to an element's original location, not its new location following a translation. The translated element's content is also translated along with it.

Scale

You may be wondering why we supplied the value 1 as the first and fourth parameters in our first matrix code snippet, but 0 as the value of the second and third parameters instead of supplying all zeros.

The reason for this is because these parameters (the first and fourth) correspond to the `scale` transform function, so to retain the transformed element's original size, the `scale` parameters are set to 1. To double the size of an element (without translating its position), we could use the following transformation matrix:

```
transform: matrix(2, 0, 0, 2, 0, 0);
```

This snippet would be equivalent to using `transform: scale(2, 2)` and would cause the targeted element to appear like this:

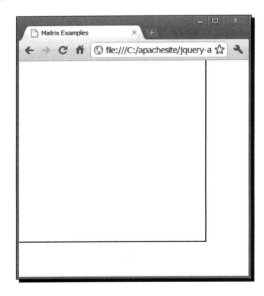

In the previous screenshot we can see that the element is now twice its original size.

The previous code symmetrically scales the target element along both the x and y axes. These values are unit-less in all supporting browsers, and the value 0 cannot be specified. Integers or floating-point numbers may be provided, and the scaling may be asymmetrical if necessary.

An interesting effect of scaling is that providing negative values cause the element to be reversed, and not shrunk, as we may intuitively surmise. So if we were to provide -2 and -2 as the first and fourth values in the previous code-snippet, the element would be reflected both vertically and horizontally, as well as being made twice its original size. We can even supply a combination of positive and negative values for this type of transformation.

A reflected element would appear like this:

The element is reversed along both its x and y axes, as if it were being viewed upside down in a mirror. This could be hugely useful if, for example, we were implementing pure-CSS reflections.

Skew

Remember the two zero values that correspond to parameters 2 and 3? These can be used as skew values, with the x axis using the second parameter, and the y axis using the third. We could skew an element (without modifying its scale or position) using the following matrix transform function:

```
transform: matrix(1, 1, 0, 1, 0, 0);
```

The following screenshot shows a skewed element:

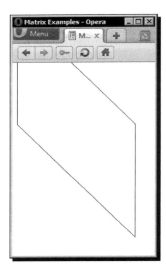

The previous screenshot shows an element skewed along the x axis. As with other matrix functions, positive values for these parameters cause transformation along the right or downwards direction, negative values along the left or up directions.

In the previous snippet, only the x axis has been skewed. A consequence of the skew is that the element has grown in size. The bounding box of the transformed element has doubled in size from 200 px (the original size of the element) to 400 px.

Regardless of this increase in size however, the flow of the document remains unaffected by the transform, and just like the other transforms, any content within the transformed element also becomes transformed.

Text appearance

Transforms have a varying impact on any text contained in the element across different browsers, with the text remaining crisp and readable in some browsers following a transform, and degrading in other browsers.

Rotation

To rotate an element using the matrix, we need to use the trigonometric functions sine and cosine to calculate the values of the first four parameters. Parameters 1 and 4 take cosine functions of the angle of rotation, while parameters 2 and 3 are sine and minus-sine functions of the rotation respectively.

Sine and cosine functions are relatively advanced mathematical constructs used to express the different relationships between the sides of triangles and the angles of triangles.

While an understanding of their exact nature is not essential to use them (JavaScript has built-in functions that will calculate them automatically), a deeper understanding of their nature and use will only help when working specifically with rotation.

For a basic introduction, see the Trigonometric Functions Wikipedia article at: http://en.wikipedia.org/wiki/Trigonometric_functions.

To rotate an element by, for example, 37 degrees we would use the following transform:

```
transform: matrix(0.7986355, 0.6018150, -0.6018150, 0.7986355, 0, 0);
```

Our rotated element should appear like this:

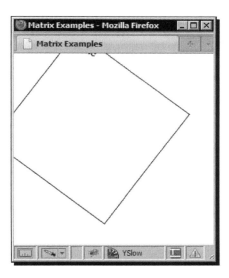

As we can see, the edges of the rotated element appear outside of the viewport. Care should be taken to correctly position elements that are to be rotated so as to ensure that there is adequate space to display the element in its entirety if necessary.

Calculating the sine and cosine functions of the angle of rotation can easily be done using a scientific calculator, or of course, JavaScript itself programmatically.

Working with transforms

Using the short-cut transform functions such as `rotate()`, or `skew()` is easier and more convenient than using the matrix. However, this ease of use comes at a price—we're limited to only using one of them at a time on a single element. If we were to try and use more than one of them in a CSS statement, only the last one defined would be applied.

If we need to apply several different transforms to an element, we can use the matrix function, depending on which transformations we need to apply. For example, we can skew an element, while also translating and scaling it using something like the following:

```
transform: matrix(2, -1, 0, 2, 300px, 0);
```

In this example, the element would be skewed along the x axis, doubled in size and moved 300 px to the right. We couldn't rotate the targeted element in the previous code-snippet at the same time as doing these things.

Even if we supply two matrix functions, one for the skew, scale and translate, and a second for the rotation, only the rotation would be applied. We can however rotate and translate, or rotate and scale an element simultaneously using a single matrix function.

jQuery and transforms

We can use jQuery's `css()` method in setter mode to set CSS3 transforms on selected elements, and we can use it in getter mode to retrieve any transform functions set on an element. We just need to ensure that we use the correct vendor prefix, such as `-moz-transform` for Firefox, or `-webkit-transform` for Webkit-based browsers. Opera also has its own vendor prefix, as do newer versions of IE.

One thing to be aware of is that while we can set a specific transform function, such as `rotate()`, on a selected element, we can only get the value of the `style` property in its matrix format. Look at the following code:

```
$("#get").css("-moz-transform", "rotate(30deg)");
$("#get").text($("#get").css("-moz-transform"));
```

This would result in the following:

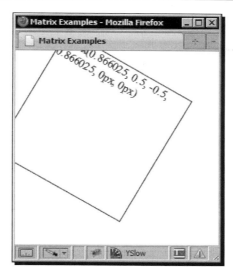

In the previous screenshot, we see that the rotation we applied in the first line of code using the `rotate()` transform function is returned with the second line of code as a matrix function.

Using the new cssHooks

The cssHooks file that we used earlier in the book (see `https://github.com/brandonaaron/jquery-cssHooks`) also has some CSS3 2D transforms behavior included. While it is beneficial from a learning perspective to create these effects manually, as we do throughout the remainder of this chapter, remember to use this file to save yourself time and effort in the future.

Internet Explorer transforms

Internet Explorer, versions 8 and below, do not support the CSS3 `transform` style property at all. These browsers do however provide a proprietary Matrix filter that can be used to generate (almost) the same effects as those provided by the W3C CSS3 version.

IE9 has recently been released in preview/beta format and has added support for true CSS3 2D transforms.

The `filter` property is used in a very similar way to the CSS3 version. For example, to rotate an element by 15 degrees, we could use the following CSS:

```
progid:DXImageTransform.Microsoft.Matrix(
  M11=1.4488887394336025,
  M12=-0.388228567653781,
  M21=0.388228567653781,
  M22=1.4488887394336025,
  SizingMethod='auto expand'
);
```

This code produces the following effect in IE8:

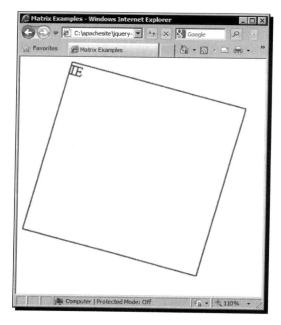

As you may notice in the previous screenshot, the size of the element has increased considerably. This is due to the `sizingMethod` being set to `auto expand`. Another thing you may notice is that two of the parameters are reversed in IE's implementation of the matrix (parameters `b` and `c`).

Instead of hiding some of the content outside of the viewport, IE has repositioned the element so that it remains entirely visible. This may or may not be beneficial depending on the circumstances of a particular implementation.

Setting the `auto expand` parameter causes the image to increase in size, which is a slight inconvenience to say the least. However if we don't set this, the element will be clipped, as shown in the following screenshot:

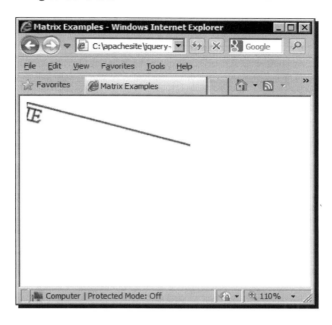

Clipping pretty much destroys our simple box (and the content is still scaled), as we can see in the previous screenshot.

CSS3 3D transforms

All of the transform functions we have looked at so far are two-dimensional, operating on just the x and y axes. Transforms that operate in three dimensions, along x, y, and z axes have also been proposed.

3D equivalents of all of the transform functions exist and usually just take an extra parameter which corresponds to the vector of each dimension, and the angle. For example, a 3D rotation could be added using this code:

```
transform: rotate3d(0, 1, 0, 30deg);
```

As with 2D transforms, there is an all-encompassing matrix function that allows us to implement any of the other transforms and allows us to combine some of them together on a single element.

If, like me, you thought the 2D transform matrix, with its six parameters, was complex and perhaps a little hard to understand, wait till you start using the 3D matrix, which has 16 parameters in total!

At present 3D transforms are only supported in Webkit-based browsers, so we won't be looking at these in any further detail. But hopefully they'll be appearing in more browsers sooner rather than later.

Animated rotation with jQuery and CSS3

In this example, we'll set up an animation that rotates an image using the `rotate()` transform function. Because this is supported by the majority of common browsers it's actually really easy to implement, and can be a great effect that enhances the appearance and behavior of the page it is used on.

Time for action – animating an element's rotation

We'll just be rotating a simple image in this example, so this is the only visible element we need in the `<body>` of the page.

1. Add the following `<img>` to a fresh copy of the template file:

```
<img src="img/color-wheel.png" id="colorWheel">
```

2. At this point we don't even need any styles as everything we need to set can be done in the JavaScript, which we'll add next.

3. In the function at the bottom of the HTML page, add the following code:

```
var img = $("#colorWheel"),
  offset = img.offset(),
  origWidth = img.width(),
  origHeight = img.height(),
  rotateStrings = [
    "rotate(",
    0,
    "deg)"
  ],

  getVendor = function() {

  var prefix = null,
    vendorStrings = {
    pure: "transform",
```

```
      moz: "-moz-transform",
      webkit: "-webkit-transform",
      op: "-o-transform"
  };

  for (props in vendorStrings) {
    if(img.css(vendorStrings[props]) === "none") {
      prefix = vendorStrings[props];
    }
  }

  if (prefix === null) {
    prefix = "filter";

    img.css({
      position: "absolute",
      filter: "progid:DXImageTransform.Microsoft.Matrix(
        sizingMethod='auto expand');"
    });
  }

  return prefix;
},
vendor = getVendor();

function doRotate() {

  rotateStrings[1]++;

  if (vendor === "filter") {

    var rad = rotateStrings[1] * (Math.PI * 2 / 360),
      cos = Math.cos(rad),
      sin = Math.sin(rad),
      driftX = (img.width() - origWidth) / 2,
      driftY = (img.height() - origHeight) / 2,
      el = img.get(0);

    img.css({
      left: offset.left - driftX,
      top: offset.top - driftY
    });
      el.filters.item("DXImageTransform.Microsoft.Matrix")
        .M11 = cos;
```

```
        el.filters.item("DXImageTransform.Microsoft.Matrix")
          .M12 = -sin;
        el.filters.item("DXImageTransform.Microsoft.Matrix")
          .M21 = sin;
        el.filters.item("DXImageTransform.Microsoft.Matrix")
          .M22 = cos;

    } else {
      img.css(vendor, rotateStrings.join(""));
    }
  }

  setInterval(function() { doRotate() }, 100);
```

4. Save the page as `rotate.html`. If we run the page in a browser now, we should see the color wheel slowly spinning around its center.

What just happened?

The first thing we do is cache a selector for the image as we'll be referring to it several times throughout the code. Note that this is the only jQuery object we create in the whole script, which as we've discussed earlier in the book, is great for improving performance.

We also set some other variables at this point including the offset of the image (its `absolute` position on the page), its original `width` and `height`, and an array containing different parts of the CSS property that we'll set, in string and integer formats.

We also set an inline function (`getVendor()`) as the value of a variable which we can use to determine which vendor prefix to use. This function first also sets some variables which will be used to store the determined vendor prefix, and an object literal containing all of the different prefixes we want to test for. We also include the native `transform` property. Although this isn't yet supported by any browser, one day it may be, so this helps future-proof our code.

The function iterates over each property in the object literal using a `for in` loop. Within the loop, we try to read the value of the `transform` property using each vendor prefix. An interesting fact is that each browser will report `none` as the value of the prefix it supports, and a falsey value such as `false`, `null`, or `undefined` for the prefixes it doesn't support. We can use this to reliably determine which browser is in use and therefore which vendor prefix we need to use. The correct vendor prefix for whichever browser is in use is then saved to the `vendor` variable ready to be returned.

If none of these tests identify a vendor prefix, then it's likely that the browser in use is a version of Internet Explorer. Internet Explorer versions 8 and below do not currently have a vendor prefix (although IE9 does feature one) and do not support the `rotate` function at all. It does support rotation via its proprietary `filter` property however.

If the vendor variable is still set to `null` at this point, we set the variable to `filter`. In order to programmatically work with the value of the `filter` property in IE, the `filter` must already be applied to the element, so we also set a filter on the element in this part of the code using jQuery's `css()` method ready for us to manipulate later in the code. We also set the `sizing mode` to `auto expand` in order to prevent the element from being clipped when the rotate is applied.

At the end of the function the `prefix` variable is returned containing a string of the vendor prefix for the browser currently in use. Directly after the function we set a variable called `vendor` which will contain the value returned by the function for easy reference.

Next we define a regular function `doRotate()` which will be used to perform the actual rotation. The first thing we do in this function is increment the second property of our `rotateStrings` array by one.

We then check whether the `vendor` variable equals `filter`. If it does, we know that the browser in use is IE and can proceed to determine the values that the proprietary `filter` will need. IE allows rotation to be implemented in two different ways. We could use the `BasicImage filter` property to rotate the image, although that only allows us to set one of four rotation values: 0, 1, 2 or 3, which correspond to 0, 90, 180, or 270 degrees. This is simply not flexible enough for our needs in this example.

So instead we use the `Matrix` filter, which gives us much more control over the degree of rotation. This is very similar to the CSS3 matrix transform, with six parameter values that are combined to generate the different transforms (a rotation in this case).

The parameters that we use in this example are `M11`, `M12`, `M21`, and `M22` which map roughly to the first four values in the CSS3 version, with the exception that values two and three are reversed in Microsoft's version.

The values of each of these properties must be computed using the JavaScript trigonometry `Math.cos` and `Math.sin` functions. We set some variables to calculate these values. The first, `rad`, converts the number of degrees of rotation into radians as these are the units required by the `Matrix` filter. The radians are calculated by multiplying the current degree of rotation (as stored in the second item in our `rotateStrings` array) by PI times 2 divided by 360.

An unfortunate problem that occurs in IE when rotating elements is that the rotated element drifts around the page as it is being rotated. This is caused by the size of the elements bounding box increasing as the element rotates. The rotation does occur around the center of the element, but because IE thinks the element has grown, the center of the rotated element is shifted on each rotation.

The `drifX` and `driftY` variables that we set allow us to determine how far the element has shifted so that we can correct it. The shift is worked out by comparing the original `width` and `height` of the element prior to it being rotated, with the new `width` and `height` following the rotation.

We also store the raw `img` element from the jQuery object using jQuery's `get()` method with an argument of `0` which returns the actual DOM node instead of a jQuery object. The `filter` must be applied to a proper DOM element.

Once we've set our variables, we then correct the drift caused by the previous rotation using jQuery's `css()` method, and then insert our computed trigonometry values into the `Matrix` filter.

Finally, if the `vendor` variable equals anything other than `filter` we can simply set the relevant vendor prefix to the items in our `rotateStrings` array. We do this by calling JavaScript's `join()` method on the array. This is much more efficient than using concatenation to create the string needed for the CSS property, and as this function will be executed repeatedly we really need to make sure it is as efficient as possible.

The last thing we do in our code is start the rotation animation off by setting an interval that calls our `doRotate()` function every 100 milliseconds. We use an anonymous function as the first argument of the `setInterval()` function which avoids requiring that we attach the function to be executed be saved to the `window` object.

Problems with IE

Aside from the fact that IE makes us work twice as hard as any other browser to set the element's rotation, it also presents us with another problem: it totally destroys the alpha layer of the PNG we are rotating. Suddenly our nice anti-aliased circle-edge becomes jagged and unsightly (view this example in IE to see the issue).

The animation is also slightly jerky in IE, and both this and the inability to use PNGs with alpha-layers in them could easily be a show-stopper for IE. If this was the case, we could easily disable the animation in IE by simply doing nothing when the `filter` property is returned by our `getVendor()` function. There are some things we could do however, to negate the problems in IE.

For example, we could simply use a PNG with no transparency, which would preserve the circle's border in IE (in this example). Or, we could lay another image over the top of the image we are rotating to hide the jagged edges.

Pop quiz – implementing CSS3 rotation

1. In this example we used an array in conjunction with the JavaScript `join()` method to create the string. Why?

    a. Because it's more fun

    b. Because it makes our code look better

    c. Because performance-wise, it's much faster than string concatenation

    d. Because otherwise the element won't rotate correctly

2. To make the animation run correctly in Internet Explorer we had to constantly adjust the `top` and `left` style properties of the rotated element in order to maintain its position. Why does the drift in IE occur?

    a. Because the size of the rotated element's bounding box is changed throughout the animation. As the rotated element is centered within its bounding box, its position changes as the box increases and decreases in size

    b. Because the alpha layer of the PNG was removed

    c. Because the `Matrix filter` property was used

    d. Because of a bug in IE's implementation of the CSS3 `rotate` property

Have a go hero – extending CSS3 rotation

The rotation effect can be used in many places, whether animated or not, but when animated as in this example, it makes a very good background as part of a larger composition of elements. Used as the background of a semi-transparent logo for example, creates a stunning effect.

Have a go at incorporating the effect into a page and using it as the background of another image. You'll also see first-hand how much this can improve the appearance of the effect in IE.

Animated skewing

Just like with the `rotate()` function, we can animate a `skew()` transform for creating attractive special effects. In this example, we'll use the `matrix()` function for all browsers, not just IE, in order to apply several transforms to an element at once.

The context of this example will be a cover-flow style widget that displays images one after the other by animating the images' skew. The user will be able to cycle back and forth through the images using links:

The previous screenshot shows how the finished widget will appear.

Time for action – creating the underlying markup and basic styling

First we'll look at the HTML that we'll be using in the example and then we'll look at the initial styling added to the elements prior to being skewed.

1. Add the following code to the `<body>` of the template file:

```
<div id="viewer">
  <div id="flow">
    <img src="img/beatles.jpg">
    <img src="img/blink.jpg">
    <img src="img/doves.jpg">
    <img src="img/flash.jpg">
    <img src="img/floyd.jpg">
    <img src="img/jurassic.jpg">
    <img src="img/naked.jpg">
    <img src="img/prodigy.jpg">
```

```
    <img src="img/xx.jpg">
    <img src="img/zabiela.jpg">
  </div>
  <ul>
    <li id="left"><a href="#" title="Move Left">Left</a></li>
    <li id="right"><a href="#" title="Move Right">Right</a></li>
  </ul>
</div>
```

2. Save the page as `skew.html`. Next in a new file add the following code:

```
#viewer {
  width:700px; height:220px; padding:100px 0 30px; margin:auto;
  border:1px solid #000; position:relative;
}
#flow:after {
  content:""; display:block; height:0; clear:both;
  visibility:hidden;
}
#flow img {
  display:block; margin-left:-165px; position:relative; top:-15px;
  left:245px; float:left; background-color:#fff;
}
#viewer li { list-style-type:none; position:absolute; bottom:10px;
}
#left { left:20px; }
#right { right:20px; }
```

3. Save this file in the `css` directory as `skew.css`.

What just happened?

We're using a simple collection of elements for this example. We use an outer container, mostly for positioning purposes so that we can center the widget in the viewport and position other elements within it.

The `<img>` elements are what we will be applying the skew animations to, so these are isolated in their own container to make selecting them in the script later on easier. We also have a list element containing two links. These will be used to trigger the animations.

The CSS is as light as the HTML. We simply position the container, the images, and the controls as required for the example. All of the fun CSS3 we'll set and manipulate using the script. You should note that this example isn't progressively-enhanced as this would deviate too far from an already quite large example, as we'll see in a moment when we add the JavaScript.

Time for action – initializing the widget

The first thing we need to do is set up the images ready to have their skew manipulated. We can also add the function that will return the correct vendor-specific prefix for the transform style property that we used in the last example. In the empty function at the bottom of the HTML page, add the following code:

```
var viewer = $("#viewer"),
  flow = viewer.find("#flow"),
  order = flow.children().length,
  oneRad = 1 * (Math.PI / 180),
  matrix = ["matrix(", 1, ",", 0, ",", 0, ",", 1, ",",
    "0px,", "0px)"],
  msMatrix = "progid:DXImageTransform.Microsoft.Matrix(
    sizingMethod='auto expand')",
  getVendor = function() {
    var prefix = null,
      vendorStrings = {
        pure: "transform",
        moz: "-moz-transform",
        webkit: "-webkit-transform",
        op: "-o-transform"
      };

    for (props in vendorStrings) {
      if(flow.css(vendorStrings[props]) === "none") {
        prefix = vendorStrings[props];
      }
    }

    if (prefix === null) {
      prefix = "filter";
    }

    return prefix;
  },
  vendor = getVendor(),
  property = (vendor !== "filter") ? matrix.join("") : msMatrix;

flow.children().eq(0).addClass("flat").css(vendor,
  property).css("zIndex", order + 1);

flow.children().not(":first").each(function(i) {

  el = flow.children().eq(i + 1);
```

```
matrix[1] = 0.7;
matrix[3] = -30 * oneRad;
matrix[5] = -10 * oneRad;
matrix[7] = 0.7;
matrix[9] = (vendor === "-moz-transform") ? "90px," : "90,";
matrix[10] = (vendor === "-moz-transform") ? "-30px)" : "-30)";

if (vendor !== "filter") {
  el.addClass("skew-right").css(vendor,
    matrix.join("")).css("zIndex", order);
} else {
  el.addClass("skew-right").css(vendor, msMatrix).css({
    zIndex: order,
    top: -30,
    left: 270,
    width: 140,
    height: 140,
    marginLeft: -100
  });

  el.get(0).filters.item("DXImageTransform.Microsoft.Matrix")
    .M11 = 1;
  el.get(0).filters.item("DXImageTransform.Microsoft.Matrix")
    .M12 = matrix[5];
  el.get(0).filters.item("DXImageTransform.Microsoft.Matrix")
    .M21 = matrix[3];
  el.get(0).filters.item("DXImageTransform.Microsoft.Matrix")
    .M22 = 1;
}

order--;

});

matrix[3] = 0;
matrix[5] = 0;
```

What just happened?

In the first part of the script we initialize our variables. If you've wondered why we always initialize our variables at the top of functions, the reason is because of a phenomenon called Hoisting. This is where variables initialized in functions get "hoisted" to the top of the function and can contain results that we aren't expecting.

The first variable we create is a cached selector for the outer container of our widget. This is the one and only jQuery object we create in this entire example. Some of the code we'll add is quite intensive in places, so keeping the number of jQuery objects we create to a bare minimum is essential for performance reasons.

Next we use the original jQuery object and the find() jQuery method to cache a selector for the flow element (the direct parent of the image elements that will be skewed) as we'll need to access or manipulate this element several times as well.

Then we store the number of image elements in the widget using the length property of a jQuery object containing the child elements of the flow element. We also store the result of converting one degree to one radian so that we can easily convert from one unit to another throughout the script without repeatedly performing the same calculation. Both the CSS3 transform matrix and IE's matrix filter can accept radians so that makes them a convenient unit to work with.

We then create our matrix array, and Microsoft's matrix property as a string. The array includes all of the individual properties as array items, including the required commas as strings. The reason we include the commas in our array is so that we can call the join() JavaScript function on the array later without specifying a separator and without having to worry about removing the unnecessary commas this would insert incorrectly.

Next we add the getVendor() function that we used in the last example. This is a convenient way to ensure the correct prefix is used when we apply the skew styling. We won't cover this function in detail as we have already looked at it earlier in the chapter. Again we call the function straight away after defining it and store the result in a variable for later use.

The last variable we create will hold a string containing either the CSS3 matrix function with all required parameters, or it will contain IE's matrix property in its most basic form, with only the sizingMethod parameter defined. If you remember from the previous example, IE can only manipulate the matrix property after it has been initially set.

At this point we can move on to prepare the first image. We select the first image using jQuery's eq() method, passing in 0 as the index of the element we are interested in. We set a class name of flat on the first image so that we can easily select it later, and also give it a higher z-index than the other images so that it is visible in its entirety.

Next we loop through the remaining images using jQuery's each() method. The anonymous function we pass to the method accepts the parameter i which is the index of the current iteration.

This will allow us to select each element in turn one after the other on each iteration of the loop. The first thing we do in the function is cache a reference to the current `<img>` using the index as an argument for the `eq()` method. We add 1 to the index value to avoid selecting the first image.

In the next block of code we set some of the items in our `matrix` array. We set the scale parameters (items 1 and 7 in the array) to 0.7 so that the skewed images are reduced in size slightly, and we set the skew parameters (items 3 and 5) to the radian equivalent of -30 and -10 degrees. This will skew the images slightly up and to the right.

We also set the translate parameters (items 9 and 10 in the array) to position the skewed elements correctly so that they stack up horizontally. If the browser in use is Firefox we have to use `px` in the value for the translate properties, but with other browsers the values should be unit-less. We use a ternary condition to check the `vendor` variable (this will contain the vendor-prefix for the current browser) and set the value accordingly.

Once we've set our array items we then check that the browser in use is not IE and provided it isn't, we apply the skew to the current element. We also set the `z-index` of the current element using the `order` variable, which is set to the length of the number of images.

On each iteration of the loop we reduce the value of this variable by one (later in this section of code you'll see the statement `index--` which decreases the variable). The `z-index` of each element will therefore get progressively lower as we process each image.

If the browser in use is IE, we apply the Microsoft `matrix` and set some different CSS on the images. The translate parameters don't work in IE, so we position the images using jQuery instead. Skewing the elements in IE also causes the elements to increase in size, so we have to drastically reduce their dimensions, which we also do with jQuery.

Once we have set the required CSS styles, we then skew the elements by manipulating the proprietary Microsoft `matrix` filters. Remember, these properties can only be manipulated on actual DOM elements, not jQuery objects, so we retrieve the raw element using jQuery's `get()` method and the index `0`.

After the `each()` loop has finished, we reset parameters 3 and 5 in the `matrix` array. This is because we will use the array again several times, so each time we should use the default values for the parameters.

Time for action – animating an element's skew

Next we'll add the function that will skew elements to the left. The function will need to be applied to two elements, the flat, or non-skewed element, as well as the one before it (to the right in this case). The function to animate the skew from right to left is as follows:

```
function skewRTL() {

  var flat = flow.find(".flat").css("zIndex", order + 1),
    preFlat = flat.next(),
    flatMatrix = matrix.slice(0),
    preMatrix = matrix.slice(0),
    flatDims = 200,
    preDims = 170,

  skew = function() {

    if (preFlat.length) {

      if (flatMatrix[3] <= 30 * oneRad && flatMatrix[5] <=
        10 * oneRad) {

        var flatTranslateX = parseInt(
          flatMatrix[9].split("p")[0], 10),
          flatTranslateY = parseInt(
            flatMatrix[10].split("p")[0], 10),
          preTranslateX = parseInt(
            preMatrix[9].split("p")[0], 10),
          preTranslateY = parseInt(
            preMatrix[10].split("p")[0], 10);

        flatMatrix[1] = flatMatrix[1] - 0.001;
        flatMatrix[3] = flatMatrix[3] + oneRad;
        flatMatrix[5] = flatMatrix[5] + (oneRad / 3);
        flatMatrix[7] = flatMatrix[7] - 0.001;
        preMatrix[1] = preMatrix[1] + 0.01;
        preMatrix[3] = preMatrix[3] + oneRad;
        preMatrix[5] = preMatrix[5] + (oneRad / 3);
        preMatrix[7] = preMatrix[7] + 0.01;
        flatMatrix[9] = (vendor === "-moz-transform") ?
          flatTranslateX - 6 + "px," : flatTranslateX - 6 + ",";
        preMatrix[9] = (vendor === "-moz-transform") ?
          preTranslateX - 3 + "px," : preTranslateX - 3 + ",";
        preMatrix[10] = (vendor === "-moz-transform") ?
          preTranslateY + 1 + "px)" : preTranslateY + 1 + ")";
```

```
    if (vendor !== "filter") {
      flat.css(vendor, flatMatrix.join(""));
      preFlat.css(vendor, preMatrix.join(""));
    } else {
    flat.get(0).filters.item(
      "DXImageTransform.Microsoft.Matrix")
      .M12 = flatMatrix[5];
    flat.get(0).filters.item(
      "DXImageTransform.Microsoft.Matrix")
      .M21 = flatMatrix[3];
    preFlat.get(0).filters.item(
      "DXImageTransform.Microsoft.Matrix")
      .M12 = preMatrix[5];
    preFlat.get(0).filters.item(
      "DXImageTransform.Microsoft.Matrix")
      .M21 = preMatrix[3];

      flatDims = flatDims - 2;
      preDims = preDims + 0.5;

      flat.css({
        width: flatDims,
        height: flatDims
      });
      preFlat.css({
        width: preDims,
        height: preDims
      });
    }

  } else {

    clearInterval(flatInterval);

    if (vendor !== "filter") {
      preMatrix[3] = 0;
      preMatrix[5] = 0;
      preFlat.css(vendor, preMatrix.join(""));
    } else {
      flat.css({
      top: -30,
      left: 260
    });
  }
}
```

```
            flat.prev().css("zIndex", "");
            flat.removeClass("flat").css("zIndex", "");
            preFlat.addClass("flat");
        }
    } else {

        clearInterval(flatInterval);
        flat.css("zIndex", order + 1);
    }
};

preMatrix[3] = -30 * oneRad;
preMatrix[5] = -10 * oneRad;

if(!flatInterval) {
    var flatInterval = setInterval(function() { skew() }, 1);
}
};
```

What just happened?

The first thing we do in our function is set the variables used by the function. We cache a reference to the current element that has the class flat and also set this element's z-index to be one higher than any of the other images to ensure it is always on top of the other images.

We also cache a reference to the next image after the flat image. In this function, this will be the image to the right of the un-skewed image. We then make two copies of the original matrix array, one for the flat element and one for the preFlat element. To copy an array all we do is use JavaScript's slice() method with an index of zero.

The next two variables we create are the initial dimensions of the flat and preFlat images. These variables are only used by IE, but because of hoisting we need to define them here and not in an IE-specific code block later in the function.

Next we define an inline function called skew() which we'll repeatedly call in order to produce the actual animation. Within this function we first check that there is an element after the flat element by checking that the preFlat object has a length. If the length is equal to zero (that is if it does not have length), we simply clear any intervals that may exist, and make sure the flat element is at the top of the z-index stack.

If the `preFlat` object does have a length however, we then check that the current `skewX` property is less than or equal to the radian equivalent of 30 degrees, and that the `skewY` property is less than or equal to the radian equivalent of 10 degrees (we can work this out by multiplying 30 or 10 respectively by our stored figure for 1 radian). The current skew properties for the `flat` image are currently stored in items 3 and 5 in the `flatMatrix` array.

Provided both conditions are true we can then proceed with the animation. Part of the animation involves translating the `flat` and `preFlat` images so that as well as skewing, they move as well (we'll also resize them, but we'll come to that in a moment).

In order to translate the images correctly we need to get their current translation, which we do first of all by defining four new variables and populating them with the current translation values from the two matrix arrays. These figures need to be numerical so we use JavaScript's `parseInt()` and `split()` functions to break the strings apart and convert the digits to integers.

Next we need to update our two matrix arrays with the new values. The right-to-left function will incrementally update the values in the `flatMatrix` and `preMatrix` arrays, and then apply the arrays to the element. So the animation will consist of rapid updates to each transform parameter.

The `flat` image also needs to be skewed as it is translated, so we increase the `skewX` and `skewY` parameters by one radian and a third of one radian respectively. Remember, in order to skew an element to the left and up directions the skew parameters should be positive, so we increase the values of items 3 and 5 of the `flatMatrix` array on each pass of the function.

The `flat` image starts off larger than the skewed images so we need to reduce array items 1 and 7 slightly each time the function runs. The `skew()` function will be called 30 times, so to reduce the scale of the flat image so that it finishes the correct size we reduce the scale parameters by `0.001` on each pass of the function.

The values we want are 30 degrees of skew on the x axis, and 10 degrees of the skew on the y axis. 10 is one third of 30 which is why we increase the `skewY` parameter by one radian divided by three.

I mentioned earlier that in Firefox the translate parameters need a unit, such as `px`, but other browsers are unit-less for these values. We use a JavaScript ternary conditional to check the `vendor` string and if it equals the Firefox vendor prefix (`-moz-transform`), we add `px` to the value. The flat image only needs to be translated on the x axis and it needs to move left by 6 pixels, so we update array item 9 with a value that is 6 less than its current value.

We also have to update the `preFlat` image so that it goes from being skewed to the right to being flat. We also have to increase the size of the `preFlat` image as they start out smaller. In a similar way to before, we update the relevant array items in the `preMatrix` so that over the course of 30 iterations of the `skew()` function they end up at the right values. The `preFlat` image also needs to be translated, but this time along both the x and y axes.

Next we check the vendor string once more and as long as it isn't `filter` (IE), we apply the transform to the `flat` and `preFlat` image by joining the array. If it is IE we have to do a little more work to apply the transformation.

We apply each of the relevant Matrix properties, `M12` and `M21` on the `flat` and `preFlat` images. We use jQuery's `get()` method with an index of `0` to obtain the actual DOM element once more. We also reduce the size of the `flat` image, and increase the size of the `preFlat` image using our `flatDims` and `preDims` variables that we initialized earlier and then jQuery's `css()` method to apply the new sizes.

IE's `Matrix` property helpfully ignores the scaling parameters when the `sizingMethod` is set to `auto expand`, but this property must be set to prevent the images from being clipped. This is why we fallback to jQuery's `css()` method.

Unusually, we are able to set fractional pixel sizes when using IE, which is fortunate as it allows us to set the size of the images correctly in order for them to end up at the right size when the animation ends.

We now come to the other part of the inner conditional. This block of code is executed once at the end of the animation when the third and fifth items in our `flatMatrix` array are greater than 30 and 10 respectively.

First we clear the intervals so that the skew is not animated further. We then check the vendor string once more, and as long as it isn't `filter` we reset the skew on the flat element to `0` (on both the x and y axes).

This is needed because for some reason, the `preFlat` image doesn't *quite* go back to exactly zero. I assume this is because JavaScript's Math functions do not allow the number to have enough decimal places to be entirely accurate. The image is only slightly off however, so this sudden switch to `0` at the end of the animation is not noticeable.

Unfortunately, translating an element at the same time as skewing it does not seem possible in IE. What happens is that IE applies the new skew, but fails to apply the new position until after the skew animation has finished, so the element is skewed and then moved in two separate steps. It doesn't look too great so instead we simply reposition the flat element without animating it at this point once the skew animation has finished.

After correcting the skew, or the position, we then remove the `z-index` from the flat element (which has now been skewed to the left) and remove the class name `flat` from it, and then add the class name `flat` to the `preFlat` element.

At this point the flat image has been skewed to the left, resized and translated, and the `preFlat` image has been skewed back to zero, resized and translated. Both the `flat` and `preFlat` images are transformed together at the same time, which is why the function is as large as it is.

Right at the end of the `skewRTL()` function, defined after the `skew()` function that will be repeatedly called by the `setInterval()` function, we initialize the 3rd and 5th values in the `preMatrix` array so that the array will contain the correct skew for the initial state of the element. When we create the array, by copying the original `matrix` array used when the widget is initialized, these items will both be set to `0`.

Before calling the `setInterval()` function on the two images to be skewed, we first check that an interval doesn't already exist. This stops the widget from breaking if the link is repeatedly clicked by the visitor. The element will be skewed more than once if the link is clicked several times in rapid succession, but the widget will continue to function and the page will not throw errors.

Time for action – skewing an element from left to right

We can now add the function that skews an element from left to flat and from flat to right. This function is very similar to the function we just looked at. Changes in the code are shown in bold:

```
function skewLTR() {

    var flat = flow.find(".flat"),
        preFlat = flat.prev(),
        flatMatrix = matrix.slice(0),
        preMatrix = matrix.slice(0),
        flatDims = 200,
        preDims = 170,

    skew = function() {

        if (preFlat.length) {

            if (flatMatrix[3] >= -30 * oneRad && flatMatrix[5] >=
            -10 * oneRad) {

                var preTranslateX = parseInt(preMatrix[9].
                    split("p")[0], 10),
                preTranslateY = parseInt(preMatrix[10].
                    split("p")[0], 10);
                flatMatrix[1] = flatMatrix[1] - 0.001;
```

```
flatMatrix[3] = flatMatrix[3] - oneRad;
flatMatrix[5] = flatMatrix[5] - (oneRad / 3);
flatMatrix[7] = flatMatrix[7] - 0.001;
preMatrix[1] = preMatrix[1] + 0.01;
preMatrix[3] = preMatrix[3] - oneRad;
preMatrix[5] = preMatrix[5] - (oneRad / 3);
preMatrix[7] = preMatrix[7] + 0.01;
preMatrix[9] = (vendor === "-moz-transform") ?
  preTranslateX + 3 + "px," : preTranslateX + 3 + ",";
preMatrix[10] = (vendor === "-moz-transform") ?
  preTranslateY + 1 + "px)" : preTranslateY + 1 + ")";

if (vendor !== "filter") {
  flat.css(vendor, flatMatrix.join(""));
  preFlat.css(vendor, preMatrix.join(""));
} else {
  flat.get(0).filters.item(
    "DXImageTransform.Microsoft.Matrix")
    .M12 = flatMatrix[5];
  flat.get(0).filters.item(
    "DXImageTransform.Microsoft.Matrix")
    .M21 = flatMatrix[3];
  preFlat.get(0).filters.item(
    "DXImageTransform.Microsoft.Matrix")
    .M12 = preMatrix[5];
  preFlat.get(0).filters.item(
    "DXImageTransform.Microsoft.Matrix")
    .M21 = preMatrix[3];

  flatDims = flatDims - 1.5;
  preDims = preDims + 1.5;


  flat.css({
    width: flatDims,
    height: flatDims
  });
  preFlat.css({
    width: preDims,
    height: preDims
  });
}

} else {
```

```
                    clearInterval(flatInterval);
                    clearInterval(preInterval);

                    if (vendor !== "filter") {
                      preMatrix[3] = 0;
                      preMatrix[5] = 0;
                      preFlat.css(vendor, preMatrix.join(""));
                    }

                    flat.removeClass("flat").css("zIndex",
                      parseInt(flat.next().css("zIndex")) + 1);
                    preFlat.addClass("flat").css("zIndex", order + 1);


                  }
                } else {

                  clearInterval(flatInterval);
                  clearInterval(preInterval);
                  flat.css("zIndex", order + 1);
                }
              };

          order = flow.children().length;
          preMatrix[3] = 30 * oneRad;
          preMatrix[5] = 10 * oneRad;
          preMatrix[9] = (vendor === "-moz-transform") ? "-90px," : "-90,";
          preMatrix[10] = (vendor === "-moz-transform") ? "-30px," :
            "-30,";

          if(!flatInterval) {
            var flatInterval = setInterval(function() { skew() }, 1),
            preInterval = setInterval(function() { skew() }, 1);
          }
      };
```

What just happened?

We won't cover the whole function in its entirety as it's very similar to before, but let's take a moment to look at what differs in this function. First, instead of selecting the next image to the right of the flat element, we select the one to the left of it using jQuery's prev() method instead of next().

When updating the skew on our `flat` and `preFlat` elements, we are skewing the element the opposite way. To skew an element to the right, we need to use a minus figure so instead of going from 0 to 30 or from -30 to 0, we are going the opposite way, from 30 to 0 or 0 to -30, so we minus the radian equivalent of 1 degree instead of adding it.

We are also translating to the right instead of to the left, so instead of removing 3 pixels each time to move the image left we add 3 pixels to move it right. We also provide different values for the dimensions variables used by IE.

This time when we set the `z-index` of the element that was previously flat, we add 1 to the z-index of the next element (to the right) to make sure it is higher than this element. However, we can't use our length variable from earlier or it will be at the same `z-index` as the `flat` element, but will appear above it as it comes after the element in the DOM.

The final difference is that when we initialize the third and fifth items in our array, we are specifying the current skew to the left and not the right, so these items are set to the radian equivalent of 30 and 10 degrees instead of -30 and -10.

Time for action – wiring up the controls

All that's left to do is add the event handlers to the left and right links at the bottom of the widget so that the different images can be viewed. After the two skew functions, add the following code:

```
viewer.find("#left a").click(function(e) {
  e.preventDefault();
  skewRTL();
});
viewer.find("#right a").click(function(e) {
  e.preventDefault();
  skewLTR();
});
```

What just happened?

All we do is add a click handler to each link which prevents the link from being followed with `preventDefault()` and then call the relevant skew function. The example should now be fully working in all common browsers, although the effect is handled rather badly by IE in general, with slower, more sluggish animations, less accurate skewing, and jittery, uncontrollable movements.

One point to note is that there is a difference between the full and minified versions of the jQuery source file which causes IE to throw errors when the minified version is used, but not when the un-minified version is used.

Pop quiz – using the matrix

1. The CSS3 matrix transform function is useful in which situation?

    a. When we want to work in radians instead of degrees

    b. When we need to animate a transform function

    c. When we want to apply more than one transform function to an element

    d. When coding for Internet Explorer

2. In the transform function `matrix(a, b, c, d, e, f)`, which parameters refer to the element's translation?

    a. `a` and `b`

    b. `a` and `d`

    c. `b` and `c`

    d. `e` and `f`

Have a go hero – extending matrix animation

It would definitely be beneficial to build this example so that it incorporated progressive enhancement. Work on an alternative, accessible layout that works with scripting disabled, and then convert the widget into the format used in this example.

You could also work on a more suitable fallback for IE, in which the example uses a simpler image viewer, perhaps one of those looked at earlier in the book.

Summary

In this chapter we look at the new CSS3 transform style property in detail, covering all of the different transform functions including:

- `matrix`
- `rotate`
- `scale`
- `scaleX`
- `scaleY`
- `skew`
- `skewX`
- `skewY`

◆ `translate`

◆ `translateX`

◆ `translateY`

We learned a lot about the new CSS3 `matrix` property in this chapter, as well as how to make use of it with jQuery. Specifically, we learned the following:

◆ We first saw the different values that these functions take and the effects that they have on elements they are applied to.

◆ We also saw that in order to animate these styles, we can use simple native JavaScript intervals or timeouts to continuously adjust the function parameters, or apply them in a rapid sequence.

◆ We learned that mostly, these transform functions can only be applied to elements individually, with only the last to be defined being applied. The matrix function however allows us to apply several of the functions to a single element.

◆ We can't rotate and skew a single element, but we can rotate, scale, and translate an element, or skew, scale, and translate it if we wish. Browser support for CSS3 transforms is very good, with only very minor differences between most browsers (such as the translate values being in pixels for Firefox and unit-less for Webkit-based browsers and Opera) except IE.

◆ IE does have its own proprietary implementation of the different transforms, although these are not implemented in a particularly useful way, such as not being able to translate elements if we don't want those same elements to be clipped. We can only hope that IE9, recently released as a beta product, will handle them better.

◆ In addition to CSS3 transforms, a CSS3 transitions specification has also been proposed, which would allow us to transition elements between different transform states using pure CSS, without the need for animating them with JavaScript at all. We didn't look at these at all in this chapter because support for them is restricted to just Webkit-based browsers or Opera at the time of writing. Beta versions of Firefox and IE also have support for them, but we have dealt only with fully-released browsers throughout the book.

◆ We saw that although we can't use the transform functions in jQuery's `animate()` method, we can easily create our own animations manually, and we can use them with other methods, such as the `css()` method. Don't forget about using cssHooks to achieve this kind of functionality too.

In the next and final chapter of the book, we'll take a look at a new HTML5 element that allows us pixel-perfect control over an area on the page—the `<canvas>` element—and how it can be used to create interactive animations.

10
Canvas Animations

In the last chapter, we looked at one of the latest CSS3 styles: the `transform`, which enabled us to create animated rotations, skews, scales, and translates. In this chapter, we're going to look at one of the new additions to HTML5—the `<canvas>` element.

The best way to think of the `<canvas>` element is to treat it like the kind of canvas on which an artist would paint. We can draw simple lines or complex shapes using JavaScript API methods, and there is also support for images and text. The canvas is two dimensional at this point, but may be extended to include 3D support in the future.

The `<canvas>` element, first proposed and used by Apple, has been implemented by most common browsers, and is considered one of the most stable elements from the HTML5 specification. However, support for it is not yet universal.

Like CSS3 transforms, the `<canvas>` element isn't supported in any current version of Internet Explorer (although it is supported in IE9), but just like transforms, there are alternatives that can be used in IE to create the same effect as `<canvas>`, which we'll look at when we come to the examples a little later in the chapter.

The best description of the `<canvas>` element I've seen states "A canvas is a rectangle in your page where you can use JavaScript to draw anything you want", from `diveintohtml5.org`, which sums it up quite nicely I feel.

Subjects that we'll look at in this chapter will include:

◆ The `<canvas>` API

◆ Drawing to the `<canvas>`

◆ Animating the `<canvas>`

◆ Using `<canvas>` with jQuery

◆ `<canvas>` in IE and the alternatives

◆ Creating a `<canvas>` based game

The canvas API

The `<canvas>` element comes with a rich scripting API that exposes methods and properties allowing us to define and control the shapes that are drawn on the canvas. The API can be broken down into distinct sections depending on what the methods do.

The canvas element

The `<canvas>` element itself has a couple of methods that can be called on it, including:

Method	Usage
`getContext(a)`	Returns an object (a CanvasRenderingContext2D object to be precise) which can then have other methods from the API called on it to manipulate the `<canvas>`. The argument specifies the type of context to retrieve. Only two dimensional contexts are available at present.
`toDataURL()`	Returns a data URL representing the image on the `<canvas>`. Optional arguments include the type of image represented by the data URL (with the default being `image/png`), and any arguments specific to the type, such as the quality for `image/jpg` data URLs.

The `<canvas>` element can be thought of as being similar to an `<img>` element that doesn't have an `src` attribute. Allowed attributes include the `width` and `height` of the element, an `id` and a `class`, among others. There are no special attributes associated with the canvas, although it can contain other elements. When the browser cannot display the `<canvas>`, it can display the element's content as a fallback. The only properties of the `<canvas>` element we have access to, are the `width` and `height`. Setting either of these properties causes the `<canvas>` to reset its contents to nothing, which can be useful when we want to clear it.

Context methods

There are two methods that relate directly to the context object returned by the `getContext()` method. These are:

Method	Usage
save()	Saves the current state of the canvas; only transforms are saved, not shapes or paths.
restore()	Restores the saved state.

We can also set a couple of global properties that apply to all shapes on the `<canvas>`. These properties are:

Property	Usage
globalAlpha	Sets the alpha transparency of shapes. Takes a decimal between 0.0 and 1.0.
globalCompositeOperation	Sets how shapes stack up on top of one another. Can be used to create masks and clear areas of shapes.

Native shapes

The `<canvas>` has just one native shape defined: the rectangle. One important point to note here is that the `<canvas>` element does not have an internal DOM tree—shapes or paths we draw on the `<canvas>` are not created as child elements of the `<canvas>` element and cannot be accessed with standard DOM manipulation methods. They are not individual objects, they are just pixels. Methods from the scripting API used specifically when working with rectangles include the following:

Method	Usage
clearRect(a, b, c, d)	Removes all shapes and paths from an area of the canvas. Arguments a and b specify the coordinates to begin clearing at and arguments c and d specify the width and height of the area to clear.
fillRect(a, b, c, d)	Draws a rectangle. Arguments a and b specify the coordinates to begin drawing at and arguments c and d specify the width and height of its sides.
strokeRect(a, b, c, d)	Draws the outline of a rectangle. Arguments a and b represent the starting coordinates of the shape and arguments c and d represent the width and height of its sides.

We can set the color of strokes (outlines) or fills, as well as drop-shadows using the following properties:

Property	Usage
fillStyle	Sets the color of the fill. Can be set to a CSS color, or a gradient object.
shadowBlur	Sets the amount of blur on the shadow.
shadowColor	Sets the color of the shadow. Can be set to a CSS color or a gradient object.
shadowOffsetX	Sets the relative position of the shadow along the x axis.
shadowOffsetY	Sets the relative position of the shadow along the y axis.
strokeStyle	Sets the color of the stroke. Can be set to a CSS color, or a gradient object.

These properties can be set on paths and text as well. They aren't limited strictly to the native shape.

Paths

Any shape other than a rectangle must be drawn using a path. This gives us a flexible way of drawing custom, complex shapes. Methods used for creating paths include:

Method	Usage
arc(a, b, c, d, e, f)	Draws a circular sub-path. Arguments a and b are the starting coordinates of the sub-path, c is the radius, d is the starting angle in radians, and e is the ending angle in radians. The last parameter f accepts a Boolean indicating whether the sub-path should be drawn anticlockwise or not.
arcTo(a, b, c, d, e)	Draws a circular sub-path to a specified point. Arguments a and b are the starting coordinates, c and d are the ending coordinates. Argument e is the radius.
beginPath()	Starts a new path.
bezierCurveTo(a, b, c, d, e, f)	Draws a sub-path along a Bezier curve, which is a curve featuring two control points. Arguments a, b, c, and d represent the coordinates of the two control points and arguments e and f represent the end coordinates of the sub-path.
closePath()	Closes the path by drawing a line from the current position to the starting position of the first sub-path in the current path list.

Method	Usage
`fill()`	Colors in the shape created by the current path.
`lineTo(a, b)`	Creates a new sub-path from the current location to the coordinates specified as arguments.
`moveTo(a, b)`	Moves to the coordinates specified by the arguments without drawing a new sub-path.
`quadraticCurveTo(a, b, c, d)`	Draws a sub-path along a quadratic curve, which is a curve with a single control point. Arguments a and b represent the coordinates of the control point, while arguments c and d represent the end coordinates of the sub-path.
`stroke()`	Colors in the outline of the current path list.

Paths have several properties that can be set including the style of the end of the line, or cap, or how paths are joined:

Property	Usage
`lineCap`	Can be set to either butt (the default), round, or square.
`lineJoin`	Can be set to either miter (the default), round, or bevel.
`lineWidth`	A decimal specifying the width of the path.
`miterLimit`	Determines the length between the inner point where two paths connect and the outer point before the join is mitered.

Images and patterns

The canvas allows us to draw images to the canvas in the same way that we might assign a background image to another element. We can also draw patterns based on images or gradients. This category of methods includes:

Method	Usage
`drawImage(a, b, c)`	Draws an image on the `<canvas>`. Argument a is the image to draw and arguments b and c are the coordinates to place the top-left point of the image. Note that other variants of this method exist which allow different combinations of arguments allowing images to be scaled and sliced.
`createPattern(a, b)`	Draws a repeated pattern on the `<canvas>`. Argument a is the image to use as the pattern, b is the type of repeat.

Method	Usage
createLinearGradient(a, b, c, d)	Creates a linear gradient between two points. Arguments a and b are the start coordinates of the gradient, c and d are the end coordinates.
createRadialGradient(a, b, c, d, e, f)	Creates a radial gradient between two circles. Arguments a and b are the start coordinates, and c is the radius of the first circle. Arguments d and e are the start coordinates of the second circle, and f is its radius.
addColorStop(a, b)	Adds color to a gradient. The first argument is a decimal between 0.0 and 1.0 and is the relative position within the gradient to add the color. The second argument is the color to use.

The drawImage() and createPattern() methods are very similar in that they are both used to draw an image on the <canvas>. The difference is that the pattern is repeated. The gradient methods return a gradient object which can then be used as the fill or stroke style for a shape.

Text

Text strings can be written to the canvas, but there is little styling we can perform on them as there is no associated box model with the text so that means no padding, margins, or borders. Although, we can set the font and alignment (and the fill color or stroke color using other properties). API methods include:

Method	Usage
fillText(a, b, c)	Creates solid text strings on the <canvas>. The first argument is the text to write and arguments b and c are the start coordinates of the text.
measureText(a)	Measures the specified text string and returns a metrics object with a width property.
stroketext(a, b, c)	Creates outline text strings on the <canvas>. The first argument is the text to write and arguments b and c are the start coordinates of the text.

The properties we can set on text include:

Property	Usage
font	Sets the size and the font-family of the text.
textAlign	Sets the alignment of the text. Can be either start (the default), end, left, right, or center.
textBaseline	Sets the baseline of the text. Can be either alphabetic (the default), top, hanging, middle, ideographic, or bottom.

Transformation methods

The <canvas> can have the same transforms applied to it that we saw in the last chapter, which can be applied using the following methods:

Method	Usage
rotate(a)	Rotates a shape by the specified number of radians.
scale(a, b)	Scales a shape along each axis by the specified amount, with a being the x axis and b the y axis.
translate(a, b)	Translates the shape along each axis by the specified amount, with a being the x axis and b the y axis.
transform(a, b, c, d, e, f)	The transform() method is equivalent to the matrix transform form function and can be used in the same way to scale, translate, and/or skew the shape.

Pixel manipulation

The <canvas> even allows us to work directly with the pixels in the canvas and can retrieve shapes as imageData objects, or create shapes directly by manipulating the <canvas> at pixel-level. We have the following methods for manipulating pixels:

Method	Usage
createImageData(a, b)	Creates a new, blank imageData object using the supplied arguments as width and height properties. This method can also be passed another imageData object, which will cause the method to return an (empty) imageData object the same width and height as the original.
getImageData(a, b, c, d)	Returns an imageData object containing the pixel data for the specified area of the <canvas>. Arguments a and b are the start coordinates of the area, c and d are the width and height.
putImageData(a, b, c)	Paints the pixel data to the <canvas>. The first argument is the imageData object to use, the second and third are the start coordinates of the resulting shape.

All `imageData` objects, either those we get from the `<canvas>`, or those we create with the `createImageDate()` method have several properties we can make use of, including:

Property	Usage
data	This property is a `CanvasPixelArray`, and is read-only when we get an `imageData` object from the `<canvas>`. We can also use it to set pixel data in an `imageData` object we create. The array contains four items per-pixel: the `r`, `g`, and `b` values for the pixel, and the `alpha`.
height	The `height` of the image represented by the `imageData` object. This property is read-only.
length	The `length` of the `CanvasPixelArray` in bytes. This property is read-only.
width	The `width` of the image represented by the `imageData` object. This property is read-only.

Drawing to the canvas

Drawing to the `<canvas>` programmatically is very straight forward in theory. The methods and properties are easy to use, and are quite consistent between supporting browsers. Direct pixel manipulation is the trickiest part of the API to master, but other than that there is nothing really complicated.

One thing we do find is that our code can very quickly mount up. As soon as we're drawing multiple, complex shapes, and setting various properties, our code can easily run to a few hundred lines or more even for relatively simple drawings. This is especially true when animating the contents of the `<canvas>`.

Time for action – drawing to the canvas

Let's take a look at a quick example of drawing a non-animated shape. We don't even need jQuery for this.

1. Add the `<canvas>` element to the `<body>` of our template file:

```
<canvas id="c" width="500" height="300">
  <p>Your browser doesn't support the canvas element!</p>
</canvas>
```

2. Next we can add the JavaScript that will draw to the `<canvas>`. We'll draw a Union Jack flag. Function in the `<script>` element at the bottom of the template file and add the following code in its place:

```
var canvas = document.getElementById("c"),
  context = canvas.getContext("2d");

  context.fillStyle = "#039";
  context.fillRect(50, 50, 400, 200);

  context.beginPath();
  context.strokeStyle = "#fff";
  context.lineWidth = 50;
  context.moveTo(250, 50);
  context.lineTo(250, 250);
  context.moveTo(50, 150);
  context.lineTo(450, 150);
  context.moveTo(50, 50);
  context.lineTo(450, 250);
  context.moveTo(50, 250);
  context.lineTo(450, 50);
  context.stroke();
  context.closePath();

  context.strokeStyle = "#C00";
  context.lineWidth = 30;
  context.beginPath();
  context.moveTo(250, 50);
  context.lineTo(250, 250);
  context.moveTo(50, 150);
  context.lineTo(450, 150);
  context.stroke();
  context.closePath();

  context.lineWidth = 1;
  context.fillStyle = "#C00";

  context.beginPath();
  context.moveTo(50, 50);
  context.lineTo(195, 125);
  context.lineTo(165, 125);
  context.lineTo(50, 66);
  context.fill();
  context.closePath();
```

```
context.beginPath();
context.moveTo(450, 50);
context.lineTo(305, 125);
context.lineTo(275, 125);
context.lineTo(422, 50);
context.lineTo(450, 50);
context.fill();
context.closePath();

context.beginPath();
context.moveTo(450, 250);
context.lineTo(310, 175);
context.lineTo(335, 175);
context.lineTo(450, 235);
context.lineTo(450, 250);
context.fill();
context.closePath();

context.beginPath();
context.moveTo(50, 250);
context.lineTo(200, 175);
context.lineTo(225, 175);
context.lineTo(80, 250);
context.lineTo(50, 250);
context.fill();
context.closePath();
```

3. Save the file as `canvas.html`.

4. If we run the page now in any browser except IE, we should see something like the following:

In the previous screenshot, we can see the simple arrangement of geometric shapes that make up the British flag (note that the flag is not completely to scale). Images like this are easy to produce using the <canvas> but even simple shapes can require a lot of code.

What just happened?

The first thing we do is get the <canvas> element using JavaScript's getElementById() method, and then get the two-dimensional context object from the <canvas> with the getContext() method. We can now interact with the <canvas> via the context object.

We set some of the color for the context using the fillStyle property, and then draw a solid rectangle using the fillRect() method. The arguments specified are the starting x and y location of the rectangle, and the width and height.

The filled rectangle picks up the fill style that we just set which is deep blue and will form the background of our flag. We now need to create a white horizontal and diagonal cross on top of the blue background. We can do this by drawing two thick lines across the middle of the flag, one vertical and one horizontal. We'll use paths for this, so we start a new path using the beginPath() method.

Next we set the color of the stroke to white using the strokeStyle property, and the width of the path using the lineWidth property. To draw a path we have tell the <canvas> (or the context object actually) where to start the path, which we do using the moveTo() method, specifying the coordinates to move to as arguments (the top middle of the rectangle).

To make the path, we then use the lineTo() method, specify the coordinates of where to end the path (the bottom middle of the rectangle). This gives us the vertical line. To make the horizontal path, we repeat the same process, moving to the left middle of the rectangle and drawing to the right middle.

Coordinates specified using the moveTo() method are always relative to the canvas itself with 0, 0 representing the top-left corner of the canvas. This is the same for the lineTo() method as well, even though the line that is drawn begins at the point specified by the last call of moveTo().

Next we need to make a diagonal white cross over the background rectangle and the vertical cross, which we'll do by drawing paths in the same way as before using combinations of moveTo() and lineTo() methods.

All of the paths we've added so far are part of the same path—they are sub-paths, and at this point they aren't actually visible. To make them visible, we need to either fill or stroke them, so we stroke them with the stroke() method and then close the path with the closePath() method.

For the next part of the flag, we need to draw a slightly thinner red cross over the white cross. We'll use another path for this. We set the new color style and width, and draw a new path across the center of the rectangle vertically and horizontally again.

To complete the flag, we need to add four more shapes to make the diagonal parts of the red cross. We can't use straight-line paths for these because they don't intersect, and they are all positioned slightly differently. This means that we have to draw them manually as custom shapes and fill them.

These four shapes actually make up the majority of the code, but we're basically doing very similar things as before. Each shape is made by drawing sub-paths and filling them. We use a new path for each shape to preserve the anti-aliasing of the lines. If we used one big path for all four shapes, the edges of the shapes would be jagged.

Pop quiz – drawing to the canvas

1. What arguments are required for the `fillRect()` method?
    a. The x and y location of the rectangle
    b. The width and height of the rectangle
    c. The x and y location of the rectangle, its width and height, and its color
    d. The x and y location of the rectangle, and its width and height

2. What method is required to make a path visible?
    a. `strokeStyle` and `lineWidth`
    b. `moveTo()` and `lineTo()`
    c. `stroke()` or `fill()`
    d. `closePath()`

Have a go hero – creating the flag of your nation

If you're not from the UK, have a go at drawing the flag of your own nation on the canvas. We can create compositions of repeated shapes using standard JavaScript for loops, so use this to your advantage in keeping the code required for your flag as minimal as possible. If you are from the UK, try recreating a favorite logo or icon.

If part of your flag (or logo) is extremely complex, remember that we can draw images to the `<canvas>` as well as lines and shapes, so feel free to draw out the basic part of your flag using the `<canvas>` drawing methods, and then use an image for the complex part.

Canvas, IE, and the alternatives

Our flag example will work in IE9, but not in any previous version. If we run the previous example in IE8 or lower, we'll see the fallback content consisting of a paragraph of explanatory text:

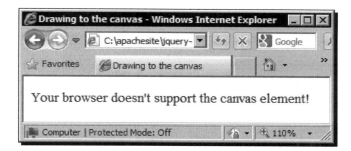

The fallback mechanism for the HTML5 `<canvas>` element is simple but effective. Any browser that doesn't understand the element simply displays any elements that are contained within it, while supporting browsers do not show any of its content except what we draw using the JavaScript API.

There is an easy way that we can allow our flag to work in older versions of IE thanks to the explorercanvas library created by Google. IE uses a proprietary technology called **Vector Markup Language (VML)** which is similar (but much older than and now deprecated) to the `<canvas>`. In fact it was Microsoft's alternative technology to **Scalable Vector Graphics (SVG)** but can also be used as a simple `<canvas>` approximation.

Using the explorercanvas library is almost as simple as downloading it and then referencing it in the page on which the `<canvas>` appears, but there is a subtle change that we need to make to our code.

 The explorercanvas library can be downloaded from Google's code repository at http://code.google.com/p/explorercanvas/.

API methods that simply do not work

The explorercanvas library does not port *all* canvas functionality to IE. A couple of methods and techniques simply will not work. These include:

- The `clearRect()` method will not work in IE
- Radial gradients do not work in IE
- Non-uniform scaling does not work correctly

Time for action – making our code compatible with IE

In this example we will recreate our flag example so that it works as intended in IE.

1. Resave the `canvas.html` page as `canvas-explorer.html` and add a reference to the explorercanvas library in the `<head>` of the page:

    ```
    <!--[if IE]>
      <script src="js/excanvas.compiled.js"></script>
    <![endif]-->
    ```

2. Now change the script at the bottom so that it appears like this (new/changed code is shown in bold):

    ```
    var canvas = document.getElementById("c"),
      draw = function(context) {

        context.fillStyle = "#039";
        context.fillRect(50, 50, 400, 200);

        context.beginPath();
        context.strokeStyle = "#fff";
        context.lineWidth = 50;
        context.moveTo(250, 50);
        context.lineTo(250, 250);
        context.moveTo(50, 150);
        context.lineTo(450, 150);
        context.moveTo(50, 50);
        context.lineTo(450, 250);
        context.moveTo(50, 250);
        context.lineTo(450, 50);
        context.stroke();
        context.closePath();

        context.strokeStyle = "#C00";
        context.lineWidth = 30;
        context.beginPath();
        context.moveTo(250, 50);
        context.lineTo(250, 250);
        context.moveTo(50, 150);
        context.lineTo(450, 150);
        context.stroke();

        context.lineWidth = 1;
        context.fillStyle = "#C00";
    ```

```
        context.beginPath();
        context.moveTo(50, 50);
        context.lineTo(195, 125);
        context.lineTo(165, 125);
        context.lineTo(50, 66);
        context.fill();
        context.closePath();

        context.beginPath();
        context.moveTo(450, 50);
        context.lineTo(305, 125);
        context.lineTo(275, 125);
        context.lineTo(422, 50);
        context.lineTo(450, 50);
        context.fill();
        context.closePath();

        context.beginPath();
        context.moveTo(450, 250);
        context.lineTo(310, 175);
        context.lineTo(335, 175);
        context.lineTo(450, 235);
        context.lineTo(450, 250);
        context.fill();
        context.closePath();

        context.beginPath();
        context.moveTo(50, 250);
        context.lineTo(200, 175);
        context.lineTo(225, 175);
        context.lineTo(80, 250);
        context.lineTo(50, 250);
        context.fill();
        context.closePath();

    };

if (window.ActiveXObject) {
  window.onload = function() {
    var context = canvas.getContext("2d");
    draw(context);
  }
} else {
  var context = canvas.getContext("2d");
  draw(context);
}
```

3. Save the new page and view it in IE. Our flag should now be visible:

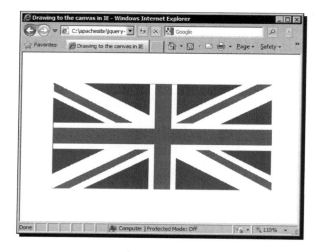

IE can be made to understand the `<canvas>` element, as we see in the previous screenshot, although its support is not completely identical to that of capable browsers. If we compare our example in IE and Firefox alongside each other, we see that IE also slightly enlarges the flag for some reason.

What just happened?

First of all we need to link to the explorercanvas library. We don't want to let normal browsers that support the native `<canvas>` element use this file as it will slow them down, so we put the `<script>` element into an IE-specific conditional comment (like we did with the `html5shiv` file earlier in the book). The `.compiled` version of the script file is simply a minified version for production use.

The next change we make is to put the methods that draw the flag into an inline function stored as a variable. This is necessary because otherwise IE will attempt to use these drawing methods before the explorercanvas library has finished initializing and will throw errors. The next part of our code also deals with this.

We use a conditional `if` statement to check for the presence of an `ActiveXObject` property of the `window` object (this will only exist in IE). If it is found, we attach an `onload` handler to the `<body>` of the page that calls the `getContext()` method and our `draw()` function once the page has finished loading, and the explorercanvas library has done its thing.

If the browser is not IE, we simply get the context and call our `draw()` function straight away. Note that we pass the context object into the `draw()` function as an argument so that the API methods work correctly. Other than these changes, our code is the same and should now function as intended in IE versions 8 and below.

Pop Quiz – supporting IE

1. We wrap the `getContext()` method in a conditional comment that checks for IE and uses an `onload` handler attached to the `<body>`. Why?

    a. The `<canvas>` can only be interacted with via the `<body>` element in IE

    b. To give explorercanvas a chance to add `getContext()` support to the `<canvas>` in IE

    c. To prevent memory leaks in IE

    d. A handler function must be used with explorercanvas

2. Which methods/techniques do now work in IE when using explorercanvas?

    a. Scaling and Bezier curves

    b. Radial gradients and quadratic curves

    c. Radial gradients, `clearRect()`, and non-uniform scaling

    d. Non-uniform scaling, PNG-based images, and stroked text

Have a go hero – extending IE support

Convert your own flag (or logo/alternative) so that it works in IE using the explorercanvas library. You'll more than likely need to make use of an `onload` event handler to ensure that the `getContext()` method isn't called until the `<canvas>` is ready to be used.

Animating the canvas

The `<canvas>` methods we've looked at so far are easy to use and nothing if not a little repetitive. Animating the objects on the `<canvas>` is where things start to get interesting. Animating is harder than simply drawing on the `<canvas>` and as we have no real way of debugging it other than trial and error, solving bugs can quickly become problematic and somewhat time-consuming.

In our flag example, there was no real benefit to using the `<canvas>`. We could have got exactly the same effect, with much less code and processing, by simply including an image of the flag on our page. However, animating the `<canvas>` is where its benefits really begin. This is where we can do *much* more than anything we could achieve with a simple image. The additional complexity that animating the `<canvas>` entails is totally worth it.

Time for action – creating an animation on the canvas

In this example, we'll draw the same flag as we did before, except that this time we'll animate the different shapes. The underlying HTML used in this example is exactly the same as in the previous examples. All that changes is the contents of the <script> element at the end of the <body>.

1. To make the working file for this example, just remove everything in the <script> element at the bottom of canvas-explorer.html and resave the file as canvas-animated.html.

2. The first thing we'll do is bring the blue rectangle in from the side of the canvas to the center of the <canvas> element. Add the following code to the now empty <script> element at the bottom of the page:

```
(function() {

  var canvas = document.getElementById("c"),

  init = function(context) {

    var width = 0,
      pos = 0,
      rectMotion = function() {

        if (width < 400) {
          width = width + 2;
          context.fillStyle = "#039";
          context.fillRect(0, 50, width, 200);
        } else if (pos < 50) {
          pos = pos + 2;
          canvas.width = 500;
          context.fillStyle = "#039";
          context.fillRect(pos, 50, 400, 200);
        } else {
          clearInterval(rectInt);
          whiteLines(context);
        }
      },
      rectInt = setInterval(function() { rectMotion() }, 1);
  };

  if (window.ActiveXObject) {
    window.onload = function() {
```

```
        var context = canvas.getContext("2d");
          init(context);
      }
    } else {
      var context = canvas.getContext("2d");
      init(context);
    }
})();
```

What just happened?

In the previous examples in this chapter all of our variables were global, which is generally a bad practice when coding for the real world. In this example our code is within the scope of the anonymous function, so the variables are only accessible within that function and are therefore not considered global.

We also use the same construct for detecting and working with IE that we did before, where we define an inline function that is either called straight away for most browsers, or once the onload event of the body is fired for IE. The function that is called is init() in this example.

Within this function we declare width and pos variables and then define another inline function called rectMotion(), which will be called repeatedly by an interval. Any shapes drawn outside of the bounds of the <canvas> do not exist, so we can't draw a rectangle out of view and then animate it into view. Instead, we gradually build up the rectangle by starting at the left edge and incrementally widening the rectangle until it is the correct width.

This is done using the first branch of the if statement, which will be executed while the width variable is less than 400. To speed the animation up, we actually increase the width of the rectangle by two pixels at a time (although the speed of the animation is also considerably different between browsers) by increasing the width variable and then using the variable as the width argument in the fillRect() method.

Once the width variable has reached 400, we then change over to use the pos variable instead. In this part of the conditional, we increase the pos variable by two (the rectangle will appear to move two pixels at a time, again for speed), reset the <canvas> by setting its width, and set the fillStyle property. We then draw the new rectangle, using the pos variable as the argument for the x axis position.

It will look as if the rectangle is being moved to the right, but this is not the case at all. We are actually destroying the rectangle and then drawing a completely new one two pixels to the right of the original.

Once the rectangle is in the correct location we clear the interval and then call the next function, (we'll add this shortly) passing in the context object. After the `rectMotion()` function, we add a final variable that contains the ID of the interval which calls the function to animate the rectangle. We use this variable to clear the interval once the animation is complete.

If you run the page in a browser at this point, the blue rectangle appears to move into the `<canvas>` from the left before stopping in the middle. Next, we need to animate the horizontal and diagonal white crosses over the blue rectangle.

Time for action – animating the white crosses

In this part of the animation, we'll draw a white line down the middle and across the center of the rectangle, and then make the diagonal cross grow out from the center to the corners. The following code should be added in between the `canvas` and `init` variables in the code so far:

```
whiteLines = function(context) {

  context.fillStyle = "#fff";
  context.strokeStyle = "#fff";
  context.lineWidth = 50;

  var width = 0,
    height = 0,
    pos = {
      ne: { x: 250, y: 150 },
      se: { x: 250, y: 150 },
      nw: { x: 250, y: 150 },
      sw: { x: 250, y: 150 }
    },
    growDiagonal = function() {

      if (pos.ne.x >= 50) {
      context.beginPath();
      context.moveTo(pos.ne.x, pos.ne.y);
      context.lineTo(pos.ne.x - 4, pos.ne.y - 2);
      context.moveTo(pos.se.x, pos.se.y);
      context.lineTo(pos.se.x - 4, pos.se.y + 2);
      context.moveTo(pos.nw.x, pos.nw.y);
      context.lineTo(pos.nw.x + 4, pos.nw.y + 2);
      context.moveTo(pos.sw.x, pos.sw.y);
      context.lineTo(pos.sw.x + 4, pos.sw.y - 2);
      context.stroke();
```

```
      context.closePath();

      pos.ne.x = pos.ne.x - 2;
      pos.ne.y = pos.ne.y - 1;
      pos.se.x = pos.se.x - 2;
      pos.se.y = pos.se.y + 1;
      pos.nw.x = pos.nw.x + 2;
      pos.nw.y = pos.nw.y + 1;
      pos.sw.x = pos.sw.x + 2;
      pos.sw.y = pos.sw.y - 1;
    } else {
      clearInterval(crossInt);
      redCross(context);
    }
  },
  growVertical = function() {

    if (height < 200 || width < 400) {
      if (height < 200) {
        height = height + 2;
        context.fillRect(225, 50, 50, height);
      }
      if (width < 400) {
        width = width + 4;
        context.fillRect(50, 125, width, 50);
      }
    } else {
      clearInterval(rectInt);
      crossInt = setInterval(function() { growDiagonal() }, 1);
    }
  },
  rectInt = setInterval(function() { growVertical() }, 1);
},
```

What just happened?

Essentially we have another inline function, which contains another function that gets repeatedly called with another interval. As we're drawing white crosses this time, we need to set some style properties (we'll be drawing both lines and rectangles in this function and so set the fillStyle and strokeStyle) as well as the lineWidth property.

We initialize width and height control variables, which will be used to control how many times the interval runs, and we also store the starting positions of the vertical and diagonal crosses in an object called pos.

We then define two inline functions, one to create the vertical cross and the other to create the diagonal cross. The `growVertical()` function is called first with an interval and we just draw one white rectangle from top to bottom, and one from left to right in the center of the background using the `width` and `height` variables to repeat the interval as many times as necessary. The interval is cleared once the rectangles are the correct size and then the `growDiagonal()` function is called with another interval.

In this function we need to draw four lines, each starting in the middle of the vertical cross. We use the different properties in our `pos` object to do this. Each time the function is executed, we move to the x and y positions specified for each line in the object and then draw towards the relevant corner. We then update the properties in the object ready for the next iteration of the function.

The properties each need to be updated by different amounts, for example, the line moving from the center to the top-left of the rectangle need to move negatively along both the x and y axes, whereas the line to move to the top-right corner needs to move positively along the x axis, but negatively along the y axis. We use a new path on each iteration of the function to preserve the anti-aliasing of the lines.

Once the lines are drawn we clear the interval and call the next function. We'll define this function now. It should be placed after the `canvas` variable, but directly before the `whiteLines()` function that we just added.

Time for action – animating the red crosses

All we need to do now is draw the vertical red cross and the four custom red shapes. Add the following code in between the `rectInt` variable declaration near the top of the `<script>` and the `whiteLines` function we defined in the previous section:

```
redCross = function(context) {
  context.fillStyle = "#C00";
  context.strokeStyle = "#C00";
  context.lineWidth = 30;

  var width = 0,
    height = 0,
    pos = {
      up : { x: 250, y: 150 },
      down : { x: 250, y: 150 },
      left: { x: 250, y: 150 },
      right: { x: 250, y: 150 }
    },

    addStripes = function() {
```

```
context.lineWidth = 1;

function makeStripe(props) {
  context.beginPath();
  context.moveTo(props.startX, props.startY);
  context.lineTo(props.line1X, props.line1Y);
  context.lineTo(props.line2X, props.line2Y);
  context.lineTo(props.line3X, props.line3Y);
  context.fill();
  context.closePath();
}

setTimeout(function() { makeStripe({
  startX: 50, startY: 50,
  line1X: 195, line1Y: 125,
  line2X: 165, line2Y: 125,
  line3X: 50, line3Y: 66
})}, 1);
setTimeout(function() { makeStripe({
  startX: 450, startY: 50,
  line1X: 305, line1Y: 125,
  line2X: 275, line2Y: 125,
  line3X: 422, line3Y: 50
})}, 50);
setTimeout(function() { makeStripe({
  startX: 450, startY: 250,
  line1X: 310, line1Y: 175,
  line2X: 335, line2Y: 175,
  line3X: 450, line3Y: 235
})}, 100);
setTimeout(function() { makeStripe({
  startX: 50, startY: 250,
  line1X: 200, line1Y: 175,
  line2X: 225, line2Y: 175,
  line3X: 80, line3Y: 250
})}, 150);
},

growVertical = function() {

  if (height < 100 || width < 200) {
    if (height < 100) {
      context.beginPath();
      context.moveTo(pos.up.x, pos.up.y);
```

```
            context.lineTo(pos.up.x, pos.up.y - 2);
            context.moveTo(pos.down.x, pos.down.y);
            context.lineTo(pos.down.x, pos.down.y + 2);
            context.stroke();
            context.closePath();

            height = height + 2;
            pos.up.y = pos.up.y - 2;
            pos.down.y = pos.down.y + 2;
          }
          if (width < 200) {
            context.beginPath();
            context.moveTo(pos.left.x, pos.left.y);
            context.lineTo(pos.left.x - 2, pos.left.y);
            context.moveTo(pos.right.x, pos.right.y);
            context.lineTo(pos.right.x + 2, pos.right.y);
            context.stroke();
            context.closePath();

            width = width + 2
            pos.left.x = pos.left.x - 2;
            pos.right.x = pos.right.x + 2;
          }
        } else {
          clearInterval(crossInt);
          addStripes();
        }

      },
      crossInt = setInterval( function() { growVertical() }, 1);
    },
```

What just happened?

Again, we have an outer inline function (called redCross()) containing some properties that set the color and line styles, and some nested functions that will be used to draw the red cross and the four custom shapes. As with the previous function, we declare width and height control variables, and an object called pos containing the starting positions for the lines that make up the cross. The cross is drawn first with the growVertical() function.

This function is very similar to the function in the last section of code. We draw four lines starting in the middle of the rectangle which radiate to the top and bottom center, and the right and left center.

The four custom shapes are drawn using a single master function that accepts a configuration object specifying the start point (passed to the moveTo() method), and the points that make up each sub-path (passed to the lineTo() methods). We then use the setTimeout JavaScript function to create each shape one after the other, using the object passed to the master function to specify the relevant points on the canvas to draw each shape.

This is all the code we need, so when we run the page now we should see the animation of the flag being drawn. The code works in all browsers, including IE, but as I mentioned earlier, the performance does vary considerably between browsers, with Webkit and Opera browsers running smoothly and very quickly, Firefox somewhere in the middle, and IE crawling along almost intolerably slowly.

Animating the <canvas> is all about conditional if statements, intervals, and timeouts. As we saw, the code itself is quite straight-forward. We just need rather a lot of it in order to produce even simple animations.

Pop quiz – animating the canvas

1. Why did we store each call to setInterval() in a variable?

    a. For performance reasons

    b. In order to clear the interval when appropriate

    c. Because of the closure created with the anonymous function as the first argument to the function

    d. So that we can pass arguments to the function called by the interval

2. In the first function, where we drew the blue rectangle, we set the width of the <canvas> each time the rectMotion() function is called by the interval. Why?

    a. To make sure the <canvas> was big enough to contain the rectangle as it grew

    b. To correct a bug in Internet Explorer

    c. To reset the state of the <canvas>, ensuring there was only one rectangle at each point in the animation

    d. As a requirement for setting the fillStyle property

Have a go hero – creating canvas animations

Go back to the static version of the flag you drew of your home country (or the logo or image of your choice) and convert it so that the different parts of the flag are animated into existence.

Creating a canvas game

The best animations are those that are interactive and engage the user, and this is exactly how a game can be seen, as one continuous, user-driven animation. The power of the `<canvas>` element is really highlighted when it is used to create games, as we'll see over the course of this section.

We'll create a very basic clone of the arcade classic Space Invaders with a series of alien ships that slowly advance down the screen, and a user-controlled space ship at the bottom that can shoot the incoming aliens:

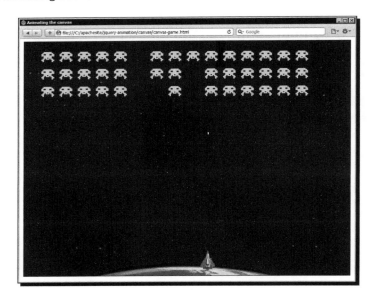

Time for action – creating the initial page

The initial page that we'll use for this example is similar to that used in the previous example, although this time we won't be supporting Microsoft's Internet Explorer so some of the initialization code isn't required.

1. Create a new page in your text editor that contains the following markup:

```
<!DOCTYPE html>
<html lang="en">
  <head>
    <meta charset="utf-8">
    <title>A canvas and jQuery Game</title>
    <link rel="stylesheet" href="css/canvas-game.css">
  </head>
```

```
<body>
  <canvas tabindex="1" id="c" width="900" height="675">
    <p>Your browser doesn't support the canvas element!</p>
  </canvas>
  <script src="js/jquery.js"></script>
  <script>
    (function($) {


    })(jQuery);
  </script>
</body>
</html>
```

2. Save the file as `canvas-game.html`. We also require a very basic stylesheet for our game. All we're styling is the `<canvas>` element itself. Create a new stylesheet containing the following style rules:

```
canvas {
  border:1px solid #000; margin:auto; display:block;
  outline:none;
  background:url(../img/bg.gif) no-repeat;
}
```

3. Save this file in the `css` directory as `canvas-game.css`.

What just happened?

The main element on the page is of course the `<canvas>` element. The only difference between this and the element used in previous examples is that we have set the `tabindex` attribute on it so that it can receive keyboard events, which is necessary for detecting and reacting to the input from the user. We're also using jQuery in this example and using the standard anonymous function + $ aliasing construct we've used throughout the book.

The styles we've used simply position the `<canvas>` element in the center of the page, give it a border, and remove the dotted outline that appears around focused elements in some browsers. We also set a background image on the element.

The background image applied to the `<canvas>` element helps to set a scene for our game, and using CSS to set a background image on the `<canvas>` element is much easier than drawing the image within it.

Time for action – the initial script

The script for the game is quite long so we'll look at it in different sections, starting with the initial structure of the script. The following code should go into the anonymous function at the bottom of the page:

```
var canvas = document.getElementById("c"),
  context = canvas.getContext("2d"),
  motionInt = null,
  dirCounter = 0,
  alienSpeed = 1000,
  aliens = [],
  alienMotion = function(dir) {

  },

  addAliens = function() {

  },

  ship = new Image(),
  shipPos = [430, 600];

  ship.src = "img/ship.png";
  ship.onload = function() {

  context.drawImage(ship, shipPos[0], shipPos[1]);

  addAliens();

  };
```

What just happened?

Essentially, all we've done here is define a series of variables and an onload event handler. The canvas and context variables are defined first, as in previous examples, in order to access and manipulate the canvas.

We also set a variable called motionInt which will be used to hold the ID of a setInterval() function later on, a variable called dirCounter which will be used to determine which direction the aliens move in, an alienSpeed variable to set the speed that the aliens move at, and an empty aliens array which we'll use to keep track of each alien on the page.

Following this we define two inline functions, one to move the aliens and one to add the aliens to the page. These are empty at the moment but we'll populate each of them next. We also create a new image, which will be the user-controlled space ship, and a `shipPosition` array which will be used to keep track of the ship's location on the page.

Once we've defined all our variables, we set the `src` of the new image object we created to represent the space ship. We then attach an `onload` event handler to the ship object, which will be executed once the image has finished loading. Within this function we draw the ship on the canvas, using the values stored in the `imagePosition` array. We then call the `addAliens()` function, which will add the aliens to the canvas. We can add the code to the `addAliens()` function next.

Time for action – adding the aliens to the page

Add the following code to the `addAliens()` inline function in the previous code block:

```
addAliens = function() {

  var alienPos = [13, 0],
  alien = new Image();

  alien.src = "img/alien.gif";
  alien.onload = function () {
    for (var x = 0; x < 15; x++) {
      for (var y = 0; y < 3; y++) {


        context.drawImage(alien, alienPos[0], alienPos[1]);

        var data = {
          img: alien, posX: alienPos[0], posY: alienPos[1]
        };
        aliens.push(data);

        if (alienPos[1] < 100) {
          alienPos[1] = alienPos[1] + 50;
        } else {
          alienPos[0] = alienPos[0] + 50;
          alienPos[1] = 0;
        }
      };
    }
  };

  motionInt = setInterval(function () {
    alienMotion("right"); }, alienSpeed);
},
```

What just happened?

We first define a new array that we'll use to incrementally set the position of each alien ship while the aliens are initially being drawn to the canvas. We define a new `Image` object for the image that will be used by all of the alien ships and set its `src` attribute. We then set an `onload` handler for the new alien image so that we can manipulate the image once it has finished loading.

We want to create three rows of 15 aliens, so within the `onload` handler we start with two nested `for` loops where the outer loop runs 15 times and on each loop, the inner `for` loop executes three times. Within the nested loops, we first draw the new alien to the canvas using the values stored in the `alienPos` array. We then create a new `data` object which stores a reference to the image object, and the x and y position of the image on the canvas. The new `data` object is then pushed into the `aliens` array which we defined earlier at the start of the script.

We then update the values in the `alienPos` array. If the second item in the array (the item with an index of 1) is less than 100, we add 50 to the value of the array item. The second item in the array corresponds to the position on the y axis of the canvas. This will give us a single column of three aliens. Note that we start the x position of the first three aliens at 13 instead of 0 so that there is a gutter between the edge of the canvas and the first column of aliens.

If the second array item is more than 100, we add 50 to the first item in the array instead, which corresponds to the x axis on the canvas, and reset the second array item to zero. This will give us 15 columns of three aliens.

Once all of the aliens have been drawn on the canvas, we set an interval that will repeatedly execute the next function, `alienMotion()`, according to the number of milliseconds contained in the `alienSpeed` variable, which initially is set to `1000` at the start of the script. The interval ID is stored in the `motionInt` variable we also created at the start of the script. We can add the code to our `alienMotion()` function next.

Time for action – moving the aliens

Our next block of code will give the aliens their motion, causing them to advance to the right along the canvas first, then down a line, then to the left, and so on and so forth:

```
alienMotion = function (dir) {

  var alienLength = aliens.length;

  if (dirCounter < 4) {
```

```
    for (var x = 0; x < alienLength; x++) {
      context.clearRect(aliens[x].posX, aliens[x].posY,
        aliens[x].img.width, aliens[x].img.height);
    }

    for (var y = 0; y < alienLength; y++) {
      aliens[y].posX = (dir === "right") ?  aliens[y].posX + 35 :
        aliens[y].posX - 35;

    context.drawImage(aliens[y].img, aliens[y].posX,
      aliens[y].posY);
    }

    dirCounter++;
  } else {
    clearInterval(motionInt);
    dirCounter = 0;

    for (var z = 0; z < alienLength; z++) {
      context.clearRect(aliens[z].posX, aliens[z].posY,
        aliens[z].img.width, aliens[z].img.height);
    }

    if (aliens[alienLength - 1].posY > 530) {
      canvas.width = 900;
      context.fillStyle = "#fff";
      context.textAlign = "center";
      context.font = "bold 36px Tahoma";
      context.fillText("GAME OVER!", 450, 350);
      $(canvas).blur().unbind("keydown");
    } else {

      for (var a = 0; a < alienLength; a++) {
        aliens[a].posY = aliens[a].posY + 29;

        context.drawImage(aliens[a].img, aliens[a].posX,
          aliens[a].posY);
      }

      motionInt = (dir === "right") ? setInterval(
        function () { alienMotion("left"); }, alienSpeed) :
        setInterval(function () { alienMotion("right"); },
        alienSpeed);
    }
  }
},
```

What just happened?

The first thing we do is store the length of the aliens array in a local variable. We'll use several `for` loops in this function so it makes sense to retrieve this value only once and compare the counter variables of the `for` loops to the variable instead of checking the length on each iteration of the various loops.

We then use an `if` statement to check whether the `dirCounter` variable is less than 4. Remember, this was one of the variables we set at the start of the script. If the variable is less than 4, we first use a `for` loop to cycle through each item in the `aliens` array and use the `clearRect()` function to remove the alien from the canvas.

We then use a second `for` loop that cycles through the `aliens` array once more, this time updating the x position of each alien by either adding or removing 35 from the current x position stored in the current item in the array.

Whether 35 is added or removed is determined by the parameter passed into the function. The first time the `alienMotion()` function is called, it will receive the parameter `right`, so the aliens will initially move across to the canvas to the right. We then draw each alien in its new position. Once the `for` loop has finished and all of the aliens have been drawn in their new positions we update the `dirCounter` variable.

If the `dirCounter` variable is equal to 4, the aliens have moved horizontally across the canvas as far as they should, so this time we need to move the aliens down the canvas a line instead of across it. In this branch of the conditional, we clear the interval that controls the horizontal movement, then reset the `dirCounter` variable back to 0. We then remove the aliens from the canvas by clearing the rectangle that each alien covers.

Before moving the aliens down a line, we first check whether the y position of the last alien in the array is greater than 530, as this is the maximum distance from the top of the canvas that an alien should get. If it is greater than this figure, at least one alien has reached the bottom of the canvas and it's game over for the player.

In this case, we clear the whole canvas, removing the space ship and any surviving aliens, and print the text **GAME OVER!** to the center of the canvas. We also use jQuery to unbind the keyboard events that control the space ship (we'll add these bindings shortly).

If the aliens have not reached the bottom of the canvas, we instead use another `for` loop to iterate over each alien in the array and move each of their y positions down by one line, and then draw each alien in its new location.

We then set a new interval, passing in the opposite direction string to the `alienMotion()` function that was used previously. These loops of four steps to the right, one step down, four steps to the left, and so on, will continue until the aliens reach the bottom of the canvas and the game is over. Next, we need to add the handlers that enable the player to control the space ship.

Time for action – adding handlers to control the ship

The following block of code should be added to the `onload` event handler for the ship image object:

```
ship.onload = function () {

  context.drawImage(ship, shipPos[0], shipPos[1]);

  addAliens();
  $(canvas).focus().bind("keydown", function (e) {

    if (e.which === 37 || e.which === 39) {

      context.clearRect(shipPos[0], shipPos[1], ship.width,
        ship.height);

      if (e.which === 37 && shipPos[0] > 4) {
        shipPos[0] = shipPos[0] - 4;
      } else if (e.which === 39 && shipPos[0] < 896 - ship.width) {
        shipPos[0] = shipPos[0] + 4;
      }

      context.drawImage(ship, shipPos[0], shipPos[1]);
    } else if (e.which === 32) {
      context.fillStyle = "#fff";
      var bulletPos = shipPos[0] + 20,
        newBulletPos = [bulletPos, 596],
        alienLength = aliens.length,
        fire = function () {
          if (newBulletPos[1] > 0) {
            context.clearRect(newBulletPos[0],
              newBulletPos[1], 3, 6);
            newBulletPos[1] = newBulletPos[1] - 2;
            context.fillRect(newBulletPos[0], newBulletPos[1], 3, 6);

            for (var x = 0; x < alienLength; x++) {
              if (newBulletPos[1] === aliens[x].posY ||
                newBulletPos[1] === aliens[x].posY +
                aliens[x].img.height) {
                if (newBulletPos[0] > aliens[x].posX &&
                  newBulletPos[0] - aliens[x].posX <
                  aliens[x].img.width + 13) {
                  context.clearRect(aliens[x].posX, aliens[x].posY,
                    aliens[x].img.width, aliens[x].img.height);
```

```
                                   aliens.splice(x, 1);
                                   clearInterval(bulletInt);
                                   context.clearRect(newBulletPos[0],
                                     newBulletPos[1], 3, 6);
                                   if (!aliens.length) {
                                     clearInterval(motionInt);
                                     dirCounter = 0;
                                     alienSpeed = alienSpeed - 100;
                                     addAliens();
                                   }
                                 }
                               }
                             }
                           }
                         } else {
                           context.clearRect(newBulletPos[0], newBulletPos[1], 3, 6);
                           clearInterval(bulletInt);
                         }
                       },
                       bulletInt = setInterval(function () { fire(); }, 1);
                   }
                 });
               };
```

What just happened?

We use jQuery to attach an event handler to the `<canvas>` element that listens for
`keydown` events. Although we're not providing support for IE and so don't need jQuery for
its cross-browser normalization when attaching events, it still makes the event handling
process much easier.

Within the function that is executed whenever a `keydown` event is detected, we check for
the presence of either the left or right arrow keys, which have a `which` property in the event
object of 37 and 39, or the space bar, which has the code 32.

If the code 37 or 39 is detected we then use a nested `if` statement to determine between
the two keys. We also check that the ship hasn't reached either the left edge, or the right
edge of the canvas.

We then use the `clearRect()` function to remove the ship and draw a new one either 4
pixels to the left, or 4 pixels to the right depending on which key was pressed. This gives the
ship left and right motion along the bottom of the canvas.

The second branch of the outer conditional deals with the space bar being pressed, which
causes a bullet to leave the ship and travel in a straight line to the top of the canvas. The
bullets will be white, so we set the `fillStyle` property of the canvas to #fff.

We also declare some more local variables here including `bulletPos` which is the current position of the bullet plus half of the width of the ship, and an array to hold the x and y coordinates of the bullet. The values for this array are set to the `bulletPos` variable for the x position, and directly above the nose of the ship for the y position. We also store the length of the aliens array as a local variable for use in a `for` loop once again.

We define an inline function along with our variables called `fire()`. This function is used in conjunction with an interval to create the motion of the bullet. Within this function, we check that the bullet hasn't reached the top of the canvas, and provided it hasn't, that is if its y position is greater than 0, we remove the bullet with the `clearRect()` function, then update the values in the `bulletPos` array and draw the bullet in its new location using the updated values from the array.

Once the position of the bullet has been updated, we then need to check whether the bullet, in its new position, has collided with an alien or not, so we use a `for` loop to iterate over each alien in the aliens array.

On each iteration we first check whether the bullet falls within the y axis of an alien, that is whether its position is less than the bottom edge of an alien, but more than its top edge. The aliens are positioned according to their top-left corner, so to work out whether the bullet has passed its bottom edge we just add the height of an alien to its y position.

If the bullet does fall within the alien on the y axis, we then check whether it falls within the space an alien is taking up along the x axis. If it does, we remove the alien from the canvas with the `clearRect()` function and splice the alien out of the array so that it stays removed.

We then remove the bullet from the canvas using the `clearRect()` function again, and clear the `bulletInt` interval. If there are no more aliens left, we clear the interval producing the motion of the aliens, reset the `dirCounter` variable, reduce the `alienSpeed` variable by `100`, and then call the `addAliens()` function to redraw the aliens at the top of the canvas.

This is effectively how the player moves up to the next level, and each time the aliens are redrawn they move faster, creating basic progression of the game. This now brings us to the end of the code. If we run the game now in a standard-compliant browser such as Firefox or Chrome, we should find that we have a perfectly playable game, implemented entirely using JavaScript and the `<canvas>` element.

Pop quiz – creating canvas-based games

1. In this example a lot of functionality that related to the player's space ship was put into an `onload` event handler. Why?

    a. Because we cannot interact with an image until it has loaded completely

    b. To make the code work correctly in Internet Explorer

    c. Because the code runs faster once the image has finished loading

    d. To help make our code more modular

2. Why did we set the `textAlign` property of the canvas to center when writing the **GAME OVER** message?

    a. Setting the alignment is a prerequisite for writing text to the canvas

    b. Because it is easier than working out the width of the text and then setting its position on the x axis in order to position the text in the center of the canvas

    c. To anti-alias the text

    d. Because it is more efficient than using padding

Have a go hero – extending the space invaders clone

Our game is a much simpler version of the original space invaders. The original arcade game had many other features including aliens that fired back at the player's ship, bases to hide behind, and one off special aliens that appeared randomly throughout the game and dropped bonuses when hit.

Certainly one thing that the game needs is a scoring mechanism, otherwise there is simply no incentive to play. Implement a scoring system that tracks a player's score throughout the game and saves the highest score to the player's machine. This could be done easily with jQuery and the cookie plugin, or using LocalStorage.

I'd also urge you, as this is the last example of the book, to implement some of the other missing features, such as giving the aliens the ability to fire back, and adding bases or shields that the player can hide beneath when the going gets tough.

Summary

In this chapter we looked at the HTML5 `<canvas>` element and saw how it can be used to create simple, static images, basic animations, and even complex interactive games. It provides a rich API that allows us to interact with it programmatically and gives us complete pixel-level control over an area of the page.

We also saw that although current versions of Internet Explorer don't support the `<canvas>` element natively, we can use a JavaScript library provided by Google to port most canvas functionality to this browser. Some animations however are still beyond IE8's capabilities even with Google's library. IE9 does support the `<canvas>` element, so hopefully the requirement of this library will soon become a thing of the past.

In this chapter, we covered the following subjects:

◆ The `<canvas>` script API

◆ Drawing to the `<canvas>`

◆ Using the `<canvas>` with Internet Explorer

◆ Creating animations on the `<canvas>`

◆ Creating interactive games with the `<canvas>`

Like with the CSS3 examples from the last chapter, there are no methods or properties in jQuery specifically for use with `<canvas>`, although they have been a number of plugins that combine the power of `<canvas>` with the ease of jQuery, and several projects that extend the jQuery `animate()` method to allow it work on objects drawn to the canvas. For more information on this, a good starting point is Steven Wittens' blog at `http://acko. net/blog/abusing-jquery-animate-for-fun-and-profit-and-bacon`.

We've now reached the end of the book. I hope that over these 10 chapters I've given you a solid foundation for producing animations using jQuery that acts as a solid starting point for you to bring your web-based UIs to life.

Pop Quiz Answers

Chapter 1

Basic animation with jQuery

Question number	Answers
1	b
2	c

Chapter 2

Using fadeIn

Question number	Answers
1	b
2	a

Using fadeOut

Question number	Answers
1	a
2	d

Using fadeToggle()

Question number	Answers
1	c

Using fadeTo

Question number	Answers
1	d
2	c

Using show and hide

Question number	Answers
1	c
2	a

Chapter 3

Viewing the queue

Question number	Answers
1	b
2	c

Adding new items to the array

Question number	Answers
1	a

Keeping the queue running

Question number	Answers
1	a

Replacing the queue

Question number	Answers
1	c
2	d

Stopping an animation

Question number	Answers
1	c
2	d

Chapter 4

Sliding elements down

Question number	Answers
1	c
2	a

Sliding elements up

Question number	Answers
1	d

Using slideToggle

Question number	Answers
1	c
2	a

Using easing

Question number	Answers
1	b
2	a

Fixing the flicker

Question number	Answers
1	c

Chapter 5

Creating an animated content-viewer

Question number	Answers
1	b
2	c

Creating expanding images

Question number	Answers
1	d
2	a

Creating a plugin

Question number	Answers
1	d
2	c

Chapter 6

Using the effect API

Question number	Answers
1	d
2	b

Using show/hide logic

Question number	Answers
1	c
2	a

Easing, color, and class animations

Question number	Answers
1	d
2	c

Chapter 7

Animating page scroll

Question number	Answers
1	c
2	a

Implementing the parallax effect

Question number	Answers
1	c
2	c

Creating a single-page website

Question number	Answers
1	b
2	c

Implementing stop-motion animation with jQuery

Question number	Answers
1	d

Chapter 8

Implementing proximity animations

Question number	Answers
1	c
2	b

Creating a marquee scroller

Question number	Answers
1	d
2	c

Chapter 9

Implementing CSS3 rotation

Question number	Answers
1	c
2	a

Using the matrix

Question number	Answers
1	c
2	d

Chapter 10

Drawing to the canvas

Question number	Answers
1	d
2	c

Supporting IE

Question number	Answers
1	b
2	c

Animating the canvas

Question number	Answers
1	b
2	c

Creating canvas-based games

Question number	Answers
1	a
2	b

Index

Thank you for buying
jQuery 1.4 Animation Techniques: Beginner's Guide

About Packt Publishing

Packt, pronounced 'packed', published its first book "*Mastering phpMyAdmin for Effective MySQL Management*" in April 2004 and subsequently continued to specialize in publishing highly focused books on specific technologies and solutions.

Our books and publications share the experiences of your fellow IT professionals in adapting and customizing today's systems, applications, and frameworks. Our solution based books give you the knowledge and power to customize the software and technologies you're using to get the job done. Packt books are more specific and less general than the IT books you have seen in the past. Our unique business model allows us to bring you more focused information, giving you more of what you need to know, and less of what you don't.

Packt is a modern, yet unique publishing company, which focuses on producing quality, cutting-edge books for communities of developers, administrators, and newbies alike. For more information, please visit our website: www.packtpub.com.

About Packt Open Source

In 2010, Packt launched two new brands, Packt Open Source and Packt Enterprise, in order to continue its focus on specialization. This book is part of the Packt Open Source brand, home to books published on software built around Open Source licences, and offering information to anybody from advanced developers to budding web designers. The Open Source brand also runs Packt's Open Source Royalty Scheme, by which Packt gives a royalty to each Open Source project about whose software a book is sold.

Writing for Packt

We welcome all inquiries from people who are interested in authoring. Book proposals should be sent to author@packtpub.com. If your book idea is still at an early stage and you would like to discuss it first before writing a formal book proposal, contact us; one of our commissioning editors will get in touch with you.

We're not just looking for published authors; if you have strong technical skills but no writing experience, our experienced editors can help you develop a writing career, or simply get some additional reward for your expertise.

jQuery 1.4 Reference Guide

ISBN: 978-1-849510-04-2   Paperback: 336 pages

A comprehensive exploration of the popular JavaScript library

1. Quickly look up features of the jQuery library

2. Step through each function, method, and selector expression in the jQuery library with an easy-to-follow approach

3. Understand the anatomy of a jQuery script

jQuery UI 1.7: The User Interface Library for jQuery

ISBN: 978-1-847199-72-0   Paperback: 392 pages

Build highly interactive web applications with ready-to-use widgets from the jQuery User Interface library

1. Organize your interfaces with reusable widgets: accordions, date pickers, dialogs, sliders, tabs, and more

2. Enhance the interactivity of your pages by making elements drag-and-droppable, sortable, selectable, and resizable

3. Packed with examples and clear explanations of how to easily design elegant and powerful front-end interfaces for your web applications

Please check **www.PacktPub.com** for information on our titles

Learning jQuery 1.3

ISBN: 978-1-847196-70-5 Paperback: 444 pages

Better Interaction Design and Web Development with Simple JavaScript Techniques

1. An introduction to jQuery that requires minimal programming experience

2. Detailed solutions to specific client-side problems

3. For web designers to create interactive elements for their designs

4. For developers to create the best user interface for their web applications

jQuery Reference Guide

ISBN: 978-1-847193-81-0 Paperback: 268 pages

A Comprehensive Exploration of the Popular JavaScript Library

1. Organized menu to every method, function, and selector in the jQuery library

2. Quickly look up features of the jQuery library

3. Understand the anatomy of a jQuery script

4. Extend jQuery's built-in capabilities with plug-ins, and even write your own

Please check **www.PacktPub.com** for information on our titles

1686291R0020

Printed in Great Britain
by Amazon.co.uk, Ltd.,
Marston Gate.